"How I wish I had grasped biblical theology long before I began to learn about it in my forties! What Jon Nielson has written in *Tracing God's Story* is a concise account of the story the divine author has written in Scripture. While this book is economical with words, it is generous with insight. It presents the story simply but not simplistically. I look forward to recommending it to those who long to have a more solid grip on the Bible's storyline."

> **Nancy Guthrie,** teacher, Biblical Theology Workshop for Women

"I am so grateful for the work of Jon Nielson. He continues to provide the church with outstanding material for the study of the Bible and theology. One of the things that makes Nielson's work rather distinctive is how well he makes the study of the Bible and theology accessible to a wide audience. In *Tracing God's Story*, Nielson does for biblical theology what he did for systematic theology in his excellent *Knowing God's Truth*. Beginning with creation, he traces God's acts of redemption all the way through to the consummation of the age. Along the way, he invites the reader to engage with the material devotionally. I am excited to get this book into the hands of members of the church I serve."

> **Todd Pruitt,** Pastor, Covenant Presbyterian Church, Harrisonburg,
> Virginia; Cohost, *Mortification of Spin*

"As in a novel, you can't just dip into a page of the Bible and get the gist. Through all the diverse writings, what's the through line? This is an outstanding and accessible introduction to the plot that keeps biblical history moving from Genesis to Revelation. I highly recommend this book."

> **Michael Horton,** J. Gresham Machen Professor of Systematic Theology
> and Apologetics, Westminster Seminary California; author, *Core
> Christianity*

"In *Tracing God's Story*, Jon Nielson takes us on a gallop through the pages of Scripture to show us how the whole grand story of redemption fits together. Neither too shallow nor too deep, this book is written at the perfect level for lay leaders in the church seeking to gain a better understanding of God's covenant faithfulness to his people across the ages."

> **Chris Polski,** Pastor, Trinity Church Kirkwood, Missouri; Visiting
> Instructor in Applied Theology, Covenant Theological Seminary; and
> his wife, **Katie Polski,** Director of Music Ministries, Trinity Church
> Kirkwood; author; speaker

"In *Tracing God's Story*, Jon Nielson presents a clear, coherent, and compelling account of the metanarrative of redemptive history, skillfully weaving the threads of God's own character with his acts of creation and providence into a tapestry of biblical theology. Not only does he provide the appropriate historical, literary, and redemptive contexts, but he also supplies the reader with cogent and salient application. I'm excited to use this resource in my church for many years to come!"

Brian Cosby, Senior Pastor, Wayside Presbyterian Church, Signal Mountain, Tennessee; Adjunct Professor of Historical Theology, Reformed Theological Seminary, Atlanta

"Understanding the great thematic threads woven throughout the pages of Scripture, accompanied with a view of the overarching grand story, grants Bible readers deeper delight in God's work and person. Jon Nielson has provided a resource that helps Bible readers do this very thing! *Tracing God's Story*, like Nielson's first volume in the Theology Basics series, is clear and simple without being simplistic. My family greatly benefited from the first volume, and I can't wait to put this second volume into the hands of my teenagers."

Jason Helopoulos, Senior Pastor, University Reformed Church, East Lansing, Michigan; author, *The Promise*; *Covenantal Baptism*; and *A Neglected Grace*

"One of the biggest challenges believers find in accessing and reading Scripture is understanding its narrative and cohesion as one unified story. Jon Nielson provides a clear, simple, and thorough overview of the story of Scripture that will make the Bible more accessible and meaningful to believers of any age. A very worthwhile and valuable resource."

Cameron Cole, Founding Chairman, Rooted Ministry; author, *Therefore I Have Hope* and *Heavenward*

"In *Tracing God's Story*, Jon Nielson helps Christians read their Bible cover to cover, with Jesus as the cohesive center. Nielson's work is clearly supported by the best of biblical scholarship, but his writing is accessible to anyone. This book succeeds as an introductory biblical theology volume that not only informs but also inspires. If you are looking for an accessible volume on biblical theology that will get you into the word—while getting the word into you—look no further than *Tracing God's Story*."

Trent Casto, Senior Pastor, Covenant Church of Naples, Florida; author, *2 Corinthians* (Reformed Expository Commentary Series)

TRACING GOD'S STORY

The Theology Basics Series by Jon Nielson

Knowing God's Truth: An Introduction to Systematic Theology

Knowing God's Truth Workbook: An Introduction to Systematic Theology

Tracing God's Story: An Introduction to Biblical Theology

Tracing God's Story Workbook: An Introduction to Biblical Theology

TRACING GOD'S STORY

An Introduction to Biblical Theology

JON NIELSON

WHEATON, ILLINOIS

Tracing God's Story: An Introduction to Biblical Theology
© 2024 by Jon Nielson
Published by Crossway
    1300 Crescent Street
    Wheaton, Illinois 60187

All rights reserved. No part of this publication may be reproduced, stored in a retrieval system, or transmitted in any form by any means, electronic, mechanical, photocopy, recording, or otherwise, without the prior permission of the publisher, except as provided for by USA copyright law. Crossway® is a registered trademark in the United States of America.

Cover design: Zach DeYoung
First printing 2024
Printed in Colombia

Scripture quotations are from the ESV® Bible (The Holy Bible, English Standard Version®), © 2001 by Crossway, a publishing ministry of Good News Publishers. Used by permission. All rights reserved. The ESV text may not be quoted in any publication made available to the public by a Creative Commons license. The ESV may not be translated in whole or in part into any other language.

All emphases in Scripture quotations have been added by the author.

Hardcover ISBN: 978-1-4335-8738-2
ePub ISBN: 978-1-4335-8741-2
PDF ISBN: 978-1-4335-8739-9

Library of Congress Cataloging-in-Publication Data

Names: Nielson, Jon, 1983– author.
Title: Tracing God's story: an introduction to Biblical Theology / Jon Nielson.
Description: Wheaton, Illinois: Crossway, 2024. | Series: Theology basics | Includes index.
Identifiers: LCCN 2023029881 (print) | LCCN 2023029882 (ebook) | ISBN 9781433587382 (hardcover) | ISBN 9781433587399 (pdf) | ISBN 9781433587412 (epub)
Subjects: LCSH: Bible—Theology. | Bible—Study and teaching. | Teenagers—Religious life. | Christian education of teenagers.
Classification: LCC BS543 .N545 2024 (print) | LCC BS543 (ebook) | DDC 230/.041—dc23/eng/20240124
LC record available at https://lccn.loc.gov/2023029881
LC ebook record available at https://lccn.loc.gov/2023029882

Crossway is a publishing ministry of Good News Publishers.

NP		32	31	30	29	28	27	26	25	24
14	13	12	11	10	9	8	7	6	5	4	3	2	1

To my wife, Jeanne,
who has walked faithfully with me
"in sickness and in health."

CONTENTS

INTRODUCTION

This book is the second in a three-part series called "Theology Basics." The first book in this series, *Knowing God's Truth*, is a basic introduction to the discipline of *systematic theology*, which simply refers to an organized approach to gathering together our beliefs about God, humanity, sin, salvation, and other subjects—all according to God's revelation in Scripture. The third book in the series, *Understanding God's Word*, will provide some basic tools for *hermeneutics*—that is, for interpreting and applying the Bible faithfully.

This book, *Tracing God's Story*, is an introduction to the discipline of *biblical theology*. In other words, we're going to take the entire Bible as one united book—one big "story"—and study it as one connected narrative of God and his saving work in the world. We will begin in the book of Genesis and end with the book of Revelation. My prayer is that by the end of this book you will have a better sense of how the entire story of the Bible hangs together as a beautiful, united narrative of the creating, saving, and restoring work of our mighty God.

Before we begin, let me say a word about the organization of the chapters. Here's what you should be ready for:

- Near the beginning of each chapter, you'll find suggested verses for you to memorize—verses linked to that chapter's topic. These memory sections are marked by the word "Remember!" Whether or not you memorize these verses is up to you, but doing so would be a great way to intentionally hide God's word in your heart as you learn more about his story.
- About ten times per chapter, you'll be instructed to "Read!" a biblical passage. After each reading, you'll find an explanation and summary of that passage. These sections will make the most sense (and be most beneficial to you) if you take time to read the passages themselves. You won't read every word of Scripture along with this book—not even close! But the reading that accompanies each section is integral to the aim of this book: to acquaint you with the story of the Bible from beginning to end.
- At the end of each chapter, you'll find a quick recap of the portion of God's story you've just studied. Then you'll see a "Pray!" section. This is an opportunity for you to talk to God for thirty to sixty seconds about what you've just learned. I encourage you to make these prayer times a priority.

I hope that *Tracing God's Story* will help you "put your Bible together" as you come to understand and treasure God's revelation to us, his people.

Chapter 1

WHAT IS BIBLICAL THEOLOGY?

Biblical theology is a discipline that seeks to discover theology (truth about God and his work) through the gradual and progressive revelation of his saving plan in the story of the Bible. This is often done by tracing certain themes or ideas through Scripture from beginning to end—Genesis to Revelation.

The core conviction of those who practice the discipline of biblical theology is that the Bible is a unified work—a book inspired by one divine author (God) and given to human beings to help them understand his broad saving plan, which ultimately was accomplished through the death and resurrection of his Son, Jesus Christ. We will see shortly how Jesus himself pointed us toward this way of understanding Scripture.

So our goal in this book is to do biblical theology. We will trace God's story of redemption as it is revealed to us progressively in the revelation of Scripture. We will begin in Genesis and end in Revelation.

For purposes of clear organization and to guide our study, we'll make our way through the Bible in eight "scenes." Here is the plan for these scenes:

Scene 1: God's Creation and a Crisis (chaps. 2–3)
Scene 2: God's Promise of a People (chaps. 4–5)

Scene 3: God's People Grow (chaps. 6–7)
Scene 4: God's Kingdom—Rise and Fall (chaps. 8–9)
Scene 5: God's People—Captive and Coming Home (chaps. 10–11)
Scene 6: God's Salvation (chap. 12)
Scene 7: God's Church (chaps. 13–14)
Scene 8: God's Eternity (chaps. 15–16)

As you can see, the titles given to these sections all begin with "God." The Bible is *his* story—the connected account of his marvelous saving work in the world that he created. By the end of this book, you should have a clearer understanding of the unity of Scripture and the beautiful story of God's redemption through his Son, Jesus Christ, which is revealed in all the pages of his inspired word.

Remember!

Take some time to get acquainted with your suggested memory verses for this opening chapter:

Brothers, I may say to you with confidence about the patriarch David that he both died and was buried, and his tomb is with us to this day. Being therefore a prophet, and knowing that God had sworn with an oath to him that he would set one of his descendants on his throne, he foresaw and spoke about the resurrection of the Christ, that he was not abandoned to Hades, nor did his flesh see corruption. This Jesus God raised up, and of that we all are witnesses. (Acts 2:29–32)

FOUNDATIONS FOR BIBLICAL THEOLOGY

We will begin by discussing some foundational arguments for biblical theology. In other words, we are going to be asking this question: Why do we believe that this is a valid way to study the Bible? This is an important question to answer because, as we will learn in the next chapter, not everyone agrees that this is a valid approach! So I will seek to explain just a few of the key foundations that establish biblical theology as the right way to engage with Scripture.

Jesus's Example

One answer to the above question is that Jesus read and interpreted the Old Testament in this way. When we practice biblical theology, we are following the lead of Jesus in the way that he looked at and applied Scripture.

READ!

Take a few minutes to read Luke 24:13–27—the account of Jesus walking and talking with two men on the road to Emmaus after his resurrection from the dead.

The disciples on the road to Emmaus were struggling to understand the events that had just taken place. Jesus, the man they had followed as the Messiah, had been killed. They were sad and discouraged because it seemed that he had failed.

Jesus confronted these men based on Scripture. He told them that it was "necessary" for the Christ to suffer and die (Luke 24:26); Scripture had told them that would happen! Then he did something amazing: Jesus opened the Old Testament Scriptures for these men—right there on the road—and explained to them the "things concerning himself" (v. 27). Luke tells us that he began with Moses (the books of Genesis to Deuteronomy) and then moved into the prophetic writings in order to show them how the Old Testament—all of it—ultimately pointed to him.

This is a crucial passage for helping us understand how Jesus interpreted Scripture. He saw himself as the main character—the one to whom the entire Old Testament pointed. Thus, biblical theology is legitimate. It is right to see the Bible as telling one great story that has its climax in the death and resurrection of Jesus.

We can draw a few conclusions:

The Bible—all of it—is about Jesus. That is not an overstatement. We can really say, according to what we see from Jesus in Luke 24, that the Bible is ultimately all about him. The Old Testament points forward to him, shows the need for him, and explains what he was going to do for God's people. The New Testament makes Jesus's work clear and plain. The Bible is about Jesus.

We cannot rightly understand the Old Testament without understanding the work of Jesus. In other words, it is bad scholarship to read the Old Testament without looking forward to the work of Jesus—the Messiah—that the Old Testament anticipates! This is what Jesus would have said. He called the men on the road to Emmaus "slow of heart" because they did not understand all that the Old Testament Scriptures had been teaching about him and his work. If we miss Jesus in the Old Testament, we simply have not studied it correctly!

We should never study the Bible without talking about Jesus. Finally, we can conclude with this important point: to study any part of the Bible without referencing Jesus—the central character of the Bible—does not do the Bible justice. We have studied it incorrectly. We need to frame our discussion of each passage of Scripture in terms of its place in the great story—a story that has its climax in the life, death, and resurrection of God's Son, Jesus Christ.

Jesus's "sermon" on the road to Emmaus lays an important foundation regarding biblical theology. How wonderful it would be to have that entire sermon recorded for us! Jesus took time to explain to the two men, from Moses and the Prophets, all the things about him in the Old Testament Scriptures. In other words, Jesus himself used "biblical theology" to see the connection between the Old Testament Scriptures and his work through his death and resurrection.

The Apostles' Preaching

Another foundation for biblical theology is the example of Jesus's apostles. We will look at just one example of the teaching of the apostles about Jesus in relation to the Old Testament. We will consider the passage from which this chapter's suggested memory verses come: Acts 2:14–41 (Peter's sermon to the crowd at Pentecost). In this passage, we will see how Peter explained the work of Jesus from Psalm 16—a psalm written by King David.

▌ READ!

Read Acts 2:14–41—the full account of Peter's great sermon at Pentecost.

Just as Jesus did biblical theology on the road to Emmaus, his apostles did biblical theology as well.

In Acts 2, Peter delivered a sermon to the crowd at Pentecost, just after the Holy Spirit had descended with power on the disciples, enabling them to share the gospel with people in many different languages. In this sermon, Peter used Old Testament Scriptures—specifically the Psalms and the words of the prophet Joel—to show what was really happening: God's promised Spirit was being poured out as Joel promised would happen in conjunction with David's descendant being raised from the dead and crowned as King (Ps. 16).

This, then, is another key passage for helping us see that biblical theology, according to Jesus *and* his apostles, is a good, right, and legitimate way to study the Bible. In fact, according to Peter, it is really the *only* way to understand the Bible correctly. We do not "get" Joel unless we see how his words were fulfilled on the day of Pentecost. We do not "get" David, in Psalm 16, if we do not see the beautiful way that his words were fulfilled in the death and resurrection of Jesus Christ.

Peter, an apostle, gives us another clear foundation for biblical theology in his wonderful sermon in Acts 2.

Old Testament "Pointers"

We can find a third important foundation for biblical theology through studying a passage from the book of Hebrews. In Hebrews 8, you will see that even the pictures, roles, and practices of the Old Testament are meant to point forward to the role and work of Jesus Christ as the Messiah.

📖 READ!

Read Hebrews 8—a rich passage that explains the priestly ministry of Jesus by contrasting it with the priestly ministry of the Levites in the Old Testament.

We could have selected any one of a great number of passages from Hebrews to illustrate this foundation for biblical theology. This book gives many examples of the ways that Old Testament pictures, practices, and roles ultimately point forward to the far greater work of Jesus Christ as the great Savior and King of God's people. In fact, the whole message of the book of Hebrews could be summed up as "Jesus is *better.*" He is better than all the systems of the Levitical priesthood, and his death is better than any other sacrifice that has ever been made!

In other words, the biblical theological foundation that we can take from Hebrews 8 is that not only did Jesus and his apostles do biblical theology, but the pictures and roles of the Old Testament *themselves* demand a more perfect fulfillment in the work of Jesus Christ, God's Son.

In this specific passage, we see the author of Hebrews (whom we cannot identify) showing us this principle in the concept and role of the Levitical priesthood of the Old Testament. He describes Jesus as the true "high priest" of God's people—the one who is "seated at the right hand" of God in heaven (Heb. 8:1). We learn about Jesus's priesthood through the role of human priests throughout history, who offered sacrifices to God for the sins of his people. Their work was meant to be a picture of Jesus's final and perfect work as the great high priest of God's people. Here is how the author of Hebrews puts it: "They [human priests] serve a copy and shadow of the heavenly things" (v. 5). He is arguing that the Old Testament priesthood was *intentionally* set up by

God to partly resemble the final saving work of Jesus Christ, the true high priest and final sacrifice for God's people.

So in light of Hebrews 8, we should look at passages from the Old Testament with the following assumptions:

- *God intentionally designed Old Testament rituals to point us to Christ.* This is clearly the argument of the author of Hebrews. The way that God set up the Levitical priesthood was not random. It was meant to show us our need for Christ's work and to teach God's people about the final salvation that was coming in God's Son.
- *We can learn more about Christ and his work by understanding the Old Testament.* A careful study of the priestly duties and functions can teach us about what Jesus accomplished for sinners on the cross.
- *Therefore, all of Scripture is valuable for showing us the beauty of the gospel.* This point flows out of the last one—biblical theology reminds us that every part of the Bible is valuable. It is all from God, and it is all meant to show us Christ in all his beauty, glory, and saving work.

So Hebrews teaches us about the Old Testament pictures *themselves.* Along with the prophecies and predictions, they are meant to make Christ visible and real to us as we read and study them.

The Unity of the Bible

There is one final foundation for biblical theology that we should consider: the connection between the way the Bible begins and the way it ends. This connection is yet another "proof" for the legitimacy of the discipline of biblical theology.

READ!

Read Revelation 21:9–22:5.

This passage from Revelation gives us a picture of the very good end of God's great story. It shows us the final dwelling place of God with his redeemed people—the holy city, also described as the new heaven and new earth, a perfect, eternal place.

As we examine this passage, one interesting point that surfaces is how so much of it is connected to all that has come before in the biblical story. Consider the following pictures that appear both in Revelation and earlier in the Bible:

- The *tree of life* shows up in the holy city (Rev. 22:2). We remember that tree from Genesis 2; God planted it in the garden of Eden, and Adam and Eve ate freely of it before the fall. After the fall, though, they were prevented from eating its fruit. At the end of the story, then, the tree returns, and God's people can eat of it again.
- The *river* shows up again, flowing through the eternal city of God (Rev. 22:1–2). We remember that there were glorious rivers flowing through the garden of Eden (Gen. 2:10–14), watering the plants and giving life to all the creatures that lived there. Here is another connection between the beginning and the end of this great story.
- The temple also shows up at the end (Rev. 21:22). But it is not a physical temple, as in the days of Solomon. In fact, there is no temple at all in this heavenly city; God himself is the temple, because he dwells with and relates directly to his people. In a way, the entire city has become God's great temple—his great meeting place with his people.

So as we look at how the ending of the Bible story contains pictures that we can gather along the way, we begin to again see an important foundation for biblical theology: the Bible story ends in a way that relates to all of what has come before. There are echoes of Genesis in Revelation, as well as pictures and events that remind us of every part of the story of God's saving work in the lives of his people in the world.

When we read Revelation in this way and see how it is so closely connected with all that has come before in the Bible story (Old Testament and New Testament), it is not very difficult to see that the Bible really does come to us as one unified story of God's great saving work in the world, a work that is centered on his Son, Jesus Christ. The Bible ends with echoes of how it began; this is God's great story, and it hangs together perfectly.

Luke 24, Acts 2, Hebrews 8, and Revelation 21–22 offer us solid foundations for biblical theology. Hopefully you have been encouraged by seeing how Jesus and his apostles understood the Old Testament as pointing forward to the saving work of Christ, with the Bible as one connected story of God's great redemption plan!

THE VALUE OF BIBLICAL THEOLOGY

Now that we have considered some foundations of biblical theology, we should consider why this approach to understanding the Scriptures is worthwhile. We will discuss the value of biblical theology as a discipline.

READ!

Read Luke 4:16–30—the account of Jesus teaching in the synagogue at his hometown of Nazareth.

In general, biblical theology can be contrasted with two other forms of theology that scholars practice:

- *Systematic theology* is "systematized," usually through categories of organization. Students of systematic theology choose a certain doctrine—the church, for example—and seek to form a systematic theology of it by looking at many Scripture passages that teach about the doctrine of the church. They are not necessarily concerned with the progressive revealing of the salvation of God or the unfolding story of the Bible. They are forming doctrines, organized in categories.
- *Historical theology* traces theological developments of thought throughout the centuries. Historical theologians usually become very well acquainted with theological viewpoints at different times in the history of the church. They study key figures such

as Augustine, John Calvin, and Martin Luther, and they seek to understand the development of theological thought over time.

While both systematic and historical theology are incredibly valuable, biblical theology offers some uniquely valuable benefits. Here are just a few:

- Biblical theology is most helpful in understanding the "big picture" of the storyline of the Bible. Since biblical theological study moves through the Bible from Genesis to Revelation, it offers the best opportunity to get to know Scripture as it developed.
- Biblical theology allows us to study the Bible as it is revealed to us—not in systematic categories, but in books—in one developing story.
- Biblical theology helps students see the centrality of the gospel in not just the New Testament but all of Scripture.
- Biblical theology helps us remember that the Bible tells the unified story of the work of one God in one world throughout all of history.

As you can see, there are some unique benefits to the particular discipline that we are engaging with in this book.

THE "JOURNEY" OF BIBLICAL THEOLOGY

Biblical theology is indeed a discipline. In order to practice it well, you need to have a picture of the full "journey" that you must take, especially if you wish to avoid certain pitfalls.

READ!

Read John 5:39.

Even some Bible scholars who believe deeply in the inspiration of Scripture find fault with people who "get to Jesus" from the Old Testament in ways that do "damage" to the history of the Bible—the actual places, people, and situations that are described. Not every tree in the Old Testament points to the cross, and just because something in an Old Testament story is described as "red" doesn't mean it's a specific prophecy about the blood of Jesus. Some people have sought to find Jesus in ways that illegitimately twist the biblical text to mean things it never meant. Because of such mistakes, we are going to seek to expose some of the problematic ways that people do biblical theology by failing to make the full journey of studying the Bible faithfully, looking to the gospel, and then bringing the text to bear in a powerful way on the Christian life today.

Step 1—Text to context. The first step of the journey of good biblical theological study is traveling from the text itself to the historical and cultural context from which the text emerges. People seeking to use a passage of Scripture in biblical theology often completely ignore this step. They almost act as if Moses, David, or the ancient Israelites were not real people doing real things in real places in history; they simply move directly from the passage to Jesus Christ.

Instead, this step should involve some careful digging into the details of the text—examining the historical situation, truly understanding the story, and getting to the bottom of the reality of the passage. Until we really understand the biblical text in its context, we are not ready to see its place in the big story of the Bible.

Step 2—Context to Christ. The next step is to move from the historical context of the text itself to its ultimate fulfillment in Jesus Christ, whose death and resurrection were the very central work in human salvation, and therefore the story of the Bible. We have to make this part of the journey after we work hard to understand the historical context and situation of Old Testament passages.

The key is finding the valid road to Jesus Christ from any given text. We can abuse Old Testament passages if we just "jump" to Jesus in random ways. The goal is to see the Bible as one grand story of God's saving work in the world; identify where any specific passage is in that progressive revelation of this saving work; and trace ahead to Jesus on the trajectory that the passage itself provides. This is not always easy to do; we will work on this in this book.

Step 3—Christ to you. Finally, truly Christian biblical theology cannot stop with simply "getting to Christ." That would make it purely academic—a lecture about how the Old Testament points to Christ. The final step of biblical theology—and of Bible study in general—is to see how any given biblical text applies to the Christian life today. Does the text demand that we repent of sin? Does it require us to worship Jesus as God's perfect King? Does the text call for obedience and faithfulness to God's word? The path to Jesus that we have taken should help us see how the text should be rightly applied to our lives today as Christians. Bible study that is about knowing God, not just knowing *about* him, will always conclude with this important step.

If we fail to take this entire journey in our study of biblical theology, we will almost certainly fall into one or more mistakes when trying to understand what the Bible means. If we miss "text to context," we will ignore important historical details and end up with a generic, misleading "impression" of a text. If we miss "context to Christ," we will ignore how each story points us toward the central theme in all Scripture. And if we miss "Christ to you," we will fail to properly apply the meaning of Scripture to our lives as Christians.

BIBLICAL THEOLOGY AND THE GOSPEL

Biblical theology is especially useful for helping us understand and believe the good news of the life, death, and resurrection of Christ for God's sinful people—the gospel.

READ!

Read 1 Corinthians 15:1–4—the clear summary of the gospel that Paul preached to the Corinthians.

Many people—even many Christians—think of the gospel as the brief message that we must believe in order to get in to heaven someday. They see it as the "ABC's" of faith—the first step toward moving on to bigger and better aspects of the Christian life. But as we look at Scripture, especially through the lens of biblical theology, we begin to see that the gospel—the good news of God's salvation through Jesus Christ—is much bigger than the ABC's of faith. The gospel is huge; it is the center of the Christian faith and life! That's why biblical theology is so helpful; it helps us better understand the gospel, which helps us live the Christian life more faithfully.

Here are a few ways that biblical theology can help expand and inform our understanding of this "big" gospel.

Biblical theology explains the fullness *of the gospel.* We would not fully understand the amazing nature of Jesus's sacrifice on the cross if we did not have all the records of the blood sacrifices of animals in books like Exodus and Leviticus. We would not understand the fullness of God's wrath against sin that was poured out on Christ if we did not have evidence of his wrath in the great flood or his judgment on Sodom and Gomorrah. We would not as fully understand our guilt before God if we did not have the witness of the prophet Hosea, whose unfaithful wife was a vivid picture of the religious "whoring" of God's people after idols and sinful practices. The Old Testament, when studied in a biblical theological way, shows us the fullness of the gospel of Jesus Christ, revealing all that he fulfilled through his death for sin and his resurrection from the dead.

Biblical theology explains the centrality *of the gospel.* A careful study of the progressive revealing of God's saving work in the world begins to show us how central the gospel must be to a right understanding of all of Scripture. Through a biblical theological perspective, we begin to see that the Old Testament cannot be rightly understood without its proper fulfillment in—and connection to—the gospel. When we see the Bible as one connected story written by God and focusing on the climax of his work in Jesus Christ, we begin to see how every part of this story ultimately makes sense only as it relates to Jesus. There is simply no other way of bringing together the sixty-six books of the Bible; they make sense as they center around the life, death, and resurrection of Christ.

Biblical theology explains the progressive revealing *of the mystery of the gospel.* Finally, the discipline of biblical theology makes sense of the way in which God reveals the mystery of his gospel progressively— that is, in gradual steps throughout history. While salvation comes by faith alone at every point of history (we see this in Abraham, who was counted "righteous" by God simply by believing his word; Rom. 4:3), the fullness of God's salvation in Jesus the Messiah has been gradually revealed and made clearer and clearer over time. The best way to really understand this process, and to study each point along the way, is to engage Scripture through the discipline of biblical theology.

Hopefully, as you study biblical theology in this book, you will under-stand the gospel in a fuller and clearer way than you ever have before.

BIBLICAL THEOLOGY AND PERSONAL BIBLE STUDY

Not only can biblical theology expand, broaden, and explain a right view of the gospel of Jesus Christ, it can have a powerful and real ef-fect on you—in your personal study and reading of the Bible. The goal of this book, you see, is not simply to help you grow in an academic understanding of the Bible. It is for you personally to grow in your understanding of your part in God's story and saving plan.

◣ READ!

Read Psalm 16—the psalm that Peter referenced in his sermon in Acts 2, the source for your memory verses for this chapter.

Biblical theology should have an impact on *you*—the way you read the Bible and apply it to your life in the right ways. What specific effects should we expect as we become more familiar with biblical theology?

Biblical theology helps you "put the Bible together." For many Christians (and perhaps for you), the Bible appears to be a collection of books that have been bound up together in the same cover but have no apparent connection with one another. It can almost seem ridiculous that the book of Judges is bound in the same book as the Gospel of John!

But biblical theology helps you "put the Bible together" in a unified way in your mind and heart. Tracing the story of God's work in the world, culminating in Jesus Christ, helps you understand the connections between Judges and John—and all the other books. Studying the Bible as one story with one author and one hero helps you see the unity of Scripture; this, in turn helps you better understand each part, as well.

Biblical theology shows you Jesus in all of Scripture. Biblical theology also helps us see how every part of the Bible either points to or explains Jesus—in his life, death, and resurrection. When we take seriously what Jesus says in Luke 24 (and John 5:39—look it up!), we begin to see that the Old Testament accounts truly demand the work of Jesus with anticipation; they show us the need for redemption, forgiveness, and salvation. In fact, some of them even foreshadow what Christ's work would look like! Biblical theology helps us see each part of the Bible in its proper role in the development of God's revelation of the mystery of salvation through his Son.

Biblical theology places you in the story. Finally, the study of biblical theology best helps you—as a follower of God today—place yourself as part of this same story of God's work in the world, a work that has been going on since his creation of Adam and Eve. Through studying the Bible as one great story, with one author and one Savior, we begin to see our own place in that story. We are living in the same scene of the story—the scene I'm calling "God's Church" (see chaps. 13–14)— as God's people who followed Jesus during the first days of the early church. Through faith in Jesus Christ, we can become part of the people that God has formed through all times and in all places. We begin to realize that we really can know and worship the God of Abraham and Moses, and that we will share eternal life with Jacob, David, and Daniel.

Hopefully you now see the difference that biblical theology can make for you as you read and study the Bible on your own. It really can change the way you look at God's word!

REVIEW

In this chapter, we've sought to be clear on our definition of biblical theology as contrasted with other theological disciplines. We've seen Jesus's own use of biblical theology, along with that of the apostles, who all viewed God's word as one big unified story with a climax in the person and work of Christ. Christians can have confidence in God's inspired word, knowing that it is given to us by God as one united story of his redeeming work in the world through Christ. It's good—and legitimate—to study the Bible in this way.

⬤ PRAY!

As you close this chapter with prayer, talk to God along the following lines:

- Thank *him for his word, which really is one unified story of his redemptive work in the world through his Son.*
- Praise *him for revealing his salvation to sinful human beings so that they can accept him and be part of his people.*
- Ask *him to help you in further understanding the Bible and the central work of Jesus Christ.*

THE OLD TESTAMENT

Chapter 2

GOD'S CREATION AND A CRISIS
PART 1

It's time now for us to begin moving through the scenes of God's big story—the story of redemption that is told throughout the pages of Scripture. While Scripture itself never states how many of these scenes there are and doesn't use them to organize itself, we are going to look at eight divisions in the story of the Bible.

In this chapter and the next one, we will dig into the first of these scenes: "God's Creation and a Crisis." As you can imagine, we will be studying the first three chapters of Genesis in the following pages as we seek to get a sense of where and how this whole story begins. If you have not studied Genesis in detail before, this will be an opportunity for you to get to know the beginning of the Bible story in a new way. If you have studied Genesis previously, hopefully this study will help you go even deeper in your understanding of this book.

Remember!

Your suggested memory verses for this chapter come from Genesis 1:26–27—the account of God's creation of human beings:

Then God said, "Let us make man in our image, after our likeness. And let them have dominion over the fish of the sea and over the birds of the heavens and over the livestock and over all the earth and over every creeping thing that creeps on the earth."

> *So God created man in his own image,*
> *in the image of God he created him;*
> *male and female he created them. (Gen. 1:26–27)*

OUR STARTING POINT

The starting point of the book of Genesis is important for us as we study the Bible. You see, the fact that the Bible begins with the creation of the world by God gives us a very important foundational truth. The account of creation sets God up as the Creator; everything else in the big story of his work in the world flows out of this foundational truth.

READ!

Read Genesis 1:1–2.

Think about a few important implications of the truth that God is the Creator:

The Creator/creature distinction. Perhaps the most basic acknowledgment that humans can make as they seek to relate to God is that he is the Creator and they are his creatures. In other words, creation sets up the great truth that God is the Creator and we are not. There is a huge distinction between everything that has been created—including human beings—and the infinitely wise and powerful Creator of the universe. Before a man or woman can begin to get to know God, he or she must start with this basic admission: "I have been created by God."

God as King. As we will see from the rest of the Bible story, the doctrine of creation sets God up as the rightful King of the universe. Many times in Scripture, God reminds his people of his creation of the world—and of the fact that this makes him the true and rightful King of it. As the Creator, God alone decides the purpose of this world and the calling of the human beings he has made. No one else can claim the right to rule over this world. The Creator, very naturally, holds all the rights as King and ruler over what he has chosen to create.

Humans as dependent. Finally, the doctrine of creation means that humans, as created beings, are ultimately dependent on their Creator for everything. They are obviously dependent on him for their very existence; they did not create themselves but were made by God for his perfect purpose. But human beings also depend on God for life—both on earth and for eternity, if God so wishes to grant that amazing gift to human beings. The doctrine of creation sets up God as the one on whom all human beings ultimately depend—for life, meaning, and salvation.

So there is a distinction between God and his creation. Creation means that God is the rightful King of all the world. And creation reminds us that humans depend on God for life now and for eternal life to come. These are extremely important starting points as we begin piecing together the entire story of the Bible.

THE ETERNAL CREATOR GOD

Now that we have considered some of the big implications of the doctrine of creation, let's focus in on verse 1 of Genesis 1 and think about what it means for the reality and eternality of the person of God. Then we need to ponder what his eternal existence means for us as we begin to seek to approach him in worship—that is, to seek a relationship with him through his Son, Jesus Christ.

READ!

Read Genesis 1:1 and Revelation 4 in light of the idea of the eternal existence of God, and the praise and worship that this truth demands.

Genesis begins with these words: "In the beginning, God . . ." This simple introduction to the book—and to the entire Bible—reminds us of an incredibly significant fact: the God who created this world and us has existed forever in glory, splendor, and power.

Think about this for a moment. There has never been a time—ever—that God has not existed. There was a time when you did not yet exist. There was a time when this entire world—the whole universe—did not exist. God, though, is eternal; he has always existed in his perfect being, glory, and holiness. This concept is far beyond our capacity as humans to completely grasp.

In the beginning, before anything existed, God was there; he chose to create the universe, the reality that we know and see all around us. So what does this mean for us as we begin our study of the big story of the Bible?

God has existed eternally as the same *God.* First, it means that God has always been the same; he has not changed throughout time but has eternally existed as exactly the same God. The Bible reveals him to us as one God in three persons—the Father, the Son, and the Holy Spirit. God has eternally existed in this way, and always will.

This idea that God never changes will become very important for us as we begin to study the Old Testament accounts of God's dealings with his people. We will need to remember that the same God who spoke to Moses and Abraham is the God who invites us to know him and worship him through faith in Christ!

God has life within himself. Next, the truth of God's eternality means that he has life within himself. No one gives life to God; he exists completely on his own. This is a difficult concept to grasp because this is true of no other being in the universe, including Satan and all the angels. God is the only being who does not depend on *any* other factor for his existence. He has existed from eternity as who he is, having life within himself, and in perfect harmony as one God in three persons.

God does not need us. This truth flows out of the last one. If God has existed eternally with life within himself, and with perfect harmony within the Trinity, then it follows that God does not need us. He did not choose to create the heavens, the earth, and human beings because of some deficiency in his existence or because he was lonely! God is completely self-sufficient—"happy" and full of life within himself. It must be that God chose to create simply for his own glory—out of the overflow of his own goodness and pleasure, which he possessed before the universe began.

We need God. This all means, of course, that while God does not need us, we desperately need him. We are finite beings; because of sin (which we will study soon in Genesis 3), we get sick, grow old, and die. Our only hope on this earth is to find a way to know this glorious Creator and to be saved through a relationship with him. Human beings desperately need this salvation. The amazing promise that we will learn as we study the Bible is that God truly offers this salvation to the humans he has created.

CREATION *EX NIHILO*

Now let's expand our focus to the first two verses of Genesis 1 as we ponder the concept of God's creation out of nothing. It is important to realize that God created the world in this way—not from pre-existing materials, but out of nothing at all. This points us again to the amazing power and glory of the God who made us.

▉ READ!

Read Genesis 1:1–2, as well as Hebrews 11:3.

The important and fundamental truth that Genesis 1—and Hebrews 11—teach is that when God created the world, he made it out of *nothing*. This doctrine is often referred to as creation *ex nihilo*, or "out of nothing." It means that when God created the universe, he did not use any materials that were "lying around" in order to form things. He literally made physical things—tangible reality—appear out of nothing. God created the world completely out of "thin air"—although there was not even air before the world existed!

Genesis 1:2 says that the earth was "without form and void." This is probably just a way of saying that there was simply nothing there except for God. Nothing had shape; there was no reality or substance in the universe apart from God.

Like the eternal existence of God, this is a concept that is simply too difficult for us to even imagine. No matter how hard we try, our human minds cannot fully grasp the idea of complete nothingness. That's why the author of Hebrews tells us that it is a matter of "faith" to believe that God indeed created the world in this way (Heb. 11:3).

These truths lead to two important questions:

How did God create the world? He did not create it with his "hands" or with any pre-existing materials. The Genesis creation account, as well as Hebrews, tells us this important truth: God created the universe by the power of his *word* (Gen. 1:3; Heb. 11:3). God *spoke* the world into existence. This simple but profound truth has incredible implications for the rest of the story of the Bible, especially as it relates to the power and effectiveness of God's word. We serve a God who commanded reality to become real. His word is incredibly powerful; it has *creative* power.

Why is ex nihilo *important?* This doctrine is crucial because it reminds us that nothing preceded God in existence—no physical beings or tangible objects. *Ex nihilo* means that everything that exists ultimately has its origin and source in God himself. He is the true beginning of all things—visible and invisible. The entire universe, including human beings, came from the powerful and creative word of the eternally existent and all-powerful God. If we do not start at this point, we will not have a good chance of understanding much of the Bible story at all!

In the next section of this chapter, we will move into the actual account of creation, as we see the way God spoke the world into existence by his great power.

GOD CREATES BY SPEAKING

So far, we've considered Genesis 1:1 and 2. In Genesis 1:3–25, which you will read in a moment, you will see creation taking shape, as God "speaks" all of it into existence. As the "days" of creation continue, you will see God giving more and more shape to his world—filling it with living things, and bringing organization to the way in which it all will work together. Hopefully you will see the beauty and wisdom of this great Creator, which is taught in this passage of Scripture and still reflected in our world today.

READ!

Read Genesis 1:1–25—the account of the first five days of creation.

As you have seen, Genesis 1 leaves no doubt as to who is the sovereign author of creation. It is God, who created all things according to his wise plan and powerful word. Now we will simply look at some important points that this passage teaches us, then touch briefly on the issue of the interpretation of the days of creation.

- God's creation by his word. As I have mentioned before, it is essential that we notice the manner in which God created every part of his world. He did it with his *word*. At every step along the way, the repeated refrain is "And God said . . ." (Gen. 1:3, 6, 9, 11, 14, 20, 24). God did not even need to get his hands dirty as he created the world. He is so powerful that he can speak reality—the physical universe—into existence. This is truly a great God, the rightful King of all.

- God's wisdom and order. Notice, too, the amazing order that God displayed as he created the world. He carefully, with great wisdom, separated the land from the waters in the perfect places and ratios (Gen. 1:9) and ordained the "lights" in the "expanse of the heavens" (Gen. 1:14) to have their proper places and times. God, we see, engages in careful planning and wise ordering of every detail of his creation.

- God's authority and power. As the account of God's creation goes on, we see that he was completely in control of every aspect. He spoke and things happened. Lights appeared in the heavens; waters swarmed with living creatures; animals began to fill the earth. God is the one with all authority and power in every inch of creation. He is sovereign, powerful, and completely in control.

One common point of debate about this first chapter of the Bible is the precise meaning of the days of creation. Some people insist that these days were literal twenty-four-hour periods. Others hold that we have freedom to accept that the days may have been time periods or ages. The Hebrew word that is translated as "day" here does have a range of meanings; it can refer to literal twenty-four-hour days or periods of time (such as the "day" of Noah, the time period in which Noah lived). Many people hold to the "day-age" theory because it seems to fit more closely with scientific studies that describe an older earth.

Whatever Christians believe concerning the meaning of these days, clearly the Genesis account describes the real physical creation of the world by God out of nothing. There is certainly no room for any evolutionary understanding of creation in this account! God created the world from nothing, and he did it by the power of his word.

THE GOODNESS OF CREATION

As you read Genesis 1:1–25, you may have noticed that one little phrase accompanies every step in God's creation of the world. Let's now focus in on that phrase. As we do, we will work hard to see the implications of the great truth that is revealed through this phrase and apply it to life in this world today.

READ!

Read Genesis 1:1–25 again.

The phrase I'm talking about first shows up in Genesis 1:10 and is repeated again and again as God continues his creation of the world (vv. 12, 18, 21, 25). Did you see it? Here it is: "And God saw that it was good." As God completed each aspect of creation, he looked at it and declared it "good." We should take this repetition seriously and consider deeply its implications for the way we think about this world. Here are just a few of these implications:

God created this world with beauty and care. We live in a world that was not "thrown together" haphazardly by a God who was trying to make something in a hurry. The fact that God stopped, admired his creation, and called it good tells us that he made it with great care, great attention to detail, and great beauty. God was very intentional about his creation; he took great care to make it exactly as he intended.

God was pleased with his creation. From this repeated phrase, we see that God was very pleased with his creation in its perfect and good beginning (before sin). He had created it, as we have discussed before, not from any need that he had for companionship or entertainment; yet he did delight in the world that he had made.

The world reflects the character of God in some way. Finally, we should see that since God called the world good, creation itself reflects his character, beauty, and order, at least in some way. We will study the uniqueness and distinctiveness of human beings from all the rest of creation; no other animal, plant, or living creature is described as being made in the "image of God." Still, the very fact that creation is described as good tells us that God left his mark on it. Everything that is good ultimately has its foundation in God himself; he is the source of all true goodness. So it makes sense that this world itself—especially in its prefall state—contained echoes of God's goodness and love in its various parts.

Of course, as we will study soon, Adam and Eve fell, and brought sin into this good world that God had created. This creation no longer is good in the perfect way that it once was, after God first made it. Still, even this fallen world can show us glimpses of the beauty, wisdom, and love of its Creator.

GOD CREATES HUMAN BEINGS

We have explored the concept of the "goodness" of God's creation and considered the implications of this goodness as we thought about how God's character is reflected in his good world. Now we will move on to the sixth day of creation, which records God's creation of human beings. Something changes here in the narrative, which signals something very different about the living creatures that God creates in this account. We will examine the uniqueness of human beings—their distinctiveness from the rest of God's physical creation.

READ!

Read Genesis 1:26–27.

Over five days, God put together a magnificent earth—glorious heavens above and land and waters below, filled with all kinds of plants and living creatures ("beasts" of the earth, according to Gen. 1:25). Then a change happened in the creation process. Things seemed to slow down. There are a few indications that something different was happening here:

- God spoke to himself; the holy Trinity (God the Father, God the Son, and God the Holy Spirit) conversed and decided to make a creature that would be far different than the others on the earth. God began: "Let us . . ." (Gen. 1:26).
- God set human beings apart from the rest of creation by giving them "dominion" over everything else (Gen. 1:26). We will discuss this concept more soon.
- The Genesis account even gives us a kind of "poem" (Gen. 1:27), which records how God created man in his own "image"—another concept that we will discuss in more detail soon.

So at this point in the Genesis narrative, we have key signs that the creation of man is different—human beings are set apart in significant ways from the rest of God's creation. What must we make of this? We must see, to begin with, that:

- Human beings are *special.* I do not mean special in a "feel-good" way—the way parents tell their toddlers that they are special. I mean that humans—in a way that differs from every other part of God's creation—are special and dear to him. God actively and personally engaged in the creation of human beings in a unique way.
- Human beings are *unique.* No matter what scientists tell us today about evolution, the intelligence of apes and dolphins, or the animal instincts of human beings, the witness of Scripture (and of our experience, of course), is that people are unique in all of creation. No other animals were given the same special attention by God during creation as human beings. They are distinct from the animal world—set apart by the Creator God as uniquely intelligent and designed beings.
- Human beings are the *focal point* of God's creation. It is significant that human beings were the final step in God's creation—the crowning act of his creative work in the world. God made them last—on the sixth day—and gave them dominion over everything

else that he had already created. The Genesis account makes it clear that while humans are certainly creatures, God has a special—eternal—purpose for them that he does not have for any other living creature that he made.

We will talk more in the next pages about the image of God in human beings, as well as the dominion and commands that God gave to them as he created them and set them on earth.

THE *IMAGO DEI*

During our study of Genesis 1:26–27, we could not help but begin to engage with the concept of God's "image" in human beings. While our discussion was focused on the uniqueness of human beings, their distinctiveness from the rest of creation, the idea of the image of God loomed over the passage.

It is this amazing reality—human beings as creatures made in the "image of God"—that we will examine carefully now. Our goal will be to understand this concept biblically as well as we can and begin to consider the amazing implications of it for the way we understand human beings and their intentional design by the infinitely wise Creator.

READ!

Read Genesis 1:26–27 again, and then read Psalm 8 as well.

In Genesis 1, the first statement that we see about the image of God in human beings comes in verse 26. God says, "Let us make man in our image, after our likeness." Then, in the summary "poem" in verse 27, the author of Genesis makes it clear that human beings—as male and female—are created in God's image.

It is important to note, as we begin this discussion about the image of God (the *imago Dei*), that there is much debate and discussion about the precise meaning of this phrase and concept. Here are just a few of the different takes on the meaning of the image of God in human beings:

- Some have equated the image of God with *rationality*—the fact that human beings are capable of higher thinking, and in this way are set apart from every other living creature on earth.
- Some, on the basis of Genesis 1:27, have equated the image of God with *gender*. They would make the case that the creation of human beings as male and female is a way that God has reflected the distinct roles and relationships within the Trinity in human relationships.
- Some claim that the image of God has to do with our *ability to create*—that our creative impulses reflect the God who made this world from nothing, and who values beauty, artistry, and order.

Most likely, the concept of the image of God in human beings is some combination of all these amazing truths.

What does the text of Genesis tell us that would help us understand what it means that human beings are made in the image of God? First, it tells us that God decided to make people in his "likeness" (Gen. 1:26). This does not mean that we literally resemble God physically. But it does mean that we reflect him in some ways (not perfectly, of course). Second, the text of Genesis tells us that human beings as "male and female" are created in the image of God. While this certainly means that both men and women carry the *imago Dei*, it probably also implies that something about our gender—and our relationships with one another—reflects the relationships and distinctions of the Trinity.

Probably the best way to summarize the concept of the image of God is to say simply that human beings "reflect" the character and reality of God in significant ways. We are not exactly like him, of course, but our personalities, capacities, and relationships point to him. Think about just a few ways that this is certainly true:

- Human beings have the capacity to *love* deeply, in a way that no other creature on earth can do.
- Human beings have the capacity for *spiritual* thought and devotion; monkeys, for example, do not worship!

- Human beings have great capacity for *reasoning* and *abstract thought*; in this way, we certainly reflect the image of the mind of God, at least in small ways.
- Human beings love *beauty* and *creativity*; think of all the paintings and works of art that humans have created over the centuries, imitating God (in a small way) in his creative work.

In many ways, human beings truly reflect the beauty and wisdom of their Creator. He has placed his image in these creatures he has made. This gives us a hint that he has something eternally wonderful planned for people. We will see this as the big story of the Bible continues.

HUMANS' ROLE IN CREATION

The final verses of Genesis 1 tell us how God "wrapped up" day six of creation. He gave a charge to human beings, giving them "dominion" in the world he had made. Our goal is to understand this charge clearly and to explore the concept of dominion that is put forward here.

READ!

Read Genesis 1:28–31—the passage that contains God's charge to the human beings he created regarding their dominion over his world and their role in it.

We learned earlier that human beings were set apart from the rest of creation—made in God's image and unique from all other living creatures. After he made them, God gave a charge to these special and unique creatures he had created. Let's study the nature of this charge and its implications for the way we view human beings and God's world today. What do we see from Genesis 1:28–31?

God charged human beings to increase the human race. First, God gave Adam and Eve the instruction to "multiply" and fill the earth (Gen. 1:28). God's goal in the creation of human beings was obviously for them to create a great race of people for his own glory and pleasure. This creation mandate from God is a good thing. From the beginning, God wanted human beings to create more human beings in order to fill the earth with people made in his image.

God charged human beings to have dominion over the earth. The second part of God's charge can be a bit more difficult to understand. God called human beings to "subdue" the earth and have "dominion" over all the other living creatures (Gen. 1:28). This is a theme that King David picks up on later in Scripture—in the psalm that you read earlier. David cries out, "You have given him [man] dominion over the works of your hands; you have put all things under his feet" (Ps. 8:6). This means:

- Human beings have a special role in ruling and reigning over this world that God has made. It is not wrong for people to rule the earth; this is a task that God has given especially to human beings, who are made in his image.
- Human beings should see themselves as "stewards"—servants of the King—in relation to the world this King has created. They are tasked with ruling it well and caring for it.
- God really does value human beings far above the rest of the physical creation. Human beings are more important to God than animals or than any other part of this earth. For that reason, he has placed them above it all.

As I noted just above, human beings are called to rule this world in loving and careful ways. Far too often, humans have sinfully abused this world; they have ruled it selfishly and wastefully. Yet the rule and dominion of human beings over the earth is God's idea. That is how he designed the world to function, and this design is a good thing.

The call for Christians, then, as they consider this charge from God to human beings, is to rule and have dominion over this earth in ways that honor the Creator. God has given this world to them, and they are to use it well, respect it, and remember that one King—one Creator—stands over them.

GOD'S REST

One final "day" of creation is mentioned in the Genesis account: the seventh day. As we think about what happened on this final day, we will consider the concept of God's "rest" from his work of creation, and the implications of this rest for us today as followers of this amazing God.

READ!

Read Genesis 2:1–3—the account of the seventh day of creation, when God rested from his work of making the world.

God did all of his work of creation during the first six days of the creation "week," then set aside the seventh day to rest. The brief passage that you read tells us this day ended with God proclaiming a blessing on the seventh day and making it "holy"—set apart for him.

It is important to understand what exactly was going on during this day of rest that God took at the end of his creative work in the world. What does it mean that God rested? How does the principle of rest operate in the remainder of the Bible story?

The meaning. The fact that God used the seventh day for rest does *not* mean that he was tired and needed to take a break from his creation work. He was not worn out by creating the world; remember, he had simply "spoken" all things into existence.

When Genesis says that God rested, it simply means that he intentionally *stopped* his work of creation. In other words, God finished his creative work. God is still working in many ways, but after the sixth day ended, God really ceased to create. So he rested from his work of creation when this world was complete (and "very good" in his eyes; Gen. 1:31).

The Sabbath. In the time of the Old Testament, when God's people, the Israelites, lived under the law of Moses, the day of rest became an important principle that guided their lives and worship. Since God rested on the seventh day of his creation, he commanded his people to take a day of rest from their work each week—a "holy" day that would be devoted not only to rest but also to the worship of their God (Ex. 20:11). You have probably read about the "Sabbath" day—and possibly even about the debates that Jesus had with the Pharisees about this day! The Sabbath principle came from God and was given to his people to guide the rhythms of their lives and give them space to rest and worship him.

"Rest" in the Bible. There is something very interesting in the creation story that we must not miss. Do you remember the phrase that wrapped up each of the previous days of creation? It was this: "And there was evening and there was morning, the _____ day" (Gen. 1:5, 8, 13, 19, 23, 31). Does that phrase appear after the description of the seventh day? No, it does not! Why is this?

The absence of this phrase must mean that we are still *living in the seventh day of creation.* God is still resting from his creation work; he is dwelling in the seventh day even now.

The book of Hebrews picks up on this theme by talking about the permanent "Sabbath rest" of God (Heb. 4:1), which we enter only by resting, by faith, in his Son. The author of Hebrews uses this picture to talk about God's eternal peace and salvation, which he gives to his redeemed people out of the overflow of his own peace and rest. To put faith in God is to enter, spiritually, into his eternal "rest."

So as we consider the passage from Genesis, we ought to understand that the God we serve is resting, even now, from his work of creating the world. He is dwelling in infinite holiness and perfect rest. By God's grace, we can enter this state of rest through faith in Jesus Christ.

The principle of rest for us. We who follow Jesus today are not under the law of Moses. This Old Testament law shows us God's holiness and should expose our sin and drive us to Christ Jesus as Savior and Lord. But we are not called to follow all of the Sabbath laws and customs as the Jewish believers were in the days of Moses.

Still, there is a good practical principle for us that comes from this Genesis account. As God gave his law to his people in the Old Testament, he commanded them to take a Sabbath day of rest in order to set aside time to worship him (Ex. 20:8–11). We, too, should make sure that we are setting aside intentional time—resting from our work—to engage in the holy worship of Jesus Christ our Lord.

Many Christians today see this Sabbath principle fulfilled in the "Lord's Day"—usually Sunday—a day when they gather with other believers in Jesus to rest from work and to worship God through singing, prayer, the preaching of the Bible, and the celebration of the sacraments.

REVIEW

In this chapter, we've started with the fundamental truths of the Bible's story: God is the almighty Creator of all things, including human beings, whom he made in his image and for his glory. As Creator and King, God defines what is right and good for all his creation. The story of the Bible begins there—and so must we as we seek to get a sense of the big picture of Scripture.

● PRAY!

As you close this chapter in prayer, ask God to remind you of his power and authority, which are demonstrated by his creation. Pray that you would remember that, as Creator, he is also the great King of all the earth. He is to be worshiped, followed, and obeyed in everything.

Chapter 3

GOD'S CREATION AND A CRISIS
PART 2

After reading about God's creation of the world, including human beings, and his appointment of the first man and woman as his stewards over the world he had made, we encounter in Genesis a beautiful picture of what life was like in the garden of Eden, the center of God's good and perfect creation. Sadly, that picture soon became distorted when sin entered the world—the "crisis" in this scene of the Bible story. As we study these events, I hope you will see more clearly the grace, generosity, and holiness of the glorious Creator of this world.

Remember!
Your suggested memory verses for this chapter are Genesis 2:23–25—the conclusion of the account of God's creation of Eve as a helper for Adam.

Then the man said,

> *"This at last is bone of my bones*
> *and flesh of my flesh;*
> *she shall be called Woman,*
> *because she was taken out of Man."*

Therefore a man shall leave his father and his mother and hold fast to his wife, and they shall become one flesh. And the man and his wife were both naked and were not ashamed. (Gen. 2:23–25)

A "RETELLING" OF CREATION

In the passage you are about to read, there seems to be a bit of a "retelling" of the creation account. In Genesis 2:4, the phrase "These are the generations . . ." is used. This phrase appears throughout the book of Genesis to introduce the different parts of the story (the "generations" of Noah, the "generations" of Abraham, etc.). So as we approach this text, we should not be too surprised to see a retelling of the pinnacle of God's creation: the forming of human beings.

READ!

Read Genesis 2:4–14—a beautiful picture of the perfect situation in which Adam and Eve lived in the very beginning, before sin entered the world.

This passage tells us that God formed Adam from the "dust" of the ground, and then "breathed into his nostrils the breath of life" (Gen. 2:7). While we do not know exactly what this means, it is certainly an action that God did not perform on any other living creature that he made. This, then, is another way in which the biblical text points to the distinctiveness of human beings from the rest of creation. When God created humans, he did it in a deeply personal way; he was intimately engaged with this "pinnacle" of his creation.

The text then goes on to show us the perfect and undamaged place that God provided for his people to live. Consider some of the descriptions of the garden of Eden that we see from this passage:

- God caused a *mist* to come up from the ground, which would water the whole earth (Gen. 2:6).
- God gave *good food* for people to eat by causing trees and plants to spring up in the garden (Gen. 2:9).
- There were *two unique trees* in the garden—the tree of life and the tree of the knowledge of good and evil (Gen. 2:9).
- God gave *rivers* that flowed through this land, as well as precious stones and gems (Gen. 2:10–14).

What is the overwhelming picture that we get as we read this account? We see the goodness of the place that God prepared for his people to live in and rule over. God intentionally and personally formed human beings in his image and set them to rule over this beautiful and perfect place. God had taken care of all the details; he had thought of everything.

It is important to note that if Adam and Eve had not sinned, they would have stayed in this place forever. But we must not get ahead of ourselves!

This passage in Genesis is meant to show us a picture of God's perfect place. As we will see much later in the story, many of the images and descriptions in this account are picked up in the description of God's perfect eternal place for his people: the new heaven and new earth, as described in the book of Revelation.

LIFE IN THE GARDEN

We sometimes wonder what life in the garden of Eden was like. What did Adam and Eve do? How did they know what they should do and not do? Genesis 2 reveals the original pattern of life that God gave to his people.

📘 READ!

Read Genesis 2:15–17—the account of the calling that God gave to Adam as he lived and worked in the garden of Eden.

The passage that we are focusing on now is a short one—just three verses. Yet it gives us some key insights into the original situation of Adam and Eve before their fall into sin. We also get a glimpse into God's great purpose for his people—a purpose that continues even now and will continue into eternity. What do we see here about Adam's call and purpose from God during these early days in the garden of Eden, before sin entered the world?

Adam was called to work. Genesis 2:15 tells us that God set Adam to work in the garden of Eden and called him to "keep" it carefully. This means that when we picture Adam in the garden, we should see him hard at work—taking care of the plants and animals, gathering food along with Eve, and enjoying the good work that God had given to him. Remember, at this point, work was enjoyable! Adam and Eve must have been thrilled with God's calling on their lives. It was good for them to have a task from God, and their work would not have been plagued with anything harmful, painful, or evil in any way. Work and play, in other words, were the *same* during those prefall days.

This is an important concept for us to grasp. God called people to work *before* the fall into sin. Work is a good thing, a gift from the Creator God. Ultimately, all human beings want to have good work that is fulfilling and enjoyable. Sadly, of course, work has now been corrupted by the fall (more on this soon).

Adam was called to live under God's word. God called Adam not just to work but also to live under the *word* of God in obedience. After the sentence that describes Adam's work in the garden, the Genesis account describes the word—the instructions—that God gave to Adam (Gen. 2:16–17). God's word was clear: Adam and Eve could eat of any tree in the garden except one—the tree of the knowledge of good and evil. They were called to obey this word of God, submitting to live under its authority and rule in their lives.

So at the beginning, God established a good pattern for his people *before* the fall: they were to do his good work as they were guided by his good word.

This pattern remains true for our lives today—and into eternity. God's people are still called to do his work as we live under the rule of his word. Life in the new heaven and earth very likely will include good work that God's people will do—with complete joy—for all eternity!

THE CREATION OF EVE

In Genesis 1:26–27, we find the account of God creating humans, both "male and female," in his image. In Genesis 2:7, we learn that God made Adam out of the dust of the ground and breathed life into him. As we come to Genesis 2:18–25, we find an account of the creation of Eve. Obviously God wants us to take his creation of human beings very seriously and to understand it well.

READ!

Read Genesis 2:18–25.

Let's seek to learn what this passage teaches us about God's design for human beings as male and female living and relating together in this world. What are some basic observations we can make from this text?

- Adam was created first. This simple fact obviously does not mean that men are more important or more valuable than women, but it is the order of creation that we find in the biblical text. The apostle Paul refers to this fact in 1 Timothy 2:13, so it has at least some importance for understanding the gender roles that God ordained.
- God created Eve from Adam (Gen. 2:21–22). This text is very clear that God took the literal flesh of Adam and used it to create Eve.

Eve came "from" the flesh of Adam; she was made of the same "stuff" as he was.

- Eve was given as a "helper" to Adam (Gen. 2:18). The passage that you read says Adam needed someone who would fit him perfectly in relationship as he worked and kept the garden of Eden. Eve was this perfect helper whom God designed for Adam.
- Eve was of the same "flesh" as Adam. Look again at Adam's joyful response to God's creation of Eve in Genesis 2:23. He declared that Eve was "flesh of my flesh." He recognized that she, like him, was fully human—made in the image of God. This allowed them to have a "one-flesh" relationship—marriage, a beautiful union between two beings made in God's likeness. We will discuss this more soon.

So what are some initial conclusions that we can draw about gender from this foundational passage of Scripture at the very beginning of the Bible? We can say, according to Genesis 2:

- Men and women are *equal* in essence. We mentioned above how Adam cried out that, at last, he had found someone who was "flesh of my flesh." Eve, then, was a human being made in God's image, just as Adam was. Women are completely *equal* with man in terms of eternal worth and in the way they reflect their Creator. There is no difference between men and women in their essence as human beings.
- Men and women have *distinctions* in roles. The account of Eve's creation begins to make clear a theme that will be developed in different parts of Scripture: men and women, while equal in essence, nevertheless have very different and distinct roles as ordained by God. This does not make one more valuable than the other; it just makes them different. Adam, for example, is never called the "helper" for Eve; that is a role that is distinct to the woman. As the Bible goes on, we get hints that this reality of

male and female (*same* in essence, *different* in role) is a reflection
of the Trinity. God the Father, God the Son, and God the Holy
Spirit are all equally *God*, yet they have very different and distinct
roles in the world.

- Men and women *complement* each other. Finally, we see that God
intends that men and women complement each other—in order
to serve and care for each other in the context of relationship. In
the very good beginning, there was no "battle of the sexes." The
purpose of distinctions was to complement—to encourage and
help each other in a perfect relationship.

God is the author of gender; it is not a human invention. He created human beings as male and female to complement each other, and
probably even to reflect the unity and distinctions that exist eternally
within the Trinity itself. As Christians, we should uphold these God-
given gender distinctions.

This passage also gives us some foundations for understanding
human marriage. Specifically, Genesis 2:18–25 tells us:

- Marriage is *God's idea*. It doesn't come fundamentally from people
but from God.
- Marriage is meant to be *between one man and one woman*. The
picture presented in Genesis 2:24 is fulfilled only as two come
together to become one flesh, made up of a man and a woman.
This was God's original and good intention, and it is still the
biblical model today.
- Marriage is the *closest human relationship*. The man and the
woman are called, in Genesis 2:24, "one flesh." This is a very
drastic and striking way to describe the unity and intimacy that
is to happen between a man and a woman in the relationship of
marriage. Marriage is a sacred union given by God. It is also a
vivid picture to help the world see the love that Jesus Christ has
for his people, the church (as we will see later).

THE FALL

You have now come to the end of the creation narrative. The earth has been made and is "very good," as God has crowned his creation with the pinnacle of his work: human beings. God has set them apart to work and keep the garden of Eden and to live under the authority and rule of his good word. This beautiful pattern is God's good intention for his creation. But then everything unravels very quickly.

READ!

Read Genesis 3:1–7—the account of the fall of Adam and Eve into sin.

Choosing Sin—and Death

In the passages that you will study for the remainder of this chapter, you are going to see the sad reality of the fall of Adam and Eve from grace into sin, as they choose disobedience and death rather than obedience to God and eternal life.

As you know, God created Adam and Eve and placed them in the garden of Eden, where they lived with good work to do. They were under the authority and rule of God's word. While God certainly talked and related much with Adam and Eve during those first days of creation, we do not have a record of all he said to them. They must have had some wonderful conversations and times together!

However, we know one thing that God said: Adam and Eve were free to eat of every tree in the garden of Eden except for the tree of the knowledge of good and evil (Gen. 2:16–17). God promised that if they ate of that tree, they would die. However, if they continued in obedience to God's word, Adam and Eve would live forever in this beautiful place, in close communion with their wonderful Creator.

But on a very sad day, Satan crept into God's good place and tempted Adam and Eve to sin. They freely chose to disobey God. Adam and Eve *both* listened to the lies of Satan (who had obviously already fallen from heaven by this point) and chose disobedience instead of obedience, death instead of life.

It is important to note that, before this sin, Adam and Eve were both sinless. They did not have sinful natures (as we do), and they were completely free to choose good or evil.

It is also important to understand, though, that this fall was bigger than just the bite of the fruit that Adam and Eve took. Look with me at all the sinful steps that led to this fall:

- Eve *engaged* with Satan's deception. This is the first problem in Genesis 3; Eve unwisely took time to have a conversation with this lying serpent. She should have sent him away the minute she saw him.
- Eve *twisted* God's word in her conversation with Satan. You will notice that, when Satan questioned God's command to Adam and Eve, Eve responded by *adding* something to God's word—she said they were not even allowed to "touch" the tree of the knowledge of good and evil (Gen. 3:3). But that was not part of God's command; he had told them only to not "eat" from it (2:17).
- Adam did not step up to *defend* God's word and his wife. In Genesis 3:6, we learn the surprising and devastating truth that Adam was "with" Eve during her entire conversation with Satan. He was right there, listening to the serpent's deception, and refusing to stand up for the goodness of God's word or for his wife.
- Adam and Eve ultimately wanted to *be God* rather than be ruled by God. This desire seems to have been Satan's greatest weapon as he tempted Adam and Eve; he held out to them special knowledge: they would become "like God" and know the difference between good and evil (Gen. 3:5). Adam and Eve did not want to submit to God's rule any longer; they wanted to be the gods of their own lives.

As you know, they chose to listen to Satan, ignore God's word, and eat the fruit that they were not allowed to eat. At that very moment, sin entered the world. Adam and Eve became aware of their nakedness, as *shame* (the first result of sin) began to infect their minds and hearts (Gen. 3:7). And they began to try to cover themselves as they felt *guilt* for the first time.

This was indeed a very sad day in God's creation—one with huge theological implications.

The Theology of the Fall

Let's now look again at this passage of Scripture with the goal of gathering some basic theological observations and principles based on this sad account. As we can see from our world and our lives today, the effect of this fall into sin was devastating and powerful in all of God's creation; we still feel its effects all around us. Therefore, it is important that we understand it thoroughly.

Here are some of the most important theological implications of what occurred in the garden of Eden on the day when Adam and Eve first disobeyed God:

Sin entered the world through Adam and Eve's sin. As the Genesis account—and the rest of the Bible story—proves, sin really entered the world on the day of the fall and permeated all of creation. Adam and Eve immediately began to feel shame and guilt—emotions they had never felt before. They recognized good and evil in a new way, and they immediately felt a great separation from God in place of their former intimacy with him. The rest of the Bible also makes clear that through their actions, this world became a fallen place. We will learn soon about the effects of this sin on all of creation.

Every human being is now born with a sinful nature. As the story of the Bible goes on, it becomes clear that the result of Adam and Eve's sin was not just that sin entered the world, but that sin began to plague every human being through birth. In other words, every person is now born with a sinful nature—a tendency toward sin that is natural, powerful, and unavoidable. Adam and Eve were the only human beings in history (other than Jesus) who were once without a sinful nature. Because of their sin, every other human being also sins. This is the devastating result of the fall.

Every human being now lives in a world that is under God's wrath. The result of all of this is that all human beings—and the world itself—are now under God's wrath and judgment against sin. Because God is perfectly holy, he naturally hates sin, so his wrath and judgment are the necessary results of human sin and rebellion. So Adam and Eve's sin not only brought a sinful nature into the world for every person who is born but also brought God's wrath into his creation. The apostle Paul makes it clear that every human being, apart from Christ Jesus, is under God's wrath, along with all of creation (Rom. 1).

These implications of the fall help us see theologically how to understand what happened in the fall of Adam and Eve. Their sin brought sin into creation, it brought a sinful nature to every human being, and it brought God's holy and righteous wrath down on this fallen world.

THE EFFECTS OF SIN

The verses that immediately follow the account of the fall of Adam and Eve show us the immediate effects that sin had on Adam and Eve's own sense of themselves, as well as on their relationship with their Creator. We'll see that sin immediately leads to shame and guilt, as well as a damaged relationship with God.

READ!

Read Genesis 3:8–13.

What were some of the immediate effects of sin in the lives of these people who had been created sinless?

Shame. The reality of *shame* entered Adam and Eve's hearts and lives. They were ashamed of their actions—and rightly so. Back in

Genesis 3:7, we saw the man and the woman trying to cover their nakedness; however, in 2:25, we were told that they were both naked but felt *no* shame. That had now changed.

Then, as this passage opens, we find Adam and Eve hiding from God as they hear him approaching (Gen. 3:8). Before their sin, they would have been happy to commune with God; that was what they had been created to do! But with their sin on their hearts and fresh in their minds, they were ashamed to even come out to stand before God.

Guilt. Adam and Eve were not only ashamed of themselves but also felt the real *guilt* that hung over them because of what they had done. In other words, while Adam told God that he was hiding from him because he was naked (Gen. 3:10), that was only half the story. It was not Adam's nakedness itself that made him want to hide from God; it was the very real guilt that he felt because of his sin, rebellion, and disobedience. Adam and Eve felt guilty before God because they *were* guilty before God.

Blame. The "conversation" that Adam and Eve then had with God is almost hard to read. We might hope that, after sinning by disobeying God's word and eating the forbidden fruit, Adam and Eve would have come back to God with great sorrow and repentance—begging him for grace, mercy, and forgiveness, and admitting their guilt and sin to him. That is not what happened.

First, we see Adam *blaming* Eve for giving him the fruit; he even hinted that God himself was partly to blame for giving the woman to him (Gen. 3:12)! Adam compounded his sin by blaming Eve—and God—for it.

Then Eve also refused to take responsibility for her actions, blaming the serpent, who, she said, had "deceived" her into eating the fruit (Gen. 3:13). Neither Adam nor Eve repented and stood before God with humility. Instead, they both pointed the finger of blame at others for their sin.

This was a sad day for the people God had made. We see the immediate effects of their first sin beginning to compound, multiply, and grow. Shame, guilt, and blame began to fester in the lives and hearts of Adam and Eve. Sin had entered the world and their hearts, and it was obviously there to stay—unless God did something about it.

SIN AND THE CURSE

Having considered the immediate effects of the fall upon Adam and Eve, we also need to think about God's response to it. As Genesis shows us, he brought a curse down on every part of his creation because of sin. It is important to understand that God was not doing something "out of the blue" because of the fall. He was simply acting as the holy God *must* act in response to sin; he was allowing sin to have its ugly and deadly effects in every part of the world. We are going to see the sad reality that sin really does bring death, destruction, and infection in every part of God's good world.

READ!

Read Genesis 3:14–24—the account of God's curse following the sin of Adam and Eve.

We must think about several different aspects of God's curse—the varying effects of his response to the sin of Adam and Eve.

The curse on the serpent. First, God cursed the serpent who had tempted his people toward rebellion against God and his word. He cursed the serpent itself, but he also cursed Satan, who had come to the garden of Eden in the form of a serpent. Satan, God said, would forever be at war with God's people, and God gave a hint that Satan would one day be brought down to death forever (Gen. 3:14–15). We'll think more about this hopeful hint below.

The curse for the woman. God told Eve that her sin would greatly affect her experience of bearing children: it would be incredibly painful because of life in a fallen world. He also said that Eve's "desire" would be "contrary to" her husband (Gen. 3:16), which probably means that her sinful tendency would be to rise up and rule over Adam in selfish and prideful ways. As we can see, the curse affected the very heart of the experience of all women—in their childbearing, their gender, and their relationships.

The curse for the man. God then turned to Adam and told him how the curse for sin would affect an activity that was at the heart of his existence before the fall: his work. God had given Adam good work to do at the beginning—keeping the garden of Eden. This work had been full of joy for Adam. But because of sin, his work would become painful and frustrating. The ground would not bear fruit as easily. Adam would have to struggle to provide food for his family. His core calling would be affected by his sin.

The curse for God's people. The sad result of sin for God's people was that they were driven out of the perfect place that God had made for them. Adam and Eve could no longer dwell in the garden of Eden in close proximity to the holy God, who cannot bear to be in the presence of sin. Genesis 3 ends with the man and the woman being sent away from God's place, with an angel guarding the entrance to the garden of Eden with a "flaming sword" (v. 24). The relationship between God and man had been terribly damaged; only God would be able to make it right again.

Hints of grace. We will talk much more about the biggest "hint" of grace in this passage in a moment (it is in Gen. 3:15). But there is another hint of God's grace even in the midst of God's pronouncement of his curse—one that we often miss as we read and study this account. It comes in verse 21, where we see God clothing Adam and Eve in animal skins before he sends them out from the garden of Eden. Do you remember the new shame that Adam and Eve felt because of their nakedness? God was dealing with this, graciously covering them. Many have described this as the first sacrifice in the story of the Bible—God causing animals to die "in the place" of his people to cover their shame. This certainly is a hint of the saving work that God would do in the lives of his sinful but still beloved people.

GOSPEL HOPE AFTER SIN

Before we conclude this chapter, it is important to look carefully again at just one verse—Genesis 3:15—that recounts part of God's curse against Satan, the serpent. It includes an amazing promise, especially considering where it comes—right in the middle of judgment for sin. As we think about this promise, we will see that this verse is incredibly important for understanding how God was still committed to working in the lives of his sinful people for their eternal good and salvation.

READ!

Read Genesis 3:15—a verse that you read earlier as part of the account of God's curse because of sin.

Biblical scholars and theologians often refer to the verse that we are now considering as the *protevangelium*, or "first gospel." They use this term because this verse seems to be the first place in the Bible that points ahead to a future hope for God's people—a coming final victory that God will secure over Satan through someone who will come as the "offspring," or descendant, of Adam and Eve. Consider what God promises to his people here:

- The offspring of the woman will "bruise" (or "crush," according to some other translations) the head of Satan—the serpent—in a final way. Although Satan would "bruise" the heel of Eve's offspring, his own injury would be much more severe. In fact, the crushing of his head implies his death; he would not be able to survive such an injury.
- The one who would achieve the victory over Satan would be a real offspring of Eve—that is, a literal human descendant. This

is a huge promise. God was saying that someone would come—a human being—who would achieve a final victory over Satan, sin, and death.

Because of the great promises that God makes in this verse, it has been understood by many to point forward to God's final victory over Satan, a victory that would secure salvation for his people. Jesus is the one who eventually came as the offspring of Eve—fully human and fully God—to "bruise" the head of Satan through his death for sin on the cross and his victory over death through his resurrection. This first gospel word from God is a promise about his own Son, who would one day come into the world to fix forever the mess that sin had created.

What do we learn about God from this verse? What does this "first gospel" tell us about the rest of the big story of the Bible? Genesis 3:15 teaches us:

- Despite the fall into sin, God was not finished working for his saving purposes in the lives of his people and his world. Even amid his judgment against sin, God gave a hint that much more was coming. He would not abandon the people he had made but would keep working to bring them back into a right relationship with him.
- The rest of the Bible story has a definite direction and focus. Everything that we will see happening in the coming chapters will be headed toward to final completion of what is promised in this "first gospel"—the victory over Satan by the offspring of Eve. We can see, in this single verse, where this whole story is going.
- God was just to punish sin but also gracious to provide mercy and forgiveness for his people. He would not abandon them forever, even if it meant sending his own Son into this world to solve the problem that no mere human could ever solve—the problem of sin and death.

REVIEW

In just the third chapter of the Bible, we read about the great crisis—Adam and Eve rejected God's good word and led all of creation into sin, fallenness, and corruption. Even so, the story was not over. God's first promise of gracious salvation came on the heels of the fall of Adam and Eve, reminding us that his plan for his people is good; he would not turn his back on his creation, despite sin and rebellion. The serpent crusher would come!

PRAY!

As you close this chapter with prayer, give thanks to God that the Bible story does not end at Genesis 3:7, with the disobedience of Adam and Eve. Thank God for Genesis 3:15 and for the rest of the Bible story, which point us to God's wonderful saving work for sinful people through the offspring of Eve—God's own Son, come to earth in human flesh to die for sins and rise from the dead to conquer Satan forever!

Chapter 4

GOD'S PROMISE OF A PEOPLE
PART 1

We are now ready to move into a new scene of the biblical story, one I've titled "God's Promise of a People." In this chapter, which is the first of two on this theme, we will see God's insistence on dwelling and working with his people—even after their great fall into sin. And we will see the early stages of his great salvation plan of blessing for this world.

Our last chapter ended with the expulsion of Adam and Eve from the garden of Eden—God's good place. Because of their sin and rebellion, they were sent away from God's presence and doomed to live in a world that was now under his curse because of sin. But we also saw that, even in the midst of God's judgment, there was a strong hint of divine grace that would continue as this story went on. Genesis 3:15 gave us a picture of the future victory over Satan and death that would be won by the "offspring" of Eve. In this chapter, we will see how God began working toward this end, even in the earliest generations of human beings after Adam and Eve.

> ### Remember!
>
> Your suggested memory verses for this chapter come from Genesis 15—a passage that we will study in the coming pages. These words are God's great promise to Abram, which is foundational for understanding God's purpose in the rest of the story of the Bible.
>
> *And behold, the word of the LORD came to him: "This man shall not be your heir; your very own son shall be your heir." And he brought him outside and said, "Look toward heaven, and number the stars, if you are able to number them." Then he said to him, "So shall your offspring be." And he believed the LORD, and he counted it to him as righteousness. (Gen. 15:4–6)*

SIN TAKES OVER

If we had any doubt about whether Adam and Eve's fall into sin really had an effect on the world—and people in the world—all doubts are erased by reading Genesis 4. Here we find the account of the way sin took over, not gradually but immediately—even in the lives and actions of the first descendants of the first human couple. The basic lesson of this chapter is that sin *spreads*. That is what we see happening in this account.

READ!

Read Genesis 4—the sad account of Cain and Abel, the first two sons of Adam and Eve.

How, specifically, do we see sin spreading in this chapter?

The first murder. Genesis 4 opens with the birth of two sons to Adam and Eve, who began to bear children after they were cast out from the garden of Eden. Cain and Abel grew up together and began to make sacrifices—offerings—to their Creator God. For reasons that the text does not specify, God was pleased with the offering of Abel (who brought sheep to God) and not pleased with the offering of Cain (who brought some of his crops). Cain became angry and envious, and decided to do the unthinkable: he murdered his brother in a field. To make matters worse, instead of repenting and crying out to God for mercy, he answered God with those chilling words that you probably know well: "Am I my brother's keeper?" (v. 9).

Adam and Eve's sin had been passed down to their children. Cain and Abel both entered the world with Adam and Eve's guilt hanging over them, but they also were born with a sin nature, a real "bent" toward sin—which meant that they would, necessarily, sin. This sad story shows us that sin had really entered the world to stay.

The attitude of Lamech. While you probably already knew the story of Cain and Abel well, we also see the devastating effects of sin in the prideful and violent attitude of a man named Lamech. In Genesis 4:23–24, we find Lamech—a descendant of Adam and Eve, whom we do not know much about—bragging to his wives about killing a young man. Here is yet another murderer, one who not only killed a young man but then decided to brag to his family about it. Sin had indeed spread, and it was making the world an ugly and dangerous place to live.

Progress and hints of grace. Even amid this rising tide of sin—of Cain, Lamech, and many others—God's plan continued to go forward. We see the progress that began to happen, as Lamech's sons started to make discoveries with tents and livestock, music, and metal (Gen. 4:20–22). God, in his mercy, allowed humanity to grow, expand, and develop on earth.

We also see hints of God's gracious character, which will continue to be made known as the story continues. God gave another son—Seth—to Adam and Eve. Then, during the days of Seth's son Enoch, we are told that "people began to call upon the name of the LORD" (Gen. 4:26). Sin was spreading, but God's salvation plan was just getting started.

A REFRAIN OF DEATH

In Genesis 5, we encounter the first genealogy in the Bible, as the author of Genesis records for us the "generations" of Adam. There is a common "refrain" in this genealogy that we should focus on as we read. But as you will see, there is also another important sign of God's gracious hand in this passage. This first genealogy reminds us that God's work in the world—and in the lives of his people—was continuing.

READ!

Read Genesis 5—the genealogy of Adam, which ends with Noah.

If you have been reading the Bible for a long time, you have probably read many genealogies—there are quite a few in the pages of the Bible. They function in different ways, and it is often interesting to note what the biblical authors choose to include—and *not* include—in their genealogies. The authors are almost always trying to teach us something very important and very specific through these records.

As you read the genealogy in Genesis 5, you hopefully saw a few key points that the author of Genesis wanted us to see. These points come in the refrain, as well as in the strong glimpse of grace that comes in the midst of this genealogy.

The refrain. As you remember, Adam and Eve were created to live forever. In their original situation in the garden of Eden, they existed without sin in a perfect and good relationship with God, their Creator. If they had not sinned, they could have continued in this state forever. This is an important point: human beings were made to live and serve God for eternity.

You remember, too, that God promised Adam and Eve that if they ate of the fruit of the tree of the knowledge of good and evil, they would surely die. After they did this, they did not die immediately—but death eventually came. When they sinned, Adam and Eve became corrupted by sin; therefore, death entered the world. Over time, Adam and Eve began to experience things they had never felt before. Their bodies began to grow old. They got sick. They became weaker. Finally, they both died.

The same was true for their descendants. That is why we find, in the genealogy of Genesis 5, the refrain "and he died." These repeated words are meant to hit us like a continual punch as we move through this chapter. As we read of man after man growing old and *dying*, we are reminded that this was *not* the way things were supposed to be. Sin caused all this. Adam and Eve brought sin and death into the world, and now, as a result, we see generation after generation growing old and dying.

The glimpse of grace. This refrain of death makes Genesis 5:21–24 all the more striking. Amid the genealogy of life and death, we find one man—Enoch—who did not die like all the rest. The refrain of death is missing from his section of the genealogy. Enoch is described as a man who "walked" with God; then, suddenly, he was just gone. He did not die; rather, God simply took Enoch away to be with him. What does this brief account of this righteous and godly man teach us?

The account of Enoch, in the middle of a "death list," reminds us that the God of grace and life was still at work in the world and in the lives of his people. He was still able to provide an answer to the problem of sin and death. We do not yet see clearly in this passage exactly how God would finally overcome sin, but we are reminded that he was able to do something about it. The only way for human beings to escape death eternally is through the gracious gift and power of God. God showed a preview of this power and grace through the life—but *not* the death—of the righteous man Enoch.

THE SPREAD OF SIN

As we move into Genesis 6, we find an account of the terrible and increasing corruption on earth—and we learn of God's attitude toward all this sin, violence, and rebellion against him.

📖 **READ!**

Read Genesis 6:1–8.

We have been examining how both sin and death spread into all the world—and all of humanity—in the years following the first sin of Adam and Eve in the garden of Eden. This spread did not slow down; if anything, it began to accelerate! The sad summary of all of this is that "every intention of the thoughts of [man's] heart was only evil continually" (Gen. 6:5).

The passage even tells us that God "regretted" that he had made humanity (Gen. 6:6). This does not mean that God did not have a plan for this problem. Rather, it is a way of putting God's reaction to sin in human language. God's "emotional" response to the sin of humanity was deep grief—and deep anger (v. 7).

So what lessons do we gather from this account of God's wrath against sin and the brief description of the one righteous man on earth (Gen. 6:8)?

God is angry about sin. The righteous Creator God of this universe hates sin. As sin spread and intensified, God grew angry, and he promised to bring his wrath and judgment against it. His response—to "blot out" humanity from the earth (Gen. 6:7)—proves the devastating seriousness of human rebellion against the rule of the holy God.

But there is another sense to God's anger that we cannot miss in this passage. God is not merely violently angry; he is also "grieved" by sin (Gen. 6:6). God loved the people he had created, and it grieved his heart to see them rebelling against his rule and falling into depravity.

The only hope for sinners is to find favor with God. The mention of Noah, in Genesis 6:8, reminds us that the only hope amid God's judgment and wrath against sin is to find "favor"—or grace—with the God of the universe. Noah is contrasted with the rest of humanity because he found this grace with God.

In a way, we could almost summarize the rest of the Bible story from these verses in Genesis 6. The rest of this story of God's work in the world will show us:

- God is *just*—he will bring his wrath and judgment against sin.
- God is *gracious*—he will give his grace to his true people.

GOD'S JUST WRATH

As you saw, God's anger was boiling up as sin spread and intensified; he is a just God, and he cannot stand to be in the presence of sin. Amid continual rebellion, pride, and violence, God's wrath will ultimately come down from heaven. That is exactly what happened in the time of Noah.

READ!

Read Genesis 7–8—a large portion of the account of the great flood that God sent in judgment on the world he had made.

If you were raised in Christian churches or circles, there is a good chance that you learned the story of "Noah and the ark." Perhaps you even sang a song about it, recounting how the animals came into the ark "two by two." Indeed, because of the animals and the boat, this has become a favorite Bible "kids" story in many circles.

However, the record of the great flood is no kids story. This is the account of the devastating judgment of God against the world—and the human race—that had rebelled against him in every way. Because people's sin "grieved" the very heart of God (Gen. 6:6), he brought destruction and judgment against them and the world he had made. What can we learn from this account?

God really will judge sin. This is the primary point of the account of the great flood, a point we must not miss. Anyone who tells you that the God of the Bible is only a God of grace (with no justice and wrath) is mistaken. God is gracious, yes, but he is also infinitely holy; he cannot bear the presence of sin, which is opposed to his holy and righteous character. The flood of the earth was not the final judgment, because life on earth continued after it. But it was a picture of God's final judgment of the world, which is really coming one day. The holy God of the universe really will judge sin. Human sin and rebellion are so serious that God's response to it was to deluge the entire world with water in order to "blot out" (Gen. 6:7) almost all of humanity.

God will provide a way of salvation. The ark is an incredible and vivid reminder of God's grace amid his judgment. God could have wiped out Noah and his family along with the rest of the human race, but he did not. God saved Noah, who had found "favor" in his eyes (Gen. 6:8), by instructing him to build a huge boat—an ark. In God's mercy, he also allowed for the animal kingdom to continue, as Noah brought pairs of animals onto the ark.

This is a truth in the "big story" of the Bible that, by God's grace, will not go away: amid God's judgment, he will provide a way of salvation—a way "out" from under his judgment and wrath. Noah's ark became a great picture of the final salvation that God would offer to his people in the cross of his Son later in the story.

God's story will continue, but only by his grace. You probably noticed that Genesis 8 ends with God making a "covenant" (a promise) with Noah after the flood. God promised never again to judge the earth in this way (with water); thus, this was a "covenant with creation" that God made. This did *not* mean that sin would not again increase on the earth; all we must do to see that this was not the case is to look around the world today! But it did mean that God had graciously allowed the story of this world to continue. Noah's descendants would flourish and spread into all the earth. God would need to provide a lasting way of salvation for human beings, who would again fall into all kinds of sin and corruption.

THE GRACIOUS GOD

After the flood, sin continued to spread and multiply in the world. Again God reacted in judgment—but a judgment that was not without significant mercy and grace. Here we will encounter a God who is committed to seeing his work move forward in the world and in the lives of his people.

READ!

Read Genesis 11:1–9—the account of the Tower of Babel.

Did you think that with God's judgment of the world by the flood and his preservation of Noah and his family, things would be better in the world the second time around? Were you hopeful that the next generations would provide a kind of "fresh start" for humanity—that Noah's descendants would all praise God and obey him joyfully? Well, the account that you just read in Genesis 11 must have put a quick end to any such hopes and expectations.

In Genesis 11, we see the people of the world joining together in unity—not to worship God but essentially to try to *become* God! The pride and rebellion that we witness in this passage is striking—and even humorous in some ways. We are seeing that the sinful nature of human beings runs very deep. They are "wired" to rebel against God, so they naturally choose sin and rebellion.

The tower. Genesis 11:1–9 begins with one united people, all with one language (v. 1), and ends with many different peoples, with many different languages, spread all over the earth (v. 9). In the middle is an account of all the peoples of the earth coming together to build a tower. But the tower was not the problem; it was their attitude and goal in building it. They said, very explicitly, that they were engaging in this project to "make a name" for themselves—they wanted to rise up to the "heavens" in pride and rebellion against God (v. 4). This is the first real example in the Bible of human pride in "development"—trying to build lasting cities and endeavors for human glory rather than in worship to the Creator.

God's response. In the most ironic moment in this account, God "came down" to see this tower that was supposedly going to reach into the heavens (Gen. 11:5). The project had obviously not reached to heaven; it was still puny in comparison with God's glory and power!

God's response to these people must not be seen as based in any kind of worry or fear; God is the sovereign ruler of the universe, and he was not frightened or intimidated by this project in any way! When he said that "nothing . . . will now be impossible for them" (Gen. 11:6), he probably meant that, with this kind of unified commitment to evil in the world, the sin of humanity would know no bounds. In other words, if this direction continued, humanity would self-destruct in sin.

Mercy in judgment. So as we see God bringing down his judgment on this situation—dispersing people all over the world through the confusion of their language—we should see his mercy and grace in it. God was protecting humanity from itself—prohibiting them from taking their sin to the next level—joining forces to rise against their Creator together. God was also, as we will see, setting up the next part of this story, when he would call one man, Abram, to be the first of a special people that God would personally lead, bless, and save.

GOD'S PROMISE OF BLESSING

I'm calling this scene of the Bible story "God's Promise of a People." But up to this point, we still have not quite seen the reason for this title.

But now we finally are ready to begin to see the great promise that the gracious and powerful God of the universe chose to make to the people in his world. God's response to human sin was not to finally destroy the world (although he could have very justly done this). Instead, he began preparing and forming a people for himself—a people who would belong to him in a special way and would experience his great blessing.

◤ READ!

Read Genesis 12:1-9—the account of God's call and promise to a man named Abram.

We know almost nothing about Abram other than the name of his father (Gen. 11:27). From what we do know about the other peoples and tribes of his time, there is a very good likelihood that he did not know God at all before God called him (Gen. 12)! He was probably worshiping idols—living far from God in his ways, customs, and beliefs. There is no evidence that God called Abram for any reason other than his own good pleasure.

What we do know is that God specifically chose Abram to be the first person in a new people that he was beginning to gather for himself. We also know that Abram, when confronted with God's call to leave everything (his people, his land, and his country) followed God immediately (Gen. 12:1-4). This man, believing the promise of God, became the beginning of God's great work in the world through his people. Abram became the first Jew.

So what can we gather from this account of the call of Abram? What can we learn about the great promise that God made to this man as he commanded him to leave everything and head to a completely new land? There are three main components of the big promise that God made to Abram:

The land. The first aspect of the promise that God made to Abram had to do with land. God sent Abram to a "land" that he promised to show him (Gen. 12:1)—the land known as Canaan—and later give to his descendants (v. 7). Central to God's promise to Abram was a place where God's people would dwell. You remember, of course, that Adam and Eve were kicked out of the garden of Eden by God because of their sin. Thus, God was promising to bring this new people to a new place where he would reign over them again.

The people. God also promised Abram that he would make a "great nation" out of him (Gen. 12:2). This was a strong promise of many descendants—a people that would come from Abram's line, who would follow God and serve him in the land where Abram was going. God promised, in other words, to raise up from sinful humanity a group of people who would belong to him in a special way. Abram would be the first of these people.

The blessing. Finally, as you probably noticed, God's words and promises were rich with talk of "blessing" (Gen. 12:2–3). God promised not only to bless Abram but also to bless "all the families of the earth" through him (v. 3). This was where God's promise to Abram got really, really large. We might have expected God to promise blessing to Abram himself. But this promised blessing was much bigger than him only. God was saying that the blessing that he would pour out on this new people would have a global effect; it would bring blessing to everyone in the world everywhere. This was a huge promise, one only God himself could make!

So the God who created the world, we find, was not done with the world, despite the level of sin and depravity in the human race. God had a plan—a plan that involved a people, a place, and great blessing that would come to every corner of his world through this people. Abram, probably knowing very little about God at this point, went where God told him to go. So God's story—the story of the Bible—continued.

ABRAM AND MELCHIZEDEK

Sometime after he arrived in the land God had promised to show him, Abram had a strange interaction with a mysterious figure named Melchizedek. While this interaction is a very real part of the story of Abram, it also gives us a "peek" into the future of God's plan for his people.

READ!

Read Genesis 14.

Before Abram met Melchizedek, Abram's nephew Lot and his family were taken captive by some tribal "kings" of his day. Abram—obviously a strong warrior—chased these kings down, freed Lot and his family, and brought them back safely (Gen. 14:1–16).

As Abram came back from this great victory and rescue of Lot, he was met by two men: the king of Sodom (a pagan king) and Melchizedek (Gen. 14:17–18). The king of Sodom offered Abram some "goods" from the battle, but Abram refused them humbly, not wanting to get rich from gifts from this pagan king (vv. 21–24). But the more interesting interaction was with Melchizedek.

It seems that Melchizedek gave Abram a meal and a blessing from God. In return, Abram offered a significant gift to this man—one tenth of all that he had.

Before I explain the significance of this seemingly random interaction, I want you to note some important biblical points about Melchizedek:

- The text does not describe Melchizedek's lineage or background at all. It is as if he comes completely out of nowhere into the story!
- Melchizedek served as a priest of God most high (Gen. 14:18). He was obviously an ancient worshiper and servant of the one true Creator God.
- Melchizedek was also a king; he ruled a place called Salem (Gen. 14:18), which some people have suspected to be the place that would later become Jerusalem.
- Abram honored Melchizedek by giving a tenth of his goods to him (Gen. 14:20). He obviously respected this man greatly given how he treated him.

We will come back to this mysterious figure later in the Bible story. For now, though, it is enough to see that he was, in some way, pointing forward to Jesus Christ. Melchizedek was understood, by David (Ps. 110) and the author of the book of Hebrews (Heb. 5), to be a kind of "type"—or picture—of Jesus and the way in which he would interact with God's people. Jesus, like Melchizedek, would have no strictly human roots; he would come from heaven above—God taking on human flesh. He would serve as a priest *and* a king—two positions that no human being, according to the law of Moses (which would come after Abram), could hold at the same time. This mysterious man was obviously a picture for us of the kind of leader God's people would have one day.

This strange interaction has even led some biblical scholars to conclude that Melchizedek (whose name, literally translated, means "king of righteousness," Heb. 7:2) was Jesus Christ himself, appearing to Abram in a preincarnate (before the incarnation) form. This is certainly a possibility, but it seems better to understand him simply as a man whom God used to bless Abram and to point us forward to a later part of the story of the Bible, when his own Son would enter the scene as the great, eternal Priest-King!

I hope that passages like this will help you continue to "put your Bible together" as you see the connected themes and how all the Bible ultimately centers on the person and work of Jesus Christ.

A COVENANT CEREMONY

As the story of the Bible continues into Genesis 15, we find the saving response of Abram to God's word (the same response of all of God's true people to his word). We also find a strange covenant ceremony that God initiates with Abram. We will consider the significance of this ceremony for an understanding of God's promise to Abram—and to all his descendants.

READ!

Read Genesis 15.

A bit of historical background is helpful for understanding what happened in the strange ceremony in Genesis 15. In short, the whole interaction between God and Abram was loosely based on the ancient practice of making a covenant/treaty between a conquering king and the people he had defeated (who would become his "vassals," or servants). Here is how it worked:

- The conquering king or warrior would split animals in two parts, then place the pieces apart from each other, to initiate this ceremony.
- The vassal would walk between the pieces of the split-apart animals, speaking about his commitments to obey the king, serve him, and remain loyal to him as his subject.
- By walking through the animal pieces in this way, the servant was saying symbolically that if he broke the covenant promises that he was making, the king would have the right to do to *him* what had been done to the *animals.*

In short, in this ancient covenant ceremony, the servant was swearing *on his very life* that he would keep the covenant that he was making with the king.

With that background, as we think about God's interaction with Abram as he confirmed his covenant promises to him, we are met with a big surprise. Everything in the ceremony started normally. The animals were split in half and the pieces set apart from one another. Then Abram walked between them, vowing to keep his half of the covenant, so God would be faithful to his promises, right? Wrong! Look again at what happened (Gen. 15:17–18).

When the covenant ceremony was set up, it was *God himself* who passed between the divided pieces of the animals! The "smoking fire pot" and "flaming torch" were symbols of God's presence; he moved through the ceremony in the place usually reserved for the servant. As he did this, he reaffirmed his great promises to Abram, swearing to give him the land that was laid out before him as the inheritance of his descendants.

So what did this all mean? This account shows us that in his covenant with Abram, God was swearing *on his own life* that he would keep his promises to this man. He was saying to Abram that, no matter what, he would be faithful to grow his people and give them an inheritance. There were no conditions attached to this; God made an unconditional covenant with Abram. He had set his favor and blessing on this man, and he would not withdraw it. God swore this on his own life!

As we look much further down the road in the Bible story, we see that there would come a day when God would "make good" on this unconditional promise to Abram and his descendants. You see, human beings are completely sinful; that problem has not gone away. In order for God to keep his great promises to his chosen but sinful people, God in human flesh would really have to lay down his very *life*.

The promise God made in this covenant ceremony was much bigger than just the Jewish people or the physical land; he was promising to give an eternal inheritance to all who are descendants of Abram *by faith*. Thus, this promise was ultimately a promise of salvation. We'll learn more about this as we continue to trace the story of the Bible.

A COVENANT SIGN

When God made his covenant with Abram, he attached a "sign" to it and commanded Abram to "mark" his people with it. This sign was circumcision. By the end of this section, you should understand this covenant sign more clearly and see how it connects to today's Christians, who also are part of God's covenant community—the church.

◼ READ!

Read Genesis 17:1–14—the account of God's establishment of the covenant sign of circumcision for Abram and all his family.

As Genesis 17 begins, we see something important: God changed Abram's name to Abraham (v. 5). In the Bible, the changing of someone's name is deeply significant, as names were often tied to purpose, identity, and character. The name Abraham means something like "the father of a great multitude." God was giving Abram a new name that fit better with the unconditional promise he had made to him—the promise of making Abraham the first in a great nation of people who would live in God's place under his eternal blessing.

With this new name in place, God reaffirmed his great promises to Abraham (Gen. 17:4–8). He reminded him of the great people he would bring from Abraham and promised again to make them his special people; he even promised them the land as their "everlasting possession" as they followed him (v. 8).

Then God established the covenant sign with Abraham and his people (Gen. 17:9–14). He asked Abraham for his obedience—not as a condition of his covenant but as a response to his great promise. Remember, God had already "counted" Abraham as righteous because of his faith (15:6); his obedience could not now be the reason that God would be faithful to him.

God commanded Abraham to take on himself—and to place on all the males who would be a part of his family and his people—the sign of circumcision. This would be a physical mark that would identify Abraham and the rest of God's people as truly belonging to God in a specific way.

So why circumcision? What was this sign, and what did it mean?

- Circumcision is a removal of a part of the skin on the private parts of the male. It is still practiced today, for medical and cleanliness reasons, in many parts of the world. It is almost always performed on boys when they are very young.
- Circumcision probably was not practiced by any of the surrounding peoples during Abraham's day. It would have truly set God's people apart in a significant way from the idolatrous people around them.
- Circumcision was not meant to be a way to gain favor with God; it was simply a physical and tangible way for God's people to mark themselves as belonging to him. It was a physical sign of belonging to the covenant community of God.

So we see God here asking Abraham to respond to his covenant promises by taking on himself—and his family—the covenant sign of belonging to God. This would mark them as people who lived under his great promise through faith in his word.

Today, almost all Christians see this covenant sign of circumcision as corresponding to the new covenant sign of baptism, which marks God's people as belonging to the new covenant community—not ethnic Israel, but the true Israel of God: the believing church of Christians. Even today, God wants his people to be physically marked as belonging to Jesus, even though faith is an inward and invisible thing.

REVIEW

God's insistent grace shines through this chapter of the Bible story as he initiates promises with his people—promises to bless them, grow them, and work through them to extend his saving blessing to the nations of the world. God saves Noah and his family from the judgment of the flood—and then swears by himself to make a people for his own glory from the family of Abraham. So the story continues!

PRAY!

As you close this chapter with prayer, ask God to help you remember that he is the same God who counted Abraham as "righteous" because of Abraham's faith alone. Ask him to help you be a "child" of Abraham, by faith, as you follow Jesus Christ today in everything.

Chapter 5

GOD'S PROMISE OF A PEOPLE
PART 2

As we read through the earliest parts of the story of the Bible, we see Adam and Eve's fall into sin, the massive spread of sin throughout the world, God's judgment on human sin through the great flood, and the renewed spread of sin after the flood. But the Bible also shows us the grace of God toward sinful people. Despite the sin and rebellion of the human race, God did not give up on his work in the world but kept bringing about his great and saving purposes for his people.

One of the main ways we see God's grace is through the promise that he gave to Abraham as he called him out of his land and away from his people. It was a promise that had three distinct components. Do you remember them? It was a promise of:

- a *land* that God would give to Abraham and his descendants;
- a great *people* and *nation* that God would grow from Abraham's descendants; and

- great *blessing* that God would give to Abraham's descendants, and through them to all the peoples of the earth.

In the last chapter, we saw how God gave this promise to Abraham, but we did not see any "proof" that God was going to keep his word. In this chapter, we will begin to see God's promise fulfilled. We ended the last chapter with an old man named Abraham and his old wife, Sarah, holding onto God's great promise, but not yet having any children as promised. This is where we pick up the story now.

Remember!

Your suggested memory verses for this chapter come from the conclusion of the book of Genesis. These are the faith-filled words of Joseph as he looked back not only on the evil that his brothers had done to him but also at the way God had used it for his glory and for his good purposes in the lives of his people.

But Joseph said to them, "Do not fear, for am I in the place of God? As for you, you meant evil against me, but God meant it for good, to bring it about that many people should be kept alive, as they are today. So do not fear; I will provide for you and your little ones." Thus he comforted them and spoke kindly to them. (Gen. 50:19–21)

STRUGGLING TO BELIEVE THE PROMISE

God had given a great promise to Abraham and Sarah. There was just one problem: they still had no son—and they were getting older every day. We see from the passage that you are about to read that, considering their age and situation, it was not always easy for them to keep believing God's promise.

READ!

Read Genesis 17:15–18:21.

In this passage, God promised the birth of Isaac two times. What do we learn from this passage as the story of the Bible continues?

Even Abraham struggled to believe. God came to Abraham and reaffirmed his promise to him very clearly. He even said explicitly that he was going to give Abraham a son *by Sarah.* Abraham's response, then, is surprising—and a bit disappointing. He cried out to God that God might bless "Ishmael." Who was Ishmael?

Hopefully you had an opportunity to at least glance back at Genesis 16, which gives the context for this statement by Abraham. Ishmael was Abraham's son whom he had with Hagar, Sarah's servant. Abraham and Sarah had agreed on this action because both had begun to seriously doubt that Sarah could really have a child of her own in her old age. Abraham did not think that God could give him a son through his aging wife, so he had decided to try to "help" God a bit. God had to reaffirm his amazing promise to Abraham, who was struggling to believe it.

Sarah doubted God's word. Sarah, too, had problems accepting the truth of God's word and promise. As God's angels appeared to Abraham (at the beginning of Gen. 18), they also affirmed God's promise—specifically stating that *Sarah* would have a son in the next year. Sarah, overhearing this conversation, laughed to herself at how ridiculous this was. God gently corrected and rebuked her for this response.

God remained faithful to his promise. In all of this, what do we learn about God? We see that, despite Abraham and Sarah's doubt and struggles to believe, he remained faithful to his promise. He kept moving ahead with his plan, even though he was dealing with people who were sometimes quite faithless. This is the God of the Bible—the God whose miraculous saving plan of blessing in the world moves ahead by his pleasure. He is not dependent on human faith, although he delights when people take him at his word.

Next we will see how God began to tangibly keep this great promise to Abraham and Sarah through the birth of a son in their old age.

THE CHILD OF THE PROMISE

In God's perfect time, Isaac, the child of the promise, was born to Abraham and Sarah. As the first of Abraham and Sarah's descendants, he would be the one through whom God would continue to keep his great promise of a people, a land, and blessing to all the peoples of the earth.

READ!

Read Genesis 22—the amazing and shocking account of Abraham's "almost" sacrifice of Isaac.

Abraham and Sarah were happy. They were praising God for the miraculous birth of Isaac, who had been born to them in their old age. He was the living sign of God's promise—the walking "proof" that God really did have a great plan for a people who would inherit the land and bring blessing to the nations. You can imagine the way this old couple cherished and loved this boy, who was a gift from God, and a living and breathing sign of hope for all that God would do in the world.

Then we come to Genesis 22, which records how God came to Abraham with a shocking request. He asked him to sacrifice Isaac to him on a mountain.

Before we talk about the rest of this story, we need to clarify a couple of key points:

- Abraham lived in a time when child sacrifice was probably quite common. The pagan peoples of his day would have done this to "appease" their gods. It was an awful and despicable practice of murder, done in the name of "worship" to idols.

- We know from Genesis 22:1 that God did this to "test" Abraham. This is a hint, right at the beginning of the account, that God did *not* mean for Abraham to go through with the sacrifice of his son. But Abraham did not know this; it was a real test for him.

Abraham took his beloved son (we can only imagine how difficult this was) and went to the place where God has told him to go. He tied him up and prepared for the sacrifice. Just as he raised the knife to kill his son, God called out for him to stop. He told Abraham that he had seen that he loved God even more than his own son, so God provided a "substitute" sacrifice for Isaac—a ram that was caught by its horns in a nearby thicket.

So what do we make of this strange account? What was God teaching Abraham? What is he teaching us?

First, God was indeed testing Abraham, to observe his loyalty and love for God first—even before his own son. God was reminding him that *he* was the one whom Abraham must worship, even as he loved and cherished his son. The author of Hebrews later explains to us that Abraham, as he was preparing to sacrifice his son, had faith that God would raise Isaac from the dead if he went through with it (Heb. 11:17–19). Abraham was indeed a man of great faith!

Second, God was showing Abraham—and us—that he was *not* like the surrounding deities and idols of the other nations. He was showing Abraham that he would *not* require child sacrifice from him. At the climactic moment, God provided a substitute—a ram that could be offered in the place of Abraham's son.

The strikingly ironic part of this story, when we look ahead in the big picture of the Bible, is that the substitute sacrifice that God would one day offer in the place of his people would not be a ram; it would be *his* Son—Jesus. In other words, God would one day do what he would never ask Abraham, or any of his people, to do. He would provide his own beloved Son to be the final sacrifice for the sins of his people on a cross.

FROM ABRAHAM TO ISAAC

As time passed, God's promise began to be passed from Abraham to his son. Isaac began to grow up, and it became time for Abraham to find him a wife. In the sovereign hand of God in this story, we see evidence of his care and love for Isaac, who would become the leader of the next generation of God's special people in the world.

READ!

Read Genesis 24—the account of Abraham's servant finding a wife for his son Isaac from the land of his relatives and people.

As we study Genesis 24, two main truths emerge. The first is a truth about God's sovereign hand in the details of the lives of his people. The second is a bigger truth about God's continuing commitment to his promise to Abraham.

God's sovereign hand. As you consider the chapter you have just read, think for a moment about all the amazing parts of this story that seem to just "line up," as if by chance. Consider the following:

- Rebekah just "happened" to be the one who approached Abraham's servant at the well as he waited there to see what God would do.
- Rebekah just "happened" to offer drinks to the servant's camels as well—the very sign he had asked God to give him.
- Rebekah just "happened" to be a relative of Abraham—a cousin of Isaac and part of the same tribe and clan.

Obviously, all these things did not just "happen" randomly. God was sovereignly working out the details of providing a wife for Isaac from the people of Abraham. He was in control of every detail of this story. Abraham's servant saw this, so it is no wonder that he cried out, "Blessed be the LORD, the God of my master Abraham, who has not forsaken his steadfast love and his faithfulness toward my master. As for me, the LORD has led me in the way to the house of my master's kinsmen" (Gen. 24:27). We cannot help but see, along with Abraham's servant, how God powerfully orchestrated the details of this meeting and provided the right wife for Isaac, the child of the promise.

God's promise continues. The overwhelming sense that we get from this chapter is that God's promise to Abraham—and to his descendants—would continue. He was not done working out all the details of the growth and blessing of Abraham's family; in fact, he was just getting started. He was hard at work leading Isaac to the right wife, for Isaac would continue the family line of Abraham and continue God's work to make this family into a great nation someday—a nation that he would bless and use to bring his blessing to all the families of the earth. God's great promise of a people was very much alive, and he proved this by his "hidden hand" at work in the story of Isaac and Rebekah.

Interestingly, we are introduced in this story to a sneaky character named Laban—the brother of Rebekah. You can see that he was focused on the ring and the bracelets that his sister was given (Gen. 24:30). He obviously had a greedy streak, and we get the sense that he may have had a few tricks up his sleeve. Laban will turn up again in the story; he will have an interesting part to play.

For now, though, God's promise continues; we see it being passed on from Abraham to Isaac, as God obviously was sovereignly providing a wife for Isaac and remaining faithful to his word. The people of God would continue to grow in the land that he was giving to them.

MEETING JACOB AND ESAU

We now jump ahead in the story a bit to the birth of Isaac and Rebekah's sons: Jacob and Esau. Things began to get a bit messier at this point, for these twin brothers were far from faithful and perfect. Yet we are going to see God's amazing faithfulness to his promises even as he worked through sinful and imperfect people. God was intent on blessing his people.

📖 **READ!**

Read Genesis 25:19–34—the account of the births of Jacob and Esau to Isaac and Rebekah, and the story of Esau selling his birthright to Jacob.

It is not going to take too long to see that this new generation was a "messy" one. Yet we are going to see that God's promise moved forward in his people and in the world.

What are some lessons God is teaching us in this passage?

God's imperfect people. Even the birth of these two boys offered glimpses that they were going to be far from perfect. They came out struggling (Gen. 25:22), with one seemingly ready to come out first, and then the other one pulling ahead at the last minute. Jacob came out grabbing the heel of his (slightly) older brother Esau. These were just early signs of what would be a contentious relationship between two very different sons of Isaac and Rebekah.

God's "grabber." Jacob got his name because he grabbed his brother's heel during his birth (Jacob literally means "he takes by the heel"). This name characterized his life and his actions, as he quickly proved to be a sneaky young man who did whatever he could to selfishly grab for himself what he wanted. We saw this in the passage we read; we're told how Jacob "grabbed" the birthright from his older brother Esau. Jacob caught Esau in a moment of weakness—so hungry that he would do and say practically anything to get some food. He took advantage of this and got Esau to sell him his birthright (the privileges and rights that belonged to the older son).

Esau, though, was not without fault in this transaction. He was shortsighted; he let his belly dictate what he wanted and thought only about the moment. The passage tells us that he "despised" his birthright in this way (Gen. 25:34), not rightly valuing his great privileges as the firstborn. He was obviously a man who based his actions on his physical appetites rather than with his heart and head.

God's promise continues. Yet despite these far-from-perfect people, God's promise was going to continue. The *big* promise of Genesis 12:1–3 was going to form a foundation that would continue throughout the entire book of Genesis—and really through the entire story of the Bible.

In Genesis 26, God confirmed the continuation of his promise to Abraham to Isaac (vv. 1–5). God was committed to keeping his great promise—the promise of a people, a place, and great blessing to them and, through them, to the world. This was an unconditional promise, and God meant to pass it on from generation to generation. After Abraham, Isaac would carry God's promise to him as God's people continued to grow. We are seeing, again, that God is insistent in his blessing on his people.

JACOB—THE GRABBER

Jacob the grabber kept living up to his nickname. When he and Esau were older, Jacob's mother helped him steal Esau's blessing as the first-born. It is a shocking story of deception, but amazingly, God used it as part of his great plan for his people. This, of course, does not excuse the lies and sneakiness of Jacob and Rebekah.

READ!

Read Genesis 27—the lengthy account of Jacob's deception of his father, Isaac, with the help of his mother, Rebekah.

As we study the account of Jacob grabbing the blessing of Isaac from his older brother, Esau, we cannot help but see the sneakiness and deception of this young man. And yet, even this episode has a place in the big picture of God's promise and work in the lives of his people.

The story. It's easy to see where Jacob learned at least some of his deceptive tendencies; Rebekah was quite sneaky and tricky. She heard Isaac send Esau away to hunt for game with which to make him a meal, after which he would give him his great blessing. Rebekah hatched a plan, and Jacob went along with it completely.

Jacob, clothed with Esau's garments (Isaac could barely see by this point), approached Isaac with food that Rebekah had prepared. He told his father that he was Esau, and that he had come to receive his blessing from Isaac. Isaac was a bit skeptical, but he ultimately fell for it; he blessed Jacob, telling him that he would be "lord" over his brothers (Gen. 27:29) and would possess God's great blessing (v. 28).

By the time Esau got back from hunting, Isaac had given his blessing to Jacob. Not surprisingly, Esau was furious, and began planning to kill Jacob. This chapter ends with Rebekah again using deception to plan to send Jacob away for his own safety.

Jacob the man. What do we learn about Jacob through all of this? We certainly learn that he was close with his mother and had picked up her deceptive tendencies. He allowed her to influence him to grab the birthright and the blessing from Esau, his older brother. Jacob, we see, was a deceiver—a man who did not seem to have a moral compass, but who did whatever he needed to do to get what he wanted.

As we will see, God had some work to do in Jacob's life. He was the son of Isaac and the grandson of Abraham, so God's promise would continue through him. But God would also pursue the heart of Jacob, and bring him to obedience and faith.

God's promise. What is perhaps most amazing about an account like this is that it shows us that God's promise, originally given to Abraham in Genesis 12, went forward in the world even through a man like Jacob! God, in his mercy, did not take away his promise of blessing, even when things like this happened. God's promise, we see, was unconditional; he was committed to letting his blessing come to Abraham's descendants, and through them to the world—even if they were sometimes faithless and despicable people. We are, again, pointed to the amazing grace of God, who makes unbreakable promises to sinful people who need his grace.

GOD'S PURSUIT OF JACOB

God never gave up on Jacob, but kept pursuing him and ultimately changed this grabber's heart. God blessed Jacob and continued to work out his great promise through him and his family. God, we see, can change the hearts of people like Jacob and work through their lives in powerful ways.

READ!

Read Genesis 29–30—a large section of the account of Jacob as he worked for Laban and was given both Rachel and Leah (Laban's daughters) as his wives.

If you have any extra time, read through as much of Genesis 31, 32, and 33 as you can. These chapters will tell you more about the developments in Jacob's life as God continued to pursue this grabber and work in his heart and life. For now, we'll focus on some of the main events in Jacob's life during his time of working for Laban.

Wrestling with Laban. Do you remember Laban? He was Rebekah's brother, who came out to meet Abraham's servant, who had come to find a wife for Isaac. You might remember that he seemed especially impressed by the ring and the gold bracelets that Abraham's servant had given to his sister. When he saw these valuable pieces of jewelry, he was immediately in favor of the marriage. Laban, it seems, was a bit of a "grabber," too.

Jacob found a home—and a job—with Laban when he fled from his brother Esau. Jacob quickly fell in love with Laban's daughter Rachel, and Laban promised her to Jacob as a wife—if Jacob would work for him for seven years. On Jacob's wedding night, though, Laban played a terrible trick on Jacob: he gave him his older, much less beautiful, daughter Leah as a wife! Jacob was furious, but he could do nothing about it. The deceiver had met his match, and Jacob soon had two wives because of Laban's deception.

Wrestling in marriage. These two wives—jealous sisters—did not make married life easy for Jacob. They were in constant competition with one another; they even tried to have children to earn Jacob's affections. It did not help that Jacob obviously loved Rachel more than Leah. His marriage was like a wrestling match, as there seemed to be constant strife and competition between the daughters of Laban, whom Jacob had married.

Wrestling with God. Through all his time with Laban, we do not get much information about the nature of Jacob's relationship with God. But based on what happened to him later, it's possible that he was beginning to change a bit in his heart. Perhaps getting a taste of his own medicine from Laban helped humble him a bit. Perhaps he began to turn in faith to the God of his grandfather, Abraham. We simply cannot be sure what was going on in Jacob's heart during this time.

We do know, though, that after Jacob left Laban with his family, God finally met him face-to-face. If you have time, read Genesis 32, which contains the account of Jacob "wrestling" with God in the middle of the night. In many ways, this "struggle" with God was typical of Jacob's entire life; it was all a struggle, with Jacob sinning and resisting obedience and faith in God. This time, though, Jacob wrestled with God and held on to him, demanding that God bless him (we cannot quite understand this passage, so we must simply believe that God chose to make this interaction possible by his grace). God blessed him and changed his name to "Israel," telling him that he had "prevailed" in his wrestling with God (Gen. 32:28). "Israel" ultimately became the name of God's chosen people as the divine promises passed on to the next generations.

God's blessing to Jacob. Jacob's nighttime wrestling match with God seems to have been a turning point in his life, for afterward, he began to embrace God's promise and live as a man of faith in the God of his father and grandfather. God had pursued this deceiver, and Jacob joyfully became a bearer of God's promise of blessing, given years before to Abraham.

Are you seeing how the story of Genesis is a story of God's grace? Are you seeing how God is insistent on bringing his blessing to his people—even imperfect and flawed people? Are you seeing how he pursued Jacob for years, and finally changed his heart?

Hopefully this story is deeply encouraging to you. You are learning about a God who makes promises to sinful people and keeps them—simply because of who he is.

JACOB AND HIS SONS

Over time, Jacob's family absolutely exploded with growth! Jacob had twelve sons, who lived with him and cared for the many flocks of sheep that he owned. Sadly, though, like the family of Isaac and Rebekah, this family had its share of problems. Still, as Genesis continues, we see that God can make his good purposes come from very evil things that his people choose to do.

READ!

Read Genesis 37—the beginning of the narrative account of Joseph.

Think back to where this people began. God spoke to one man—Abraham—and pulled him out of his homeland (a place that was likely full of idolatry and sin). God made a huge promise to this man—a promise of a people, a land, and blessing to his descendants that would also bring blessing to all the families of the earth. Already, as Genesis 37 begins, we see evidence of God's great commitment to this promise—a promise that he was going to bring about no matter how imperfect his people might be.

Keeping the promise. Just look at how richly God had blessed Jacob; he had given him twelve sons! These sons, as you know, would become the "fathers" of the twelve tribes of Israel—the people of God. It is becoming more and more obvious to us that the promise that God gave to Abraham was being passed down from generation to generation—

from Abraham to Isaac and now to Jacob and his family. We know that this promise from God did not depend on the goodness of his people because we know about the many failures of Jacob before he ultimately put his faith in the God of his fathers. God was faithfully carrying out his work in the lives of his people from generation to generation—and working to bring his saving blessing into the world through them.

Hints of the future. As Genesis 37 begins, we see that Joseph, the second-youngest son of Jacob, had two dreams, which he unwisely shared with his whole family. The first dream was a picture of his brothers' sheaves of wheat bowing down to his sheaf of wheat. The second dream was a picture of the sun, the moon, and eleven stars (obviously symbolizing his parents and his brothers) bowing down to him. Joseph probably should have kept quiet about these dreams, but they do seem truly to have been from God. Terrible things were going to happen soon to Joseph, but God was giving a hint of where this story was going to lead, as he would bring Joseph to a position of great power and authority in Egypt.

Problems in the family. As I mentioned above, this family had problems, just like the family of Isaac and Rebekah did. In Genesis 37:3, we learn that the terrible practice of favoritism was at work in this family; Jacob loved Joseph more than all the rest of his brothers. We cannot help but wonder whether Jacob might have learned this from his own family experience: Isaac loved Esau and Rebekah loved him. In any case, parental favoritism became an ugly source of the hatred Joseph's brothers felt toward him.

As the chapter continues, we see the awful and terrible result of this hatred: Joseph's brothers sold him into slavery. The account ends with Joseph in the land of Egypt. He was sold into the service of a man named Potiphar, who was the captain of the guard of Pharaoh, the king of Egypt. At this point, Joseph's brothers surely thought that they would never see him again (they lied to their father that he had been devoured by wild animals). But God was not done. Even this evil action was part of his larger plan and purpose to grow and prosper his people, and to bring his blessing to all the families of the earth.

JOSEPH'S DIFFICULT PATH

This appeared to be the end for Joseph. It seemed likely that he would live out his days as a slave in Egypt—far from God's people and disconnected from the promise of God.

As the story continues, though, we are going to see that God had something much greater than a life of slavery planned for Joseph. All that had happened to him, in all the evil and sin, had been for God's great purpose in his life and in the lives of God's people. In the passages that you will read, we will begin to see God working in the life of Joseph, even as things seem to get *worse* for him.

READ!

Read Genesis 39–41—two chapters that help us understand a bit more about Joseph's experience in Egypt.

In addition to the reading for this section, take time to read more of the story of Joseph as you are able. This is one of the great stories in all the Bible. There is simply no human explanation for Joseph's rise to power in Egypt. God blessed, protected, and helped him at every step along the way. It was bigger than Joseph, too; God was keeping his promise to his people through his faithfulness to this man.

In the house of Potiphar. When Joseph was a slave in the house of Potiphar, God began to richly bless him; he had not abandoned Joseph in Egypt. Joseph quickly proved himself to be talented, smart, and effective, and Potiphar promoted him until he was essentially second in command over all the people in his house. Then, just as things seemed to be going so well, everything fell apart. After Joseph repeatedly rejected sexual advances from Potiphar's wife, she falsely accused Joseph of assaulting her, and he was thrown into prison.

If you were Joseph, how would you have felt at this point? He was trying to honor God by saying no to sex with a married woman because of his faith in the God of his fathers. This faithfulness had not gotten him anywhere; in fact, it had landed him in prison. Even there, though, God's work was not done.

In prison. Joseph soon began to find the same favor in prison that he had found in the house of Potiphar. The keeper of the prison, like Potiphar, recognized the special hand of God in this young man's life and put him in charge of all the other inmates in the prison. God again blessed Joseph in a special way and gave him favor in everything he did.

Part of this favor was Joseph's ability to interpret dreams, by God's help. He did this, while in prison, for two servants of Pharaoh. One of them, the chief cupbearer of Pharaoh, was encouraged by Joseph's interpretation of his dream, which told him that he would soon be returned to service in Pharaoh's household. He promised to "remember" Joseph before the king when he got out of prison. But when he was released, he promptly forgot all about Joseph. Joseph again was left in what seemed to be a hopeless situation.

In the service of Pharaoh. Finally, though, after two dreams that Pharaoh could not interpret, the cupbearer's memory was jogged, and he mentioned Joseph to the king as a man who knew God and who therefore could interpret dreams. Joseph was called out of prison, brought before Pharaoh, and called on to interpret these dreams of this king of Egypt.

The interpretation of the dreams referred to coming years of plentiful food and then coming years of famine. Joseph advised Pharaoh to prepare stores of food for the people in preparation for the years of famine. Pharaoh thought this was a wonderful idea and decided to put *Joseph* in charge of this process.

We are beginning, finally, to see God's purpose in this story (remember, we have gone through these events quickly, but these were *very* long years for Joseph). In all these terrible things, God's purpose was to bring Joseph to a place where he would actually become second in command in Egypt.

The refrain. Did you notice a refrain in these chapters? Twice in chapter 39, the author used the phrase "the Lord was with him" (vv. 3, 23) to remind us about the God who was active in every part of Joseph's life. God indeed was with Joseph—for his good and for the ultimate good of his people. We will learn what this looked like in the lives of his people as we continue our survey of the story.

JOSEPH'S RISE

Joseph's life seemed to keep getting worse—before it got better. He was sold into slavery in Egypt, where he worked hard (and was blessed by God) to grow and prosper in the service of Potiphar. Then, just as things seemed to be getting better, he was falsely accused and thrown into prison. There he interpreted the dreams of the royal cupbearer, only to be completely forgotten by this man when he was restored to his position with Pharaoh. Finally, after many long years, God brought Joseph out of prison and into a place of unimagined authority and power in Egypt—ruling at the right hand of Pharaoh himself!

Let's look now at the conclusion of Joseph's story. We will see how all these events were part of God's big plan to save his people from the great famine (predicted by Pharaoh's dream) and to bring salvation to them and many other people in many parts of the world through Joseph and his wise leadership in Egypt. We also will see how this story began to fulfill God's great promise to Abraham many years before.

READ!

Read Genesis 45 and 47 to get a glimpse of how Joseph finally revealed himself to his brothers, who came from the land of Canaan to buy food from the Egyptians.

As you read these chapters in Genesis, I hope you were encouraged by the way in which this story came together, as you saw God's big purpose in all of this finally revealed. Let's think together about how this happened and what God was doing behind the scenes this entire time.

Joseph and his brothers. Jacob sent Joseph's brothers to Egypt to buy food for the family during the great time of famine. Joseph, as you know, had been set over the entire land of Egypt by Pharaoh, to oversee the collection of food and the distribution of it to people who came to Egypt to buy it. Egypt was the only region that was prepared for this famine because God had revealed it ahead of time to Joseph.

As Joseph interacted with his brothers, he had a bit of "fun" with them first; his purpose, ultimately, was to get his younger brother Benjamin to come with them to Egypt. Finally, he revealed himself to his brothers, and they reconciled with great weeping and rejoicing. Amazingly, Joseph had no revenge agenda toward them; he easily could have had them all immediately killed for what they had done to him many years earlier. Instead, he forgave them, spoke kindly to them, and invited them to bring all the people of Jacob to Egypt to settle there.

Joseph and God's big plan. It is at this point, then, that we begin to see God's *big* purpose and plan in Joseph's life. All that God was doing—even through the evil actions of Joseph's brothers—was focused on bringing his people to Egypt so that they could be saved from death and starvation during the coming time of famine. Joseph became, in God's hand, the instrument that God used to spare the lives of many people—including the children of Abraham. Also, through this account, we see how the people of Israel were brought into Egypt. As we will see, they would flourish and explode in numbers in Egypt for four hundred years.

Joseph and a "better" Joseph. We cannot miss the fact that God's big promise to Abraham—of blessing through his people to all the nations—was being fulfilled in partial ways through Joseph's life. Think about this for a moment. Joseph—a descendant of Abraham—became God's way of bringing blessing—rescue from famine—to people from many nations in the world. God had placed a member of Abraham's family on the "throne" in Egypt, and through him came great blessing both to his people (Jacob's family) and many other peoples in the world.

However, this was only a partial fulfillment of this great promise from God. Even in this great moment, Joseph was pointing us forward to a much greater version of himself—Jesus Christ, God's own Son. He would bring salvation to God's people—and all nations of the earth— in a much more lasting way than Joseph ever could!

REVIEW

God's promise continues from generation to generation—from Abraham to Isaac to Jacob and, through Jacob's son Joseph, to the surrounding nations during the time of famine. Despite the hard and rebellious hearts of his people, God kept his promises. He was forming a family for himself, calling them to take him at his word and believe his gracious promises to them.

PRAY!

Close this chapter with prayer, thanking God for his sovereign hand in the life of Joseph, which was connected to his promise of blessing for all his people. Thank God that he is still active in the world today, still working for the good, eternal purposes of all who know him, and love and serve his Son, Jesus Christ. Pray that you would have faith in his good promises, through Jesus, even today.

Chapter 6

GOD'S PEOPLE GROW
PART 1

We are now entering the third scene of the Bible story, which I've called "God's People Grow." As we begin this section, let's think back together on what we have covered so far:

- In the first scene of the Bible story, "God's Creation and a Crisis," we covered Genesis 1–3. We learned about the foundational truth of God's creation of the world, and about the crisis of sin and its devastating effects on humanity and all other parts of God's world.
- In the second scene, "God's Promise of a People," we covered Genesis 4–50. We learned about God's continuing work in his world even after the fall of humanity into sin. From Genesis 12 on, we learned how God's great promise to Abraham shapes everything that he does in the world, as he is committed to blessing his people and blessing the world through them.

In this chapter, we are going to be covering much more biblical text than we have covered so far. In fact, we are going to cover Exodus, Leviticus, Numbers, and Deuteronomy (although we will certainly not

93

read and discuss every single chapter). We are going to see how God's promise to Abraham continued in the lives of his people. And we are going to see the way God's people grew, and how he began to work to make them his own distinct people among all the nations.

Initially, my goal is to help you grasp what happens in the Bible story during this scene, which we will study in this chapter and the next one. Here are a few key points that will be helpful to know up front:

- After Jacob brings his family to Egypt during the life of Joseph, God's people live there for four hundred years. What begins as a group of about seventy people (Jacob's children and their children) becomes a huge group of Israelites, or Hebrews—some estimate there were almost 1 million of them! As you will see in a moment, the sheer number of God's people eventually begins to make the Egyptians nervous.
- The part of the Bible story that we will cover during this chapter is the Exodus narrative, which obviously focuses on the person of Moses. Moses is one of the great leaders of God's people—one who points forward to Christ in significant ways. Moses is a type of Christ. This means that he is like Jesus in some way; he points ahead to Jesus, even though he is just a man.
- During this chapter, we will also cover—very generally—God's giving of the law to the people through Moses. We will not study every part of the law. It is important to understand that, while the law was given to God's people for them to obey, it was never the way by which they would find eternal salvation. It was more about the way they should live as God's people in the community of Israel. Obedience to the law was important, of course, but salvation with God has always been about faith in him (then, as now).

In a moment, we will turn to the opening chapters of the book of Exodus and begin thinking about God's people in Egypt and the deliverance that he ultimately provided for them through Moses. It is important that, as you begin this new chapter, you remind yourself that you are continuing to learn about the same story—the one big story of God's work in the world by his grace through his people. This is the same God who made the world, gave his grace to Noah, made promises to Abraham, and then worked through Moses to deliver his people from slavery in Egypt. This is the same God whom we can follow and serve today through faith in his Son, Jesus Christ!

Remember!

Your suggested memory verses for this chapter come from Exodus 34—a passage in which God revealed his character to Moses in a special way.

The LORD passed before him and proclaimed, "The LORD, the LORD, a God merciful and gracious, slow to anger, and abounding in steadfast love and faithfulness, keeping steadfast love for thousands, forgiving iniquity and transgression and sin, but who will by no means clear the guilty, visiting the iniquity of the fathers on the children and the children's children, to the third and the fourth generation." (Ex. 34:6–7)

A NEW PHARAOH IN EGYPT

The book of Exodus opens four hundred years after the story of Joseph, which concluded our last chapter. Do you remember how Joseph summarized God's plan in his life and the lives of his people? As the book of Genesis concluded, Joseph told his brothers that they had intended evil for him (by selling him into slavery) but God had meant it all for good (Gen. 50:20). God intended to bring his people to Egypt during the years of famine and to use Joseph—one of God's people—to save them and many other people from many different nations. God was fulfilling his promise of blessing to and through Abraham—at least in a partial way—through the life of Joseph.

But as Exodus begins, it quickly becomes clear that Egypt will not be the final place for this people God is so richly blessing. The book begins with a very ominous phrase, which we will read just below, and it soon becomes clear to us that God will need to provide for his people once again.

READ!

Read Exodus 1—a chapter that describes the situation of God's people in Egypt.

In many ways, the first chapter of Exodus sets up everything that will happen in the story of Moses and God's people. Our goal, then, is to rightly understand the situation of God's people so that we can prepare for all that will happen as the Bible story continues.

God's promise. The first thing that we notice in Exodus 1 is the amazing fulfillment of God's promise to Abraham, which happened amid God's people in Egypt. Verse 7 tells us that "the people of Israel were fruitful and increased greatly," so that they filled the land of Egypt.

Do you remember when God told Abraham to look up at the night sky and said that his descendants would be like the stars in number (Gen. 15)? Abraham, although he was married to an old and barren woman, took God at his word; he believed him. Now we see God keeping that promise. Abraham's descendants were multiplying and growing in an amazing way in Egypt.

God's people's problem. Did you notice the ominous verse in this passage that warns us about what will come next? It is Exodus 1:8—"Now there arose a new king over Egypt, who did not know Joseph." Remember, Joseph had experienced great favor with Pharaoh many years earlier. He had become the second in command in all the land. That was what had brought the people of Israel to Egypt in the first place.

But as time went by, the Egyptian rulers had become less and less comfortable with an ever-increasing number of Israelites in their midst. Pharaoh felt threatened by them and responded by making them all his slaves. The passage that you just read recounts Pharaoh's harsh treatment of the people of Israel. He set taskmasters over them and put them to work doing hard manual labor. Pharaoh was extremely cruel to them. We know, from later in the story, that God's people begin to cry out to him for help.

God's blessing. Even though God's people had a serious problem, two very big hints of God's blessing emerge from this passage—first regarding his people and then regarding those who were not naturally his people:

- First, God's people continued to multiply and grow even under the oppression and cruelty of Pharaoh (read Ex. 1:12 again). Pharaoh simply could not keep God's people down!
- Second, God blessed some of the Hebrew women who refused to murder the male children of the Israelites as Pharaoh had commanded them to do. It seems that many of the people in Egypt had begun to recognize the power of God and his hand on his people.

There will be much more to this story, as we will see in the coming pages. God's people had grown, but they were living in oppression and slavery. It was time for the next step in God's plan for them.

A SPECIAL CHILD

In Exodus 2, we get the first glimpse of God's answer to his people's problem. Here we are introduced to a baby boy who would grow up to be a great deliverer for God's people. Even in this account of his childhood, it is obvious that God's hand was on this young man in a very special way. God had something very good in store for his people, who were stuck in slavery in Egypt.

READ!

Read Exodus 2—the birth narrative of Moses.

As I mentioned, Pharaoh not only had subjected the Israelites to slavery but also had proclaimed a "death order" on every Israelite boy born in Egypt. The command was to put all male children to death (although we saw that the midwives feared God and did not obey this order). The Israelites had to be very careful to keep the births of male children secret.

One family, from the tribe of Levi, had a baby boy. Fearing for the life of her child, his mother decided to place him in a basket and send him away down the Nile River, trusting God to take care of him. Can you imagine living in such a situation, where you come to think that this is the only choice you have to spare your child's life?

Amazingly, the baby was drawn out of the water by one of the daughters of Pharaoh, who decided to raise him as her own son. She named him Moses. Moses's sister, who had followed him down the river, persuaded the daughter of Pharaoh to let Moses's own mother serve as his nurse. Clearly God's hand was on the life of this baby boy; he grew up as a prince in the house of Pharaoh himself.

As Moses grew, though, he became aware of the situation of his people in Egypt. One day, he saw an Egyptian beating one of his fellow Israelites. Moses reacted quickly, killing the Egyptian and hiding his body. Moses did not get away with this, though; his action became known, and he had to flee for his life. He ended up in the land of Midian—far from Egypt—where he took a wife and settled down. It seemed, at this point, as if the story of Moses might be over.

But there is a hint as this chapter ends that this man, on whom God's hand had been so evident, would have a role to play in the lives of God's people in the years to come. The author of Exodus tells us of the "groaning" of the people of Israel (Ex. 2:24) as they cried out to God for rescue from slavery. God saw his people, so he knew they needed help. We are left wondering if Moses might have something to do with the way in which God would answer the groaning of his people.

In a way, we cannot help but look at this truly miraculous birth narrative of Moses as pointing us forward to a far greater birth narrative. One day, many years later in God's great story, his own Son would enter the world as a baby boy, born to a young virgin named Mary, and he would grow up to be the great Savior and deliverer of God's people. In the story of Moses, God is showing us a pattern of how he was going to work in the lives of his people to bring his blessing and salvation to them. He would do it by providing a deliverer, who would release them from slavery and death.

MOSES CONFRONTS PHARAOH

In Exodus 3, we see that Moses was called directly by God (via a burning bush) to return to Egypt. He had to go to Pharaoh and bring the people of Israel out of slavery so they could serve God on Mount Horeb in the wilderness of Sinai.

READ!

Read Exodus 5—the account of the first interaction between Moses and Pharaoh after Moses went back to Egypt.

After Moses returned to Egypt, he went to confront Pharaoh to demand that he let the Israelites go.

Moses before Pharaoh. At Moses's confrontation with Pharaoh, he probably wished he had stayed back in Midian! Pharaoh essentially laughed in Moses's face and denied his request to release the people of Israel so that they could worship God in the wilderness. But it seems he was angry rather than amused, because he increased the burden of work on the Israelites, forcing them to find the straw they needed to make bricks (an important component of their mode of construction). Even the leaders of Israel were upset with Moses, and Exodus 5 ends with Moses turning to God in what seems almost like anger and despair. It was not a promising beginning for Moses as the leader of God's people.

Pharaoh's response. Pharaoh's response to Moses and to God was—as we will see—an indication of his hard and sinful heart. He would stubbornly refuse to release God's people from slavery (probably because the Egyptian economy had come to rely, in large part, on the slave labor of the Israelites). Yet God would have glory over Pharaoh; his work for his people, through Moses, was only beginning.

Scan ahead in the story just a bit to Exodus 6:1. Here we see that God responded to Moses's complaint with a promise about what he soon would do in Egypt. He was not done keeping his promise to Abraham; he soon would lead this people out of the land and set them up to become a blessing to all the nations of the world.

GOD'S DELIVERANCE

In this section, we are going to cover a lot of ground in a short time as we learn what happened next in this story of God's work in the lives of his people. Through the plagues in Egypt and the final salvation picture of the Passover, God's commitment to keeping his great promises to Abraham—promises of a great people, a land, and blessing to them and, through them, to all nations of the earth—becomes even clearer.

◼ READ!

Read Exodus 11–12, the account of the final plague on Egypt, the "Passover" of God, and the Israelites' exodus from Egypt. If possible, read even more of the biblical text so that you will understand the story better.

These chapters are among the most exciting in the whole Bible story as God acts in power to overcome Pharaoh's hard heart and free his people from their slavery in Egypt.

The plagues. You saw that Pharaoh responded angrily and stubbornly to Moses's request to release the people of Israel from slavery. God's response was to send plagues—judgments—on Egypt in response to

Pharaoh's sin and stubbornness. These plagues, as we see from the Exodus account (chaps. 7–10), came in the following order:

- Egypt's water was turned to *blood.*
- Egypt was filled with *frogs.*
- Egypt was filled with *gnats.*
- Egypt was filled with *flies.*
- Egypt's *livestock* died.
- Egypt's people were covered with *boils.*
- Egypt was devastated by *hail.*
- Egypt was filled with *locusts.*
- Egypt was covered in *darkness.*

With each plague, Pharaoh continually refused to release God's people from slavery. He proved to be stubbornly opposed to God's plan for his people—his promise to Abraham that he was working to fulfill for them. Pharaoh sinfully set himself up against both God and his people.

The final plague. The final judgment that God brought on Egypt was by far the worst: he took the life of every firstborn child in the entire land. This was a vivid picture that God gave to his people—and to all of Egypt: sin against the God of the universe ultimately results in death. Pharaoh had been playing a very dangerous game with the Creator God, and he would now pay for his stubbornness with the loss of his firstborn son.

The Passover. God's people, though, were given a way out of this judgment. As God prepared to bring this plague on Egypt, he instituted something called the Passover—a meal and a ceremony that would mark his people and place them safely under God's special sign. As you saw from Exodus 12, this included a very detailed process, meal, and ceremony that God asked his people to go through. God was carefully and intentionally reminding his people that they were to be set apart from other people in Egypt—set apart for worship of him, and therefore spared from his terrible judgment that was coming on the land. God intended the Passover to become a continual feast for his people so that they would always remember this day.

The sign. So what was the Passover sign specifically? God's people, as you saw from Exodus 12, were asked to prepare a special meal as they got ready to go out from Egypt. Every family was asked to kill a lamb (one without any blemishes or defects) and to smear the blood of that lamb on the doorposts of their houses so that God would see it and "pass over," not bringing judgment against them. The people obeyed, and death did not come to their houses.

The New Testament tells us that this Passover sign was pointing forward to a much greater sign of blood—the blood of God's own Son, Jesus, who would be called the perfect "Lamb of God" (John 1:29, 36). This Old Testament sign spared God's people from the tenth plague in Egypt; the blood of Jesus would spare God's people—who put their faith in him—from the eternal judgment and punishment of hell. So the first Passover was a big moment for God's people, and for the entire story of the Bible!

PHARAOH'S OPPOSITION TO GOD

Even after the Israelites actually left Egypt, the story was not yet over. Pharaoh quickly changed his mind about letting God's people leave and decided to go after them. But God did not stop working to save and deliver his people, because he was intent on keeping his great promises to them by his grace.

READ!

Read Exodus 14—the account of the miraculous crossing of the Red Sea. Then read Exodus 16—an account of the life of God's people in the wilderness and the way in which God provided for their needs.

We are continuing to move quickly through this portion of the story. That means you are reading only a part of it (Ex. 14 and 16). If you have time, read Exodus 15 as well, which records the great song of Moses after the Israelites' Red Sea crossing.

The Red Sea. The Passover sign, you remember, was a picture of God's deliverance of his people. The blood of the lamb was meant to be the great sign of sacrifice that can deliver people from God's wrath and judgment. It pointed forward in the Bible story to the sacrificial death of Jesus Christ for God's people. The apostle Paul calls Jesus the "Passover Lamb" (1 Cor. 5:7), who was slain for sinners to spare them from judgment.

The Red Sea crossing was the completion of God's saving actions for his people. He had taken them out of Egypt, but as we see from Exodus 14, after the Israelites had actually left Egypt, Pharaoh quickly changed his mind about releasing them (probably because he realized that his slave labor force had left his country). So Pharaoh chased God's people with his army and caught up to them near the Red Sea. But the Egyptians could not get near the people all night because God caused a great darkness to fall upon them. Even so, Moses and the people cried out to God for help.

In the morning, God performed one of the greatest miracles in the history of the world for his people: he separated the Red Sea before them, and God's people began crossing over on dry ground. As Pharaoh's forces followed them in, God (through Moses) brought the waters of the sea rushing back together after the people had crossed over, and all the Egyptians were destroyed. God brought a great salvation to his people on this day—in miraculous fashion—and they were finally completely freed from slavery and set apart to be God's special people. This became a climactic saving event that Moses sang about. God's people would look back on it for centuries as a picture of God's mighty actions for them.

The provision of God. As God's people began life in the wilderness, it was obvious that his work on their behalf was not nearly done. He began to care for his people in the desert as they prepared to worship and serve him there. He gave them quail to eat, as well as "manna" (a kind of bread) that came down from heaven each morning. God began actively and carefully providing for the needs of his people as they came into the wilderness.

The grumbling people. Go back now and reread Exodus 14:11–12 and 16:2–3. Did you notice those verses during your first reading? God had done amazing things in the lives of his people—first through the plagues and the Passover, and then through the miraculous crossing of the Red Sea. Still, right after each of these events, God's people were extremely quick to begin grumbling and complaining. This is amazing, isn't it? They did not believe that God could keep on taking care of them, and they even asked Moses to send them back to Egypt!

This grumbling is a big hint of what is to come as this story continues. God had grown his people in Egypt and rescued them from slavery, but they were still sinful and stubborn. As the Bible story continues, we will see that they—and *we*—need something to deal with the deep-seated problem of sin in our lives and hearts.

APPLYING GOD'S LAW TODAY

In many ways, the passage you will read next begins to reveal God's purpose for his people as he called them out from slavery in Egypt and into service to him. In it, we will begin to see how God started to "set apart" a special people for himself—the great nation that he had promised so many years before to Abraham, and that he had promised to bless greatly and lead into a land of their own.

The Old Testament law, as you know, is constantly debated, especially with regard to how it should be applied to the lives of Christians today. I hope this discussion will give you a clearer picture of how it was meant to function in the lives of God's people *then*. You will then be in a better position to see how God's law should be understood by Christians today.

READ!

Read Exodus 19–20—the account of God's people finally gathering in the wilderness (to "serve" God) and receiving his good law, which came to them through Moses.

God's people had come out from slavery in Egypt; God was keeping his promise to Abraham, making this people into a great nation and preparing to bless them and bless the world through them. What would be next? What would God do in the lives of his people in the wilderness?

God's goal. There was a phrase that Moses—on God's behalf—kept repeating to Pharaoh throughout the Exodus narrative. Did you notice it? Look back and read through the accounts of a few of the times when Moses went before Pharaoh, and note the words that God gave him to speak. Here is the phrase: "Let my people go, that they may *serve* me" (Ex. 7:16; 8:1, 20; 9:1, 13; 10:3). That was the whole focus of God, it seems; he wanted to get his people out of slavery in Egypt so that they could "serve" him in the wilderness.

We might think, then, that God had a great "project" for his people to do in the wilderness or that he really wanted to hear them sing praises to him in worship. In a way, this was true; God did want the obedience of his people, and he wanted to use them to bring his blessing to all the peoples of the earth. But what exactly did God have in mind for the service of his people in the wilderness?

The law of God. Exodus 19, which you just read, records the people gathering around Mount Sinai, getting ready to serve God in the wilderness. God had called them out of slavery in Egypt, and they were now being set apart as God's special people in service to him. What happened next (at the beginning of Ex. 20)? God *spoke.* He gave his law—his good *word*—to his people. This is what God had wanted to do all along. He had intended to save this people, deliver them from slavery, and then bring them into his service by giving them the gift of living under his good word.

Understanding the law. What we have just discussed is the key to understanding the Old Testament law of God correctly. You see, the law was *never* intended to be a way for someone to "earn" favor with God in a saving way—or become part of his true people. We know this because God saved his people and delivered them from slavery in Egypt *before* he gave them the law!

What was the purpose of the law, then? God gave it to his people to guide them as they lived as his "set-apart" people under his good word. It was to instruct them about how to live in the presence of their holy God, who is perfect in every way. Salvation with this God is always by faith, through his grace and mercy; we know this from Abraham, who was saved by God through faith long before this law was delivered to his descendants.

We will not read through all the law, but you should study the books of Leviticus and Deuteronomy at some point soon. When you do, remember this important discussion. Remember the right place of the law—it is God's good word, given to guide people whom he has already delivered and made into a special nation for his own glory.

GOD'S PEOPLE REBEL

When God gave his good law to his people at Mount Sinai, it seemed to be the beginning of a beautiful new nation—and a beautiful new relationship between Israel and God. But sin remained in the lives and hearts of God's people, even after they had seen him act so mightily and gloriously on their behalf. We see this in the sad account of the golden calf—the decision of God's people to bow down to a mute idol rather than give their worship to the true, holy, and invisible God.

READ!

Read Exodus 32—the sad account of the creation and worship of the golden calf by Aaron and the people.

Moses was up on the mountain, receiving God's law—the good word that he was giving to his people to guide their lives as they followed him. But Moses took longer than they hoped, and they began to get restless and doubt God. They began to want visible objects—idols—that they could worship. This is where Exodus 32 begins.

The golden calf. Aaron, the priest for the people and Moses's brother, may have had good motives for what he did. He was trying to stop a rebellion of the people against Moses and God, and he may have been trying to give the people a visible "picture" of God with which they could identify. However, he did a foolish thing that led God's people into terrible idolatry and rebellion against the God who rules his people by his word.

To please the people and keep them happy while they waited for Moses to come down, Aaron invited them to donate their gold jewelry to him. He then melted it all down and created a statue of a calf. Then he invited the people to worship this image as the "god" who had brought them out of Egypt.

When Moses came down from the mountain, where the true God had been giving him his good word for his people, he found the people bowing down in worship before this golden cow!

The anger of God and the mediation of Moses. Obviously, God was angry at his people for this sinful idolatry. God is invisible, holy, and infinite; he could never be represented by an image like this. Punishment would come for God's people because they had sinned against him with their idolatry.

Interestingly, though, God allowed Moses to play a kind of mediatorial role—standing between God and the people as he pleaded for God's mercy and forgiveness for them. There would be judgment for this terrible sin, but Moses mediated for God's people and reminded God of his grace and mercy.

The lesson. So what do we learn from this sad account? What should we take from this story about God's people turning to worship an idol made of gold, even as Moses, their leader, was on the mountain receiving the good word for them from their Creator God? We should learn that:

- God's people's sin was serious. It would ultimately destroy God's people unless he solved it in an eternal way. The people who so recently had been gloriously saved and delivered by the holy God had turned quickly to idolatry. We are learning that people are bent toward worshiping visible things—idols made by human hands—rather than the true, holy, and invisible God who communicates with people through his good word.
- God's people needed a better priest. Aaron, who should have stood up for the holiness of God and prevented the worship of this idol, instead became the ringleader for the people in their sin. He made the golden calf, supported the people's worship of it, and then tried to deflect blame from himself when he was questioned by Moses. God's people obviously needed a better religious leader than Aaron—an eternal one.
- God's people needed a better mediator. Even the godly leader Moses could not be their final mediator—the one who would permanently turn away God's wrath from a sinful people. Moses gave only a faint glimmer—a hint—of the role that Jesus Christ would need to play for God's people. He would "go between" sinful people and the holy God in a permanent and lasting way. He would finally deal with their sin and bring God's forgiveness to them.

SINNING AND WANDERING

It would be very nice if we could say that Israel's sin was a one-time occurrence that never happened again. Sadly, that was not the case. In your next reading, you will learn about the great lack of faith on the part of the Israelites that kept them out of the promised land for forty years. You will see that, in general, the people were still not ready to fully take God at his word and to believe deeply that he always keeps his promises to his people.

READ!

Read Numbers 13–14.

It was finally time. God's people had been brought out from Egypt—released from their slavery and bondage to Pharaoh. God had done this in miraculous ways, through plagues of judgment against Egypt and through the climactic crossing of the Red Sea by the people. God also had given his people his good word—his law—which was meant to guide them in their new "set-apart" life in community and relationship with the holy God, and with one another. Now it was time to prepare to enter the land that God had promised to Abraham and his descendants.

Think for a moment about how God's faithfulness to his promise to Abraham was continuing. God had promised to make Abraham a great nation; this had happened, as almost a million Israelites went out from Egypt as God's special nation. God had promised Abraham a land; God was now getting ready to bring his people into Canaan as their inheritance. God had promised Abraham that he would bless his descendants, and that they would be a blessing to the nations of the world; God had given his people his word, which would show them how to live as his people and prepare them to be a blessing to the world. In that context, what happened next was very sad.

Spies sent out. As the preparations for the invasion of the land began (other, sinful peoples lived in the land that God was going to give to his people), Moses sent out twelve "spies" to go into the land and bring back a report about it and the people who lived there. The spies returned and told the people about the abundance of the land, but also about the immense strength of the people there, as well as their fortified cities. Only two men—Joshua and Caleb—gave a favorable report, and they reminded the people that God was powerful enough to keep his promise and give them the land.

Failure of faith. Sadly, the people listened to the ten spies with the negative report, not to the two faithful ones. At the beginning of Numbers 14, you read about the people weeping all night at these spies' frightening report and even wishing that they had "died in the land of Egypt" rather than have to go into battle against such frightening opponents in Canaan (vv. 1–2). Joshua and Caleb tried to speak up for God and his purpose, but the people would not listen; in fact, they tried to stone these faithful men!

God's people sinned in terrible ways in this account. They doubted God's word. They failed to believe his promises. They acted as if the peoples of the land were more powerful than their mighty God. As we see, God was not pleased with this response.

Wandering years. In God's punishment of his people, we see a certain amount of grace. He threatened to wipe them out and begin building a new people from Moses! But Moses interceded for the people and begged God to forgive them and show mercy to them, and God listened to him. Ultimately, the punishment for the people's sinful lack of faith was that they would wander in the wilderness for forty years, waiting to enter the promised land (Num. 14:34). The unbelieving older generation would die in the wilderness, and God would bring the younger generation into the land. God would keep his promise to Abraham—but not yet.

So as we end this chapter, we leave God's people wandering in the desert, waiting for the day when God would bring them into the land. He would remain faithful to this stubborn and sinful people.

REVIEW

What God promised to Abraham about the growth of his descendants began to happen; Israel grew in strength and numbers in Egypt, and was delivered from slavery by God's hand through his servant Moses. God brought this people under the guidance of his word—only to see them rebel and falter in faith yet again. Yet even in the wilderness wanderings, God never abandoned his gracious promises to his people, despite their sin.

PRAY!

As you close this chapter with prayer, give thanks to God for his faithful work in the lives of his people—then and now. Thank him that he is even now keeping his great promise to Abraham—to bless all the nations of the world through his descendants. The New Testament makes it clear that all who have faith in Jesus are children of Abraham; this means that, as you share the good news of Jesus with those around you, you are bringing God's blessing to the world as a spiritual descendant of Abraham! Talk to God about this today. Pray that he would give you courage to bring his gospel "blessing" to the world!

GOD'S PEOPLE GROW
PART 2

As we continue in the scene of the Bible story that I've chosen to call "God's People Grow," we are finally about to witness the entrance of God's people into the promised land—but under a different leader, Joshua. This chapter will cover a lot of ground: we'll begin at the opening of the book of Joshua and continue to the end of the book of Judges. Along the way, we will see God's continuing faithfulness to a people who proved to be constantly faithless, sinful, and in need of a true and perfect King to rule over them.

Remember!

Your suggested memory verses for this chapter come from the commissioning of Joshua, which you will read more about below:

Only be strong and very courageous, being careful to do according to all the law that Moses my servant commanded you. Do not turn from it to the right hand or to the left, that you may have good success wherever you go. This Book of the Law shall not depart from your mouth, but you shall meditate on it day and night, so that you may be careful to do according to all that is written in it. For then you will make your way prosperous, and then you will have good success. Have I not commanded you? Be strong and courageous. Do not be frightened, and do not be dismayed, for the LORD your God is with you wherever you go. (Josh. 1:7–9)

A NEW LEADER FOR GOD'S PEOPLE

At the end of our last chapter, we left God's people wandering in the desert for forty years as punishment for their sin. God still intended to keep his great promise to Abraham, but he would not put up with a failure of his people to believe his word. God decided to let the older, faithless generation die out in the wilderness as he waited to bring the younger generation into the promised land under the leadership of Joshua.

READ!

Read Joshua 1:1–9—a passage that contains your suggested memory verses for this chapter.

The older generation that died in the wilderness included Moses, whose death led to a leadership transition for God's people.

The failure of Moses. While Moses was perhaps the greatest human leader God's people ever had, he failed to completely honor and obey God in everything just as the rest of the people did. Numbers 20 tells us that during God's people's sojourn in the wilderness, Moses struck a rock to bring forth water for the people (instead of just speaking to it, as God had commanded) and spoke as if *he* was the one bringing forth the water, not God. Because of Moses's sin, God told him that he would not be the one to bring his people into the promised land.

This was sad, but it is a good reminder for us. Even Moses was not the perfect and final leader that God's people needed. God one day would raise up an even greater leader for his people—a perfect and eternal leader, who would perfectly honor God amid his people. Moses's failure reminds us that Jesus Christ was coming—later in the story of the Bible—to be this perfect leader for God's people.

The rise of Joshua. In the passage you just read, you saw the initial call and commissioning of Joshua by God. God reaffirmed his promise about the land to Joshua and commanded him several times to be "strong and courageous" (Josh. 1:6, 7, 9) as he led God's people into Canaan. We will talk more about Joshua's leadership below, but it is important to remember that, many years before, he had been one of the two men (along with Caleb) who had stood up to the people of Israel after spying out the land and affirmed God's power and promise to bring them into the land despite mighty enemies. He had long been a man of great faith, and now he was the one God had chosen to succeed Moses in leading his people.

The conquest/land. It will be hard for us to understand the book of Joshua if we do not deal with the concept of "land," which is the key theme in the book. The first half of the book deals with the conquest of the land, and the second half deals with the division of the land among the tribes of Israel. Here are a few key points to remember as we move into this phase of the story:

- Canaan was the land that God had promised to Abraham. Thus, in the book of Joshua, we see God continuing to keep this promise from many years earlier.
- We must not see the conquest of the land as an unjust war against "innocent" people who lived there. The Canaanites were evil

people who opposed God and his people, sacrificed children in idolatry, and were involved in many other sinful practices. God's people eventually destroyed many of these people in battle, and this was God's way of bringing his judgment against many of these peoples after many years of showing patience toward them. We will talk more about this difficult theme as we move on.

- "Land"—or "inheritance"—continues to be a very big theme throughout the Old Testament. In fact, it carries right through to the New Testament, where the idea of "inheritance" for God's people gets much bigger than a mere physical place. The New Testament begins to point Christians toward the greatest place—the new heaven and new earth that God will prepare for all who follow, love, and worship Jesus Christ.

JOSHUA'S FAITHFUL LEADERSHIP

Let's focus more specifically on Joshua as a leader. As we will see, he stepped up immediately to lead God's people, and he did this faithfully and well. In doing so, he pointed forward to a much greater leader for God's people who would enter the story later. We will see, too, how Joshua 5 reminds us that Joshua was not that perfect and final leader for the people of God.

READ!

First read Joshua 1:10–18, then read Joshua 5:13–15.

As we consider Joshua as a leader of God's people, we will examine the beginnings of his leadership role, the people's wholehearted response of commitment to him, and the interesting account of Joshua being confronted by a far greater leader before whom even he had to bow down in humility, repentance, and worship.

Joshua's leadership. In the first passage that you read, you saw Joshua stepping up immediately, in obedience to God, to lead God's people and prepare to help them enter the promised land of God. After Joshua's commissioning (Josh. 1:1–9), he immediately began preparing the people and letting them know that the conquest would soon begin. He reminded them of God's promises to them and encouraged them with the words that God had given to him (vv. 12–15). Joshua showed no hesitation; he was ready to faithfully follow God and lead God's people well.

The people's response. The people gave an encouraging and hopeful response to Joshua as their new leader. Unlike the older generation (which had died in the wilderness), the next generation responded with faith and commitment as they swore allegiance to Joshua and prepared to follow him into the land. They even reaffirmed God's call to their new leader, reminding him to be "strong and courageous" (Josh. 1:18) as he led them. This was a bright new day for the people of God.

Joshua's leader. In the second passage you read, you saw something very interesting. On the eve of the attack on Jericho—the first major city that needed to be conquered in Canaan—Joshua was confronted by a man who held a drawn sword in his hand. Joshua, a trained warrior, approached this man and asked him to identify himself as friend or foe. As the man answered, it became clear that he was not a man at all; he was "the commander of the army of the LORD" (Josh. 5:14)—perhaps the second person of the Trinity himself! Joshua, finally aware that he was being confronted by someone far greater than himself, took off his shoes and bowed down in worship at the feet of this heavenly being. God's leader for his people, it seems, needed to be led by God first!

Two "paths" to Jesus from Joshua. These brief passages that you just read show us how this part of the Bible story connects to Jesus in two ways:

- First, Joshua was a mighty leader and warrior who pointed to Jesus as a type—a Christlike figure who showed, in a powerful way, that Jesus would act on behalf of God's people.

- Second, Joshua was a man—one who also needed to fall on his knees in humility, repentance, and worship before the holy God. He was not the final and perfect leader for God's people. That leader would have to be God in human flesh.

ENTERING THE LAND

When we come to Joshua 6, we see it finally happening—Joshua and God's people beginning the conquest of Canaan. God was keeping his great promise to Abraham to give his descendants the land, and he was doing what he could not do in the previous generation of Israelites because of their lack of faith in him. Under Joshua, it was time for God to move ahead with his great work in the lives of his people.

READ!

Read Joshua 6—the account of the Israelites' conquest of the great city of Jericho.

Joshua was finally ready to lead God's people into the promised land—Canaan. First, they would need to conquer the strong and fortified city of Jericho. This may have been one of the cities that had terrified God's people forty years earlier, when the Israelite spies brought back a discouraging report about the strength of Canaanite cities.

As the people prepared for battle, Joshua followed God's careful, and somewhat strange, instructions to the letter. The people marched around the city six times; they then marched around it seven times on the seventh day, and the priests blew their trumpets loudly. At that point, the walls of the city simply collapsed. The Israelites went in, defeated the people, and began their conquest of the land.

So what was that first great victory in the promised land meant to teach us?

God keeps his promise. First, this victory shows us—again—God's commitment to faithfully keeping his promise to his people. After the people had spent forty years wandering in the desert, God was still going to keep the promise that he had made so many years earlier to Abraham. He was going to take his people into Canaan and give them this land as their inheritance. He was going to bless them there and prepare them to be a blessing to all peoples of the earth.

God fights for his people. Second, this victory—especially the nature of this victory—was meant to remind God's people that *he* was the mighty warrior who would do battle on their behalf. While God's people did eventually do some fighting, as they entered Jericho, God chose to give his people a victory in such a fashion that they had no choice but to acknowledge that he was the only one responsible! The Israelites did not make the walls fall; God's miraculous power did it. God was reminding his people, even during this great victory, that *he* was the source of their power.

As we close this discussion, it is important that we not neglect the comment that the author of Joshua makes about Rahab. She was a prostitute from Jericho who helped the Israelite spies escape when they had come to spy out the land. Go back and read Joshua 6:25 again. What happened to Rahab? She was spared, and she eventually became a part of God's people because of her faith (Heb. 11:31)!

We will find out much later in the Bible story that Rahab would marry into God's people and become an ancestor of the great King David. What is God teaching us at this point? He is showing us, even as we see his people entering the land that he was giving to them, that his eternal plan was not *only* about ethnic Israelites. It actually would include Gentiles—"sinners"—like Rahab, who would put their faith in him and be saved by his grace. This is very good news for you and me!

THE CALL TO CONQUEST

Let's now jump ahead to the end of the book of Joshua, where we find an account of the end of Joshua's life and his final words to the people of God. It will become clear from this account that, although Joshua's life was almost over, the conquest of the land was not yet complete. Joshua commanded God's people to keep pressing forward—driving out the people who held the land. We will see, from the rest of the story, how well the people did in fulfilling this call.

READ!

Read Joshua 23–24—the record of Joshua's final two speeches to God's people near the end of his life.

As we consider Joshua's final words to the people of God, we learn a few important lessons regarding the big story of the Bible.

Joshua's faithfulness. First, we see Joshua's faithfulness as a good leader of God's people. You remember his call and commissioning from God because you are (hopefully) memorizing some key verses that come from that call (Josh. 1:1–9). At the end of the book of Joshua, it becomes clear that Joshua had kept his call and commissioning very faithfully. While Joshua was certainly human, and a sinner, he was also a faithful leader of God's people, for he led them according to God's word in every way. At the end of his life, he was able to affirm his faithfulness before the people and call them to continue walking in the pattern of obedience to God's word that he had modeled for them. God's people have had few leaders so faithful as Joshua!

A continuing call. Second, part of Joshua's "farewell speech" was a call for God's people to move forward in the full conquest of the land (a task that was still unfinished at the time that Joshua died). Joshua reminded God's people of God's great promise to drive out the peoples of the land before them if they would only keep pushing ahead and working to rid the land of those peoples (with all their sin and idolatry). God's charge to the people through Joshua was clear: do not stop the conquest until the people of God possess the entire land!

We should stop here and acknowledge that this call to conquest is, for some people, one of the most difficult aspects of the Bible. It was, of course, a call from God to his people to defeat other nations in battle. It was a call to "holy war," and it involved combat and loss of life. How do we deal with such violent parts of the Bible?

We begin by recognizing that God's people were acting on *God's* behalf in these times. They were not going out on their own to kill for fun; they also were not selfishly taking land out of their own greed. God was using his people to bring judgment on others who had opposed him and his word for centuries—people with whom he had been patient as they continued to sacrifice their children to idols, practice sexual immorality, and act with brutal violence toward the people around them. These were not innocent people; God had promised to bring judgment against them centuries earlier.

Also, we need to see that, from the perspective of God's people, God's call to conquest was ultimately about the purity of their worship to God. Joshua's speech makes this clear to us; God's motivation as his people entered the land was for them to establish right worship of him— obedience to his word, unhindered by idolatry and the sinful practices of the peoples of the land. God wanted his people to be purified—set apart—for him and for right worship of him. That was—and is—God's good goal for his people.

The incomplete conquest. Sadly, after Joshua died, the conquest—even though it was commanded by both Joshua and God—was not fully completed. In the next section, we will turn forward in the Bible story to the book of Judges, which begins with the account of God's people failing to fully drive out the peoples of the land. As you can imagine, disastrous results came from this failure.

The book of Joshua, though, ends on a high note. God's people were a great nation, and they were now in the land that God had promised to Abraham many years earlier. They seemed poised to live under God's blessing and be a blessing to the peoples of the earth.

MEETING THE JUDGES

The failure of God's people to drive out the peoples of Canaan is explicitly displayed as the book of Judges opens. We quickly see that this failure damaged their worship, their relationship with God, and the blessing that they were meant to experience in God's good place. Judges presents a "cycle" that begins during the Israelites' early years in the promised land. But God would not abandon his people, even as they kept turning away from him and choosing sin rather than obedience.

◣ READ!

Read Judges 2:6–3:6—the account that picks up after Joshua's final speech to God's people and goes on to explain what happened after his death.

The opening chapters of Judges present a sad reality: the people of God failed to completely drive out the inhabitants of the land of Canaan. Almost immediately, this failure influenced their worship and obedience to God; they started to worship the gods and idols of the land, and they turned their backs on the gracious and powerful God who just years before had led their ancestors out of slavery in Egypt. In response to this sin—and in order to bring his people to their senses—God raised up other nations to conquer them in battle and oppress them. His goal was always to bring them to repentance, but they were stubborn and kept turning away from God and his good word.

During this time period, the "Judges cycle" began. This cycle is repeated many times in the book of Judges; we will study just a few examples. Here is a basic description of the cycle that we see repeatedly:

- Step 1—God's people turned away from him—usually toward the worship of Baal or another one of the false gods of the peoples of the land.
- Step 2—God raised up another nation and allowed them to oppress his people in order to bring them to their senses and discipline them for their sin and rebellion.

- Step 3—God's people finally cried out to God for help; they asked him to deliver them from their oppressors and enemies.
- Step 4—God raised up a "judge" for his people—usually a mighty warrior whom God empowered to defeat the enemy and restore peace to God's people, as well as some level of faithfulness to God's word.
- Step 5—God's people were faithful to him during the lifetime of this judge.
- Step 6—The judge died, and the people quickly fell back into sin and idolatry. Then the whole cycle began again.

As you will see, the book of Judges clearly shows us God's *grace*; he would not finally and permanently abandon his people and his plan for them, even as they continually turned away from him to sin and rebellion. God kept raising up judges who got them out of trouble with their enemies.

The book of Judges, though, also clearly shows God's people's need for a *king*—a permanent and godly king who could lead them in right worship of God in a lasting way. During the time of the Judges, God's people were only loosely tied together as a nation in the land that God had promised them. But they were not living well under God's blessing, and they were certainly not bringing blessing to the nations around them!

MEETING GIDEON

One of the most well-known of the judges is Gideon. He appears early in this book and is, in many ways, a perfect example of the judges whom God raised up for his people. As you will see, he was not as capable a leader as Joshua was, but God was able to use him for the deliverance of his people, who again had fallen into sin and idolatry, and had been captured and oppressed by the Midianites.

READ!

Read Judges 6–7—the bulk of the story of Gideon.

Gideon was an unlikely hero for God's people. Just consider some of the ways that the author shows us Gideon's lack of courage, commitment, and strength in Judges 6:

- Gideon saw himself as the "least" in his family, and saw his family as part of the "weakest" clan in his tribe of Israel (v. 15).
- When the angel of God approached Gideon, he was beating out wheat in a winepress (not where this was normally done) so that he could hide the wheat from the Midianites, who had been taking all the food of God's people.
- Gideon doubted God and did not want to accept the call to lead God's people.
- Gideon struggled to believe the words of the angel, and even "tested" God several times to make sure that he was really telling the truth.

Despite all of Gideon's weaknesses and doubts, though, this was the man God chose to deliver his people from the Midianites. God's people had called out to him for help, and he was going to provide a very unlikely hero for them.

During the days of Gideon, because of his people's sin and idolatry, God had given them into the hands of the Midianites—a people in the land of Canaan. The Midianites' oppression of God's people was brutal—they would come down and steal the crops of God's people, making life extremely difficult for them. So God called Gideon—this weak and fearful man—to deliver his people.

But it was not just by calling a weak man that God determined to prove himself to his people. Think again about the details of the battle against the Midianites that you read about in Judges 7:

- God intentionally limited Gideon's army to three hundred men, who would fight against a Midianite army of thousands.
- God equipped this "army" of Gideon with clay pots and torches rather than weapons of war.

- God himself threw the Midianite camp into confusion during the night, and they ran away before Gideon's army of three hundred men.

In other words, this was one of the easiest victories in the history of the world! Gideon used terrible military strategy (from a human perspective) and was vastly outnumbered by the Midianite army. But God showed his people that he was the Lord. He was the warrior. He was the one who could bring unlikely and miraculous victory against their enemies with no human army to speak of. Gideon won a victory that was totally due to the hand of God; he had no ground on which to boast.

So the story of Gideon is a story of an unlikely hero using terrible military strategy but gaining a miraculous victory over an army of thousands that was oppressing God's people. God again came to the rescue of his sinful people through the work of a judge. Sadly, if you read ahead to Judges 8, you will find that Gideon was certainly not the lasting leader God's people needed, as he led the people into more idolatry. By the time Gideon was dead, God's people were ready to turn back toward sin and rebellion against God's word.

MEETING SAMSON

If Gideon is one of the best-known judges, Samson is probably one of the most well-known figures in all of Scripture. He was a man of incredible and miraculous strength (given to him by God), and God used him to deliver his people in wonderful ways. Even so, Samson embodied the struggle of God's people with sin during this period; even though God used him, he could not control his appetites and urges.

READ!

Read Judges 13–16—the entire account of Samson, a great judge of God's people.

Near the end of the book of Judges, the author twice makes an important point: "In those days there was no king in Israel. Everyone did
what was right in his own eyes" (17:6; 21:25; he also stresses the point
that there was no king in 18:1; 19:1). This is the theme of the book of
Judges. God's people were in the land, but with no king ruling over
them, people were ultimately doing whatever they wanted to do. By
the end of the period covered in this book, the land of Israel was in
chaos, and God's people clearly needed a true and better leader than
any of the judges who had come along.

As we look at the account of Samson, we need to consider how God's
work in and through him pointed—positively—to the much greater
deliverance that God would bring to his people through Jesus. We
should also see, though, that Samson was closely tied to God's people
during this time—struggling with sin just like they were.

Samson represents Christ. Let us consider, first, how the ministry
and life of Samson gave a hint of what God would one day do for his
people through his own Son.

First, we have a miraculous birth; a son was born to a couple who
had no children (this should remind us of Abraham and Sarah, to
whom God gave a child of promise). The angel of God told this couple
that their son would be a great deliverer and leader for God's people.
As we will see later in the story of the Bible, Jesus also is introduced to
us in a narrative of a miraculous birth, establishing him as the great
Savior of God's people.

Second, as Samson enters his adult years, we see him doing battle
against the Philistines—the enemies of God's people during those
days—in incredible ways. At one point, he killed a thousand Philistines with only the jawbone of a donkey. God had truly blessed
this man with superhuman strength, which he used against God's
enemies. Like Samson, Jesus would battle the enemies of God, cast-
ing out demons and defeating Satan, sin, and death through his death
and resurrection.

Third, the book of Judges tells us that in his death, Samson killed more people than he had killed during his entire lifetime; he gave God's people rest and relief from the enemy Philistines. Jesus, too, would be held captive by sinful people, and through his sacrificial death, would defeat the hold of sin on God's people and defeat death itself forever.

Samson represents God's people. Throughout the course of the narrative, though, we also see that Samson battles not only the Philistines but also the sinful desires of his own heart. Most of the time, he does not even seem to battle them; he just gives in to them.

Samson at one point visited a prostitute. At another point, he had a relationship with a woman named Delilah, who turned out to be an evil and wicked woman who gave him up to his enemies.

The point is this: God used Samson in mighty and powerful ways, but Samson himself was much like the rest of God's people during this time. He was constantly turning toward sin, even as God continued to work powerfully in and through his life. Samson was a judge who resembled the people whom he led.

THE BOOK OF RUTH

Before we conclude our quick survey of Judges, we should look briefly at the account in the book of Ruth—which emerged during the same time as the events and stories we have been studying. You are going to see how this account fits into the big story of the Bible—the story of all that God was doing in and through his people as he continued to fulfill his great promises to Abraham.

READ!

Read all of the book of Ruth (or as much as you can).

It is easy to forget, as we read and study the little book of Ruth, that this story is set during the time of the judges, which we have just been studying. Yet this is what the book tells us as it begins. All the events of this amazing account occurred during a time of great sin in Israel—a time when everyone was doing as he or she saw fit, because there was no king ruling over them. What can we learn from this beautiful little book?

Worthiness. First, we should see clearly through the book of Ruth that God's people are called to be "worthy" (Ruth 2:1; 3:11) even during times of great sin and rebellion. The character of Boaz is a bright spot during the dark time of the judges. He was a man who kept the law of God because of his faith in God, even though there was no king in the land forcing him to do this. The way Boaz treated Ruth—a poor woman—was in line with the law of Moses, which provided for "gleaning" in fields (Lev. 23:22), and commanded God's people to take care of the widow, the orphan, and the foreigner in their midst (Deut. 24:19). Boaz clearly was a worthy man for us to emulate and learn from.

Redemption. Second, the theme of redemption shines brightly in the book of Ruth. Boaz was called a "redeemer" (Ruth 2:20) for Naomi's family; this means that he was a relative who could take care of a widow, raising children to continue the name of her dead husband. This is what Boaz did for Naomi and Ruth. He "redeemed" Ruth, taking her as his own and preserving the family line of Naomi. There was nothing in this for Boaz; he did it simply because it was the right thing.

Gentile inclusion. Third, the author of Ruth goes out of his way to remind us that Ruth was a Moabite. In other words, she was not part of the people of Israel; she was a Gentile. Yet God showed favor to this Gentile woman, who turned in faith to him and wanted to be a part of his people (see Ruth 1:16–17 for Ruth's commitment to Naomi and to Naomi's people and God). Because of Ruth's faith, she was brought into God's people and even became an ancestor of the great King David. Even in the time of the judges, we see here a glimpse of God's promise to Abraham that all the peoples of the earth would be blessed through him!

The king. Finally, the story of Ruth ends with the important and central work of God through all these events. What was God doing in the details of the lives of Boaz, Naomi, and Ruth? He was sovereignly orchestrating a marriage that would lead to the birth of the man who would one day be a good and faithful king over his people: David. In fact, the book ends with this point. The author tells us that Boaz was the father of Obed, who was the father of Jesse, who was the father of David (Ruth 4:21–22). Ruth, the Moabite who put her faith in God, became the great-grandmother of King David!

In all of this, God showed himself to be faithful to his people— to bring them the king that they needed to finally begin to break the judges cycle.

GOD'S PEOPLE AND A BIG MESS

Much has happened during this scene of the Bible story. God's people have come out of Egypt, where they had grown and multiplied, and God has brought them (through Joshua) into the land that was promised to Abraham hundreds of years before. God is faithful to his people; there is no doubt about that!

Still, not all is right in Israel; at the end of the book of Judges, the story is still unfinished. God's people have become a great *nation*; that part of the promise to Abraham is surely being fulfilled. God's people are in the *land*; God is keeping that promise as well. But God's people are not living under his *blessing*; they continue to fall back into sin and idolatry even as God keeps on sending judges to deliver them again and again. Because of this failure, they are certainly not bringing God's blessing—the blessing of knowing and worshiping him—to the nations around them. Instead, they are worshiping the idols of these nations. Something else is needed to solve this sinful mess.

READ!

Read Judges 20–21—the chaotic conclusion of the book of Judges, which is really no conclusion at all.

We keep referencing the great promise God made to Abraham hundreds of years before the Exodus and the time of the judges. This is appropriate and good, as this promise was unconditional, and it serves as the foundation for everything that happens in the rest of the Bible story. God's promise was about a *people*, a *land*, and *blessing* to this people and, through them, to the nations of the world. That promise is being fulfilled, but it is still very obviously incomplete during the period of the judges, as I mentioned above.

However, there is another promise that we should also remember—one that came to God's people long before Abraham was born. It is the promise of God to his people in Genesis 3:15—the "first gospel" word that we see in the Bible. This was a promise that, one day, a descendant of Adam and Eve would "bruise" (or "crush") the head of Satan forever and solve the problem of sin and death for God's people. As we progress through the Bible story, we are seeing that the true problem—the recurring "plague" in the lives of God's people in this story—is their own sinfulness and rebellion. If God is going to keep his promise finally and perfectly to Abraham, he is going to need to provide a way for sinful people to receive his saving blessing. They will not be able to receive it through their own goodness and obedience.

So where do we go from here? What is next for the people of God as the story of the Bible continues?

The human king. The conclusion of Judges and the story of Ruth showed us that God's people needed a king to rule over them. It was part of God's plan to bring them a king—someone who could lead his people well and keep them faithful to the word of his law. In the next chapter of the Bible story, we will see the rise of the kingdom of Israel under the great King David and King Solomon. Under their leadership, Israel would become greater than it had ever been before.

The divine King. Even so, we will see that someone far greater than David or Solomon would still be needed. While these kings would establish new heights of glory for God's people—and would bring fulfillment in many ways to God's promises to Abraham—they would not finally answer God's "gospel" promise in Genesis 3:15. That promise would need to be addressed by a King who is not merely human. God's great King, Jesus, would still need to enter this story—and this broken and sinful world.

REVIEW

God's servant Joshua led the next generation of God's people into the promised land, fulfilling that aspect of God's promise to Abraham. After Joshua, though, the period of the judges of Israel again revealed the stubborn, sinful, and idolatrous hearts of God's people. God had been faithful to them, but they remained not fully faithful to him. It was clear that God's people needed a good and faithful king to rule over them and help them believe and obey God's word.

PRAY!

As you close this chapter with prayer, give thanks to God for his continual gracious and faithful work in the lives of stubborn, sinful, and rebellious people. Thank him that his work did not stop during the period of the judges, but that he chose to be faithful. Thank him that his saving work in the world continued until he sent his own Son into the world to be the great King and Savior that his people ultimately needed.

Chapter 8

GOD'S KINGDOM— RISE AND FALL
PART 1

Following the growth of God's people and their conquest of the promised land, the next major development in the Bible's big story was the founding of Israel's much-needed monarchy. That brings us to the next scene in the story, which I'm calling "God's Kingdom—Rise and Fall." We'll cover this scene in this chapter and the next, exploring a large chunk of biblical material in the books from 1 Samuel to 2 Chronicles. We won't read every single book in that section of Scripture, but I hope that these two chapters will give you a good grasp of what happens in this part of the story.

Our study will take us into the time of the kings of Israel—the period of the monarchy, which began under King Saul and then continued through the line of David. Some of the most well-known stories in the Bible are found in this part of the Bible—the accounts of David and Goliath, Solomon and the queen of Sheba, and the battle between Elijah and the prophets of Baal on Mount Carmel. Our goal in these two chapters will be to place these wonderful stories in their right context, in the big story of the Bible. You see, Bible stories are *more* than just stories—they are part of the big picture of God's saving work in this world. They all connect as part of the beautiful work that he began with a promise in Genesis 3:15 and that he will complete in and through his Son, Jesus Christ.

As our last chapter ended, it was clear that God's saving work in the lives of his people was far from complete. God's faithfulness had been evident; he had made them into a great nation during their time in Egypt and had brought them into the promised land under the good leadership of Joshua. But although God raised up judge after judge to lead his people temporarily, the people insisted on falling back into sin and idolatry. It seemed that God's people needed a *king*—someone who could rule over them powerfully and keep them close to God. The monarchy of Israel would be the next step in God's progressive work in this world on behalf of his people.

Here are a few of the major "characters" we will meet in this scene of the Bible story:

Samuel. Before the kings started reigning, God blessed his people with the last—and the best—of the judges. Just below, you will be introduced to Samuel—a man who led God's people with faithfulness, courage, and truth. Samuel pointed to Jesus Christ as he fulfilled (faithfully, but imperfectly) the roles of prophet, priest, and king (judge) for God's people, at least for a time.

David. Probably the best king we will meet in these chapters will be David, who was called "a man after [God's] own heart" (1 Sam. 13:14). Under David's rule, the kingdom of Israel was firmly established. He was a mighty warrior, a poet/psalmist, and a lover of God, God's people, and God's word. It was to David, as we will see, that God made some very big—and eternal—promises about the lasting nature of his reign over God's people through his descendants.

Solomon. While David was a wonderful king, the kingdom of Israel reached its greatest height under Solomon, who brought glory and splendor to Israel in a way that God's people had never seen before. Under Solomon, as you will see, the kingdom of Israel came closest to a perfect fulfillment of God's promise to Abraham in Genesis 12—the nation, in God's place, being blessed by God and bringing his blessing to the ends of the earth. Solomon's reign was the absolute height of the Israelite monarchy.

Sadly, we will also see, over the next two chapters, that even Solomon, at the height of his reign, was not able to permanently bring God's blessing to God's people and to all the nations. He was a failure, too, and the kingdom began to unravel quickly after his death—even in the very next generation. By the time we get to the end of the next chapter, we will still be waiting for the ultimate fulfillment—the eternal answer—to God's big promise to his people.

Remember!

Your suggested memory verses for this chapter come from 1 Samuel 15—a scene in which Samuel reminded Saul of the true worship of God, which is not sacrifice but obedience.

> *Has the Lord as great delight in burnt offerings and*
> *   sacrifices,*
> *   as in obeying the voice of the Lord?*
> *Behold, to obey is better than sacrifice,*
> *   and to listen than the fat of rams.*
> *For rebellion is as the sin of divination,*
> *   and presumption is as iniquity and idolatry.*
> *Because you have rejected the word of the Lord,*
> *   he has also rejected you from being king.*
> *   (1 Sam. 15:22–23)*

MEETING SAMUEL

As you know, the book of 1 Samuel begins in the period of the judges. God's people had been caught in a continuing cycle of sin, slavery, deliverance, temporary obedience, and then sin (such as idolatry) again. Something needed to change if God's people were ever going to live faithfully and permanently in obedience to him and spread his blessing to the surrounding nations.

As the book opens, we can see that God was beginning to provide this change that his people needed. He began to do this through the person and leadership of a man named Samuel. He would become the last and greatest judge of God's people, as well as the one who would anoint the first two kings of God's people in Israel.

READ!

Read 1 Samuel 1 and 3.

We will begin by looking at Samuel's birth and the start of his ministry.

The need. At the birth of Samuel, God's people were again in a very bad place. Take a moment to read 1 Samuel 2:12–26, if you have not already. Do you see what was happening in Israel during this time? The sons of Eli, the high priest over God's people, were doing terrible and wicked things as they "led" God's people in worship. They were stealing meat from the sacrifices of God's people—meat that should have gone to God, not them. They were also involved sexually with some of the women who worked as helpers in the temple. These "spiritual leaders" of God's people, who were meant to serve as mediators between God and his people, as their priests, were despicable and sinful men. God's people were in dire need of godly leadership.

The birth. The birth of Samuel, then, was meant to show us that God had a plan to give his people a godly leader to guide them in obedience and worship of God. Samuel's birth fit into the biblical pattern of God providing a son to a barren woman, linking it with other great births in God's story (Isaac's, Samson's, etc.). After Samuel was born, his godly mother, Hannah, devoted him in service to God in the temple with Eli, in accordance with the promise she had made to God in prayer before she became pregnant. So Samuel grew up in the temple, serving God under Eli and learning how to lead God's people in worship. He was trained as a *priest* for God's people.

The call. In 1 Samuel 3, you read of God's beautiful nighttime call of Samuel. Did you notice how this chapter begins? First Samuel 3:1 tells us that the word of God was "rare" in those days. That was about to change. God was raising up a *prophet*—Samuel—who would bring his word to his people in a powerful way. As we see from what God told Samuel in chapter 3, this word—at least to begin with—had to do with the wickedness of Eli's sons and their coming judgment by God. The chapter ends with the word of the Lord beginning to go out to all Israel through the ministry of Samuel, as everyone began to acknowledge him as a true prophet of God.

The ministry. So what would Samuel's ministry for God's people look like, according to these beginnings in 1 Samuel? Samuel would be a *priest*; he would mediate the relationship between God and his people by helping the people worship God rightly through sacrifices and obedience. Samuel also would be a *prophet*; he would faithfully bring God's word to God's people in a powerful way as he led them. He also would be the last and greatest *judge* as he ruled God's people during a time when there was no king in Israel. This would be a great man—a better leader than God's people had enjoyed in a long time.

SAMUEL AND JESUS

Samuel was called by God to be a prophet, priest, and judge/king over the sinful people of Israel. A passage from 1 Samuel 7 sheds light on this threefold calling. As we see Samuel fulfilling these roles for God's people, we will also look ahead to the way in which Jesus perfectly fulfilled the same three roles—much later in the story—for the people of God.

▐ READ!

Read 1 Samuel 7:3–17—a passage that summarizes and describes the faithful and powerful ministry and leadership that Samuel provided for God's people during his days as their judge, prophet, and priest.

What does this passage teach us about Samuel's roles in the lives of God's people?

Samuel as judge. Samuel is explicitly described as "judging" (1 Sam. 7:6) the people of God. He also had a significant role in leading and directing them in battle against the Philistines, who were the main enemies of God's people during this time. Under Samuel's leadership of the people, they won a great victory over the Philistines, and God drove these enemies back during his entire "career" as judge.

Samuel as prophet. Samuel also spoke God's word to God's people. As the passage that you just read begins, we see Samuel speaking words of conviction and challenge—from God—to the people (see 1 Sam. 7:3–4). According to God's word, Samuel prophetically called the people to put away the idols they were worshiping and to serve God alone. They obeyed the word of this faithful prophet, a word that had come from God himself.

Samuel as priest. Finally, we see Samuel acting as a priest in this passage. Amid the military challenge against the Philistines, God's people begged Samuel to cry out to God in prayer on their behalf (1 Sam. 7:8). After this request, we see Samuel offering a sacrifice and praying on behalf of the people (v. 9). He was acting as their priest—making a sacrifice for their sin and mediating between them and the holy God.

Samuel and Jesus. The ministry of Samuel practically begs us to connect it to the bigger picture of God's saving work in the world—a work that would be finally fulfilled and completed through the ministry of his own Son. Jesus would not enter the scene for more than a thousand years, but Samuel's leadership and ministry over God's people during his faithful life offered a glimpse of what the ministry of the greatest and most faithful leader would look like

Jesus would be a *prophet*; he would speak God's word to God's people in a divinely powerful way. Jesus would show how all of God's law was fulfilled in him, and he would lead God's people to a right understanding and obedience of his good word through faith in him.

Jesus would be a *priest*; he would offer the greatest and the final sacrifice for the sins of God's people on the cross. He would also be the sacrifice, laying his body down as the perfect Lamb, dying for sin. Jesus, as we see from the New Testament, also has a continuing priestly role for God's people: he still mediates and "pleads" for God's people at the right hand of God.

Jesus would be the great *King*—the eternal ruler of God's people and the final Judge of all the world. He would establish and begin his reign through his death on the cross and his resurrection from the dead, by which he would conquer sin and death forever for all who would repent and believe in him. He will reign forever, enthroned over God's people to rule them perfectly.

As this story continues, remember to look ahead to Jesus, who is the perfect fulfillment of all the pictures that we get in the Old Testament accounts.

THE PEOPLE WANT A KING

Now let's think about the shift toward the monarchy that is recounted in 1 Samuel 8. Here we see that the people asked Samuel to give them a king to rule over them, and we are introduced to the man who was the answer to this request: Saul.

📖 READ!

Read 1 Samuel 8 and 9—the account of the request of God's people for a king, and the choosing of Saul by Samuel (through God).

What do we learn from these chapters that tell us about the beginning of the monarchy in Israel?

A confusing tension. First, we see a very confusing tension in this passage. On the one hand, we know (from Deut. 17, which you can look at if you have time) that God gave provisions in his law for the kings who would rule over his people one day. In other words, God knew that all of this was coming! He had even planned for it by giving his people careful instructions for how a king should act and lead. So in one sense, this was certainly all part of God's plan.

On the other hand, Samuel was truly upset about the people's request for a king, and God said that this request signaled a rejection of him. What do we make of this? If God had planned for this to happen all along, why was Samuel so upset by this request from the people?

The answer to this tension seems to lie in the attitude and motives of the people making this request. Look carefully at what they said as they asked Samuel for a king (see 1 Sam. 8:5, for example). What was behind their request? They wanted to be like all the other nations! They were not motivated by a desire to be led well by a king who loved God and could teach them God's word. They simply wanted to have a king just as other peoples did. This choice was not altogether disconnected from the people's tendency toward idolatry—a sin of the nations around them. This is why the people's request was sinful and displeasing to Samuel.

The "people's choice." It became clear that Saul, the first king of Israel, was exactly what the people were looking for. It seems they were looking for a "figurehead"—someone whom they could admire and who would "look the part" of a king—and they found it in Saul. First Samuel 9 begins by telling us that he was more handsome than anyone in Israel;

he even stood head and shoulders above everyone else in height. Saul was, in every way, a kingly figure—at least physically. He was exactly what the people envisioned for a king who would lead them and fight their battles for them.

A promising beginning. Take a moment and skim over 1 Samuel 11. There you will see that Saul had a very promising beginning to his reign. He won a great victory over the Ammonites, who were oppressing the people of Jabesh-Gilead. Saul, it seemed, would be a great military leader.

We can imagine that God's people were excited about their new leader. The monarchy was beginning, and the nation of Israel was ready to grow and become strong. But would this promising beginning last? Would Saul be the king that the people had been waiting for?

SAUL'S FAILURE

Sadly, as you read and study 1 Samuel 13 and 15, you will see that Saul's reign fell into a downward spiral almost from the outset. It did not take long, we see, for Saul to begin to reject God's word! This pointed to the need for an even better king—both immediately and far down the road in the story of the Bible.

READ!

Read 1 Samuel 13 and 15—two accounts of Saul's blatant failure to obey God's word and lead his people well.

Things quickly began to go wrong in the life and heart of Saul, and therefore in his reign. What do we find as we study these passages from 1 Samuel?

An attempt to be a priest. First, in chapter 13, we see Saul, during battle preparations, becoming impatient with Samuel, who had told Saul to wait until he, the priest, was there to make a sacrifice, in accordance with God's law. Saul, though, did something terrible—something that was against all the instructions of God. When Samuel did not show up quite on time, Saul conducted the sacrifice himself. He failed to obey the word of Samuel, and therefore the word of God.

What did this mean in the big picture of the Bible story? In 1 Samuel 13, we find a human king who also tried to act as a priest, but whose sacrifice was rejected because he failed to perfectly obey God. Saul was not permitted to act as both king *and* priest for God's people. Even as a king, he was called to obey God's word, and he failed to do this.

A failure to obey. In chapter 15, we see a different situation, but a very similar result. As Saul went into battle against the Amalekites—an ancient enemy of God and his people—he was given a very specific command from God: destroy *everything*. This may seem like a harsh command, but it represented the judgment of God against the Amalekites that had been promised since the time of Moses—hundreds of years earlier. God's command was his way of bringing his righteous judgment against these violent and idolatrous people through the king he had placed over his people.

Sadly, Saul again refused to fully obey the word of God. He left the best of the captured animals alive after his victory over the Amalekites. He even left their king alive, as a kind of "spoil" from the battle. Then, when Samuel showed up, Saul claimed to have fully obeyed God. When Samuel confronted him, Saul blamed the people for making him do this (which was simply not true). This king of Israel was spiraling into sin, failing miserably to be the kind of ruler the people really needed. Samuel told Saul that the kingdom would be ripped from his hand, and that God would raise up a man after his own heart to rule his people.

So while Saul's reign would continue for several more years, his legacy was over before it even began. The people's choice for the kingship turned out to lack the heart of a king—a heart ready to obey God's word and lead God's people faithfully. It would only get worse for Saul as he plunged into anger, depression, and even witchcraft by the end of his life. His story is a sad one—a story of a man who refused to put himself under God's word.

THE UNEXPECTED KING

Saul had rejected God's word and God's rule; he was not the kind of king who could lead God's people with faithfulness and bring his blessing to all the nations through them. God's people needed a far better king than Saul.

In the passages that you will read next, you will see the beginning of a new line of kings—one that will continue, ultimately, forever (at least in some way). God led Samuel to the home of a man named Jesse—and to his youngest son, who was out in the fields watching the sheep. David was someone whom no one expected as God's next king for his people. But David had the heart of God's king.

READ!

Read 1 Samuel 16 and 17—the account of Samuel's anointing of David as the next king of Israel, and then of David's great victory against the Philistine giant Goliath while he was still a young man.

After God rejected Saul as king, he moved quickly to establish a new kingly line for his people. As we consider the passages you just read, a few major observations emerge:

God's king is unexpected. First, consider the fact that the way in which the next king was identified was almost totally different than the way Saul was chosen. You remember that Saul "looked the part" in every way. He was handsome, tall, and strong—just the way people thought a king *should* look. David, though, wasn't even the most impressive person in his own house. One by one, Jesse brought his sons before Samuel, who was impressed by the looks of David's older brothers (even Samuel, it seems, was at least somewhat focused on outward appearances, at least at first). Finally, though, the youngest brother—David, the shepherd boy—was called in from the fields. Samuel anointed him as God's next king and assured Jesse that God "looks on the heart" (1 Sam. 16:7). It was this young, unexpected man who had the heart that God desired for the king who would rule his people.

God's king is a representative savior. In 1 Samuel 17, we quickly see that while David may not have had the most impressive outward appearance, he truly did have the heart of a king. Goliath, a giant Philistine warrior, was tormenting and provoking God's people, and even the most impressive fighting men of Israel were too terrified to stand up to him. David, while visiting his brothers in the army, became incensed at the way this giant was defaming God and mocking his people, so he told King Saul that he would fight him.

As the story continues, it becomes clear that this young man—already anointed as the next king of Israel (although nobody knew it yet)—would act as a kind of "representative warrior/savior" for God's people. As the Israelite army stood frightened and huddled on the sidelines of the battlefield, young David ran out boldly to the giant, armed only with a sling and some stones. By God's strength, he killed Goliath, cut off his head, and led God's people in a great victory over their enemies. It would be a while before David took the throne over Israel, but this representative battle was a little taste of the kind of warrior king he would be for God's people in the years to come.

God's king points to a greater King. So David began to rise—in power and prominence—over God's people. Saul would do his best to kill David, but he was God's chosen and anointed king; he would rule one day, and God would begin a new line of kings through him. Under David and his son Solomon, God would begin to fulfill his great promise to Abraham in a bigger way than ever before.

It is important to remember that David—the anointed king and the representative savior of God's people—pointed to a much better King. David, at each step along the way, reminds us to look ahead in the story to the true Son of David—Jesus Christ, God's perfect King for his people. As wonderful as King David would be, he still would be a sinner who needed God's grace. He would not be the final answer for the sinful people of God.

A BIG PROMISE TO DAVID

Let's jump ahead in the story of David to a key moment in his life— and in the big story of God's saving work in the world and his people. If you are not familiar with God's promise to David in 2 Samuel 7, note it now! It set the stage, with yet another great promise from God, for what he would continue to do in and through David.

READ!

Read 2 Samuel 7—the account of David's intention to build a temple for God, and God's response to him through a great promise.

We are skipping over much of the story of David as we move into 2 Samuel 7. We simply do not have time to cover all the years that David spent in the wilderness, running from King Saul, who desperately wanted to kill him. David learned to trust God more deeply during those wilderness years, and God faithfully preserved the life of his chosen and anointed king for his people.

Finally, as we see in this passage, God had secured the kingdom under the rule of King David. He had defeated his enemies and taken the throne in Jerusalem over a united people of God. Israel had never reached such heights of power and influence—and it was only beginning.

David's idea. As the kingdom of Israel came into a period of peace and prosperity under King David, he began to look at the "dwelling" place of God—the place of worship for God's people. They were still worshiping God in a big tent, but David now lived in a great house as the king of Israel. This did not seem right to David, so he decided to build God a "house"—a place of worship where his people could come before him to offer sacrifices and prayers to him. Nathan, a prophet of God, told David to go ahead with this plan.

God's response. However, God told David that he did not need him to build a house. He said that David's son Solomon would build a house, and besides, no house could hold the God of the universe! So David would not build a house for God; instead, God told David that he would build a "house" for him. This house of David, according to God, would be a royal line that would continue *forever.* God told David that he would never lack a son to rule over God's people, and he promised to establish the kingdom of David's son forever.

The meaning of this promise. We need to understand how massive this promise from God to David was. This was a promise that, long after David's death, a literal "Son of David" would rule over God's people forever. This was a promise of a "forever kingdom" with a "forever King." It is no wonder that David responded to this promise of God with humble praise and worship. He could not believe the favor that God had shown to him, and he prayed to God with gratitude and joy.

Because God promised a forever kingdom with a forever King, this promise still holds today; God is still keeping this promise to his people. But how?

God is doing it through the eternal reign of his Son, Jesus, who is ruling now, and will forever. Jesus came into the world as God in human flesh. Humanly speaking, he was descended from David. Jesus is, in that sense, the Son of David, through whom God is keeping his promise to his people of this forever kingdom. Do you see why this was such a huge moment in the big story of the Bible? God was promising to work through David's line forever!

KING DAVID'S FAILURE

We've just seen a great moment in the big story of the Bible, when God gave a great promise to the man after his own heart. But not long after that great moment, we come to the sad account of the failure of this great king to whom God had made his great promise. The story of David's sin with Bathsheba—and David's attempted cover-up—is a vivid reminder to us that even the best human king is far from perfect. David, too, needed to receive God's grace for his sins; he needed a great Savior.

READ!

Read 2 Samuel 11 and 12—the account of David's sin with Bathsheba and his murder of Uriah, and then of his confrontation by Nathan the prophet.

Were you surprised by the sad account you just read? Was it shocking to you? It should be, at least at some level. But it should also be an important reminder that even David was not the final answer for God's people. They still needed to look forward to an even better King—one who would rule perfectly, without any sin.

Wandering on the roof. As 2 Samuel 11 opens, we find David wandering on his roof during the time of year when "kings go out to battle" (v. 1). The author seems to be gently suggesting to the reader that this roof was *not* where David should have been. Rather, he should have been leading his people in war, securing the borders of Israel, and continuing to push back the enemies of God's people. Instead, he was bored. To have something to do, he went walking on the roof—and from there he saw a woman bathing. Overcome by lust, David did what he could do (because he was the king) and had this woman (Bathsheba) brought to him. He had sex with her, and then sent her away. This is a terrible example of a man following only his physical appetites and taking something that he wanted.

Sin on top of sin. What happened next in this account teaches us a very important lesson: sin almost always leads to more sin! Bathsheba became pregnant, and David felt the need to try to cover up the fact that he was the father of her unborn child. So he called her husband,

Uriah, home from battle and tried to get him to have sex with his wife. Uriah, though, was so righteous and honorable that he refused to go home to his wife while his friends and brothers were still fighting the battles of Israel.

So David did something even worse than all that he had done before—he arranged for Uriah to be put to death by commanding the army to draw back from him in battle, causing him to be surrounded by enemy soldiers. Uriah was killed, and David took Bathsheba as his own wife. Chapter 11 ends with the ominous statement that God was very angry about what David had done (v. 27).

God's word convicts. We must wonder if David thought he had gotten away with these sins. He seemed to go on with life as usual, with Bathsheba as his new wife. It took God's word, through the prophet Nathan, to convict David of his sin and wake him up to the reality of what he had done. Nathan told him the story of a rich man who stole the only lamb of a poor man to serve at a feast. David was incensed with anger, but then Nathan pointed at David and said, "You are the man!" (2 Sam. 12:7). We will see soon how David responded to this exposure of his sin and the conviction that God's word brought to him through the prophet.

The lesson. What do we learn from this account? We see that even the very best human leaders of God's people are flawed and sinful. David, the king with a heart for God, was capable of doing terrible things—even adultery and murder. David needed a Savior, which meant that all of God's people needed to look for a greater Savior and King than David!

DAVID'S REPENTANCE

Like King Saul, David sinned in terrible ways against God and his word. However, something set David apart from Saul. David, as we see from Psalm 51, repented of his sin with all his heart, and sought forgiveness and mercy from God. It will be good for us to look carefully at David's repentance and see what we can learn from it since we also approach God as sinners.

READ!

Read Psalm 51—the psalm written by David after he was confronted by the prophet Nathan for his sin against Bathsheba and Uriah.

We have seen that David sinned in truly shocking ways. Perhaps the only thing more shocking than David's sin was his heartfelt and overwhelming repentance before God, which we see from Psalm 51. This repentance reminds us why David was called a man after God's own heart. His conscience was afflicted as he understood what he had done against God and his people, and he cried out to God for mercy. We see that David, unlike Saul, really did love God and really was sorry for his sin. God would grant forgiveness and mercy to David as he turned to him in repentance, looking for grace.

What does full repentance look like, according to Psalm 51?

- First, repentance is the full "ownership" of one's sin. David did not blame anyone else—or even his own circumstances—for what he had done. He admitted that he was the one who had sinned; he was responsible for a great evil. David spoke openly about his guilt and acknowledged it before God.
- Second, repentance is the acknowledgment that sin is, first and foremost, a "vertical" issue—between human beings and the holy God. David says something very shocking in this psalm: "Against you, you only, have I sinned" (Ps. 51:4). Of course, David had sinned against Bathsheba and Uriah as well as God. But he realized that sin is ultimately an issue between the sinner and God. He stood guilty before the holy God, so he needed to turn to God first.
- Third, repentance involves getting to the root of the sin. After David had called out to God for mercy and forgiveness in

Psalm 51, he then asked God to "create" in him a "clean heart" (v. 10). He also asked God to "restore" the "joy" of his salvation to him (v. 12). David recognized that his sin was a symptom of a heart that needed to be more fully given over to God in joyful worship. He wanted God to continue to change his heart so that he would be less tempted to sin in such striking ways.

- Fourth, repentance means turning outward into witness after the experience of God's grace. In Psalm 51:13, David talked about turning to "teach transgressors" (other sinful people) the ways of God. David wanted to experience God's forgiveness, mercy, and grace, and then teach others about the God who shows mercy to sinners and forgives their sins.

King David, the great king of God's people, needed to repent for his sin. And repent he did! Psalm 51 shows us a king who, although far from perfect, really did have a heart after God's heart. He cried out for mercy and grace, and found both by faith in this great God. We know, too, from the big story of the Bible, that this prayer from David for grace from God was fully answered through the death of the great "Son of David." Jesus, the great King, died for King David's sins on the cross too.

REVIEW

As Samuel anointed Saul (who failed to follow God) and then David (a man after God's own heart), we see many of God's promises partly fulfilled. God's people were in the land, gathered under God's word and under the rule of a godly king. Even so, David's failures remind us that he was sinful and fallen—just like all of God's people. Our hopes begin to look beyond David to a forever King—and an eternal kingdom.

● PRAY!

As you close this chapter with prayer, give thanks to God for the way this unit has shown us how he kept his great promise to his people—a promise made many years earlier to Abraham! God's people were in the land, under the leadership of a great king, and were beginning to experience God's blessing in new ways. Thank him, also, that God was planning to bring his own Son into the world to keep his biggest promise to them perfectly.

Chapter 9

GOD'S KINGDOM—
RISE AND FALL
PART 2

The founding of Israel's monarchy marked a time of both great blessing and great sin, as we saw in our previous chapter, the first of two in which we are considering the scene of the biblical story we are calling "God's Kingdom—Rise and Fall."

On the positive side, the kingdom of Israel came together under the great leadership of King David. God had brought his people into his good place—Canaan—and had given them a good ruler. Under David, God's people began to live under God's blessing as never before, and it seemed that they were poised to bring his blessing to the other nations of the world. Many aspects of God's great promise to Abraham were coming together.

But King David was far from perfect. He did sinful and terrible things in his adultery with Bathsheba and his attempt to cover it up by murdering her husband. David would not be the final and eternal King that God's people needed; he, too, needed to repent and find God's great forgiveness and mercy. Still, it was to David that God gave his great promise of a forever kingdom; one of his descendants, God told him, would rule God's people forever.

So David's son Solomon was born. He would inherit the throne of Israel after his father and would take Israel to even greater heights. It's not hard to imagine that God's people during this time wondered if Solomon might be the eternal King that they needed.

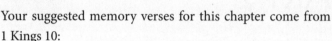

Remember!

Your suggested memory verses for this chapter come from 1 Kings 10:

And she said to the king, "The report was true that I heard in my own land of your words and of your wisdom, but I did not believe the reports until I came and my own eyes had seen it. And behold, the half was not told me. Your wisdom and prosperity surpass the report that I heard. Happy are your men! Happy are your servants, who continually stand before you and hear your wisdom! Blessed be the LORD your God, who has delighted in you and set you on the throne of Israel! Because the LORD loved Israel forever, he has made you king, that you may execute justice and righteousness." (1 Kings 10:6–9)

BUILDING A HOUSE FOR GOD

In 2 Samuel 7, we saw that David wanted to build a temple for God—a house of worship for him. God told him no and instead promised to make David's family into a great "house"—a forever kingdom, over which one of David's descendants would rule forever. God also promised that David's son Solomon would be the one to build the temple.

READ!

Read 1 Kings 7 and 8—the account of Solomon's preparation and dedication of the glorious temple that he made for the worship of God.

By the time of the events recorded in 1 Kings 7 and 8, David had died, and his son Solomon had taken over the throne in Israel. As Israel prospered greatly during a time of peace, King Solomon turned his heart to building a house for God—a great place for his people to worship his name. What do we notice from the passage we just read, and what was the significance of this temple that Solomon built?

First, Solomon dedicated great resources to this place for the worship of God. First Kings 7 describes the fine materials that went into its construction. Interestingly, however, it was not quite so big and glorious as his own palace.

Second, Solomon prayed a great prayer to God as the temple was "dedicated" to him for worship. I hope you read this prayer very carefully; it was a beautiful plea to God to bless his people, remember his mercy toward them, and even help other people turn in faith to him. Solomon essentially asked God to keep his great promise to Abraham as the temple was inaugurated. Second Chronicles 7, another version of this account, tells us that God's presence came down powerfully and "filled" the temple (v. 2); God chose to meet with his people in this place in a powerful way.

Third, the significance of this temple was that it would become, for God's people, the primary place for them to meet with their God. Blood sacrifices would be made there for sin, and God would allow sinful people to draw near to him in worship. This physical temple would not stand forever, but its inauguration was a great moment in the history of the people of Israel, for it pointed to a much greater meeting place between God and man at the cross of Jesus Christ.

This, then, is a high point in the big story of the Bible. In a moment, though, you will see how the story climbs one more time to its "peak" in the Old Testament.

THE BLESSING OF GOD UNDER SOLOMON

God descended with glory on the new temple, and it became the place where God's people met with him for worship during the days of Solomon and long after. This was a great blessing for Israel. But God did not stop there. As we read on in 1 Kings, we see even more clearly the great blessing of God on his people—and through his people—during the days of Solomon. Through this account, more than any other in the Old Testament, we see God keeping all his great promises to Abraham. This season of blessing would not last, of course, but because it did happen, we need to focus on this partial fulfillment of God's promise of blessing to his people and, through them, to the world.

READ!

Read 1 Kings 10:1–13—a passage that is probably the high point of the entire Old Testament.

Think about how far God's people had come since God first made his promise to Abraham hundreds of years before the days of Solomon. To just one man, living in a land called Ur, God made a huge promise—a promise of a *people*, of *land*, and of *blessing*—to this people and, through them, to all the peoples of the earth.

As we have traveled through the story of the Bible so far, we have seen God keeping the first two parts of this promise. The people of Israel multiplied greatly during the four hundred years that they spent in Egypt. Then, under the leadership of Joshua, they came into the land that God had promised to Abraham many years before. But God's people still had not seemed quite able to bring God's blessing to the peoples of the earth, in accordance with God's promise to them. In fact, rather than bringing the blessing of their God to other nations, they seemed much more prone toward worshiping the idols of the nations around them.

But the passage you just read shows us how all of God's promises to Abraham came together in a beautiful and powerful way during the reign of King Solomon in Jerusalem. Let's think about this together.

First, think about the promise of a *people*. God's people had become incredibly numerous and powerful. They were ruled by a mighty king, and God had subdued their enemies through the great military victories of Solomon's father, David. The people were powerful, secure, and at peace.

Second, think about the promise of a *land*. God's people held and ruled Israel, with the beautiful city of Jerusalem as their capital. In this city, their king dwelled in a glorious palace, and they met with God in a beautiful temple through worship and sacrifice. God's place was wonderful.

Third, think about all that happens in this passage regarding the *blessing* of God—first to his people and then, through them, to the nations. The queen of Sheba—a Gentile monarch from a faraway land—came to King Solomon because she had heard of his incredible wealth and wisdom. As she tested him with difficult questions and saw every part of his kingdom, she was absolutely amazed; the text tells us that her experience took her breath away.

Do you see what was happening? The blessing of God on his people was spreading to all the peoples of the earth. God's people—and God's king—were finally poised to become a blessing to all nations. Monarchs from other nations were coming to Jerusalem to see and experience the wisdom and blessing of God there. It seems, based on this high point, that God's people were finally ready to live as a light to the nations under the great blessing of God.

SOLOMON'S DOWNFALL

Sadly, Israel did not remain at its high point for long. In the *very next chapter* of the biblical story, we begin to see the failure of Solomon as the king of God's people. In the passage that you will read next, you will see the sin and idolatry that crept into King Solomon's heart and life, which reminds us that God's people were still waiting for a far better King.

READ!

Read 1 Kings 10:14–11:8—the sad account of Solomon beginning a downward trend into sin.

Before we dig into the passage you just read, take a few minutes to read one more brief passage: Deuteronomy 17:14–20. What do you see in Deuteronomy 17 regarding God's specific instructions for kings?

Positively, the kings were to read God's law every day so that they might live by it (Deut. 17:18–20). Negatively, God listed three things that the kings were not to acquire for themselves (vv. 14–17):

- excessive numbers of *horses*
- many *wives*
- excessive amounts of *silver* and *gold*

With that background, think back to the passage that you just read about Solomon. What did Solomon do? He ultimately disobeyed every one of these specific prohibitions from God. He had an excessive amount of gold and other precious things. He had an excessive number of horses to go along with a huge military force. Finally, and probably most dangerously, he had roughly a thousand wives—many of whom worshiped foreign gods and idols, and who turned his heart away from the true worship of God.

Here is the point: in Moses's time, God had looked ahead to the period of the monarchy and had given commandments for the kings who would rule his people. Those commandments would keep the kings dependent on *him* as the true King of the people (by prohibiting them from getting too rich or relying too much on military power) and would keep them worshiping *him* as the true God of the people (by prohibiting them from taking many foreign wives, who might turn their hearts toward idolatry). Solomon, at the very height of his kingship and at the high point of the Old Testament, began to break God's commandments one by one as the king of God's people.

What does this tell us? We are beginning to see that even Solomon—the great son of David, who built the glorious temple for the worship of God—was not the final and perfect King that God's people needed. There would be someone even greater than Solomon—someone who would be not just great but perfect. That King would be able to lead God's people in a forever kingdom, where there would be no more sin, idolatry, or death at all.

A DIVIDED KINGDOM

The effects of Solomon's sin soon began to be felt in the life of his family and in the lives of everyone living in God's kingdom. Just one generation after Solomon, the great kingdom of Israel split into two parts—never to be fully joined again. This was the sad beginning of a descent into a new cycle of sin for God's people—one that would lead all the way to exile, which would come as a punishment from God.

READ!

Read 1 Kings 11:9–12:33.

Solomon's son, Rehoboam, was in line to take the throne after the death of his father. He was the grandson of David, only two generations removed from the man to whom God promised a "forever kingdom," with a descendant ruling over God's people forever. Rehoboam, though, would *not* be that king!

Grace and judgment. The passage you just read begins with God's words to Solomon about his sin. Because of Solomon's failure, God promised to "tear" part of the kingdom from his rule (1 Kings 11:11); he would bring his judgment on Solomon's house because of his idolatry and disobedience. Yet even in this, God was gracious. He promised to not do this during the reign of Solomon, out of love for his father, David. Still, this sin of Solomon was serious to God, and it would not be ignored.

A foolish choice. As Rehoboam rose to power after the death of his father, Solomon, it became clear very quickly that this man was nowhere near the leader that David or Solomon had been. At the beginning of his reign, the people came to him with a request; basically, they asked him to rule them with more gentleness and grace than his father had (evidently another failure of Solomon was that he made things hard for God's people, and worked them harshly in his service). Rehoboam got good advice from the older men of Israel, who told him that if he showed grace and gentleness to the people, they would be loyal to him forever. His young colleagues, though, told him to be tough with the people—to answer them harshly, to show them who was in charge. Rehoboam unwisely listened to his young and foolish friends.

A great divide. Because of Rehoboam's answer to God's people, ten of the twelve tribes of Israel (all except for Judah and Benjamin) decided to follow a far more evil man—Jeroboam—instead of Rehoboam. They broke off from the rule of Rehoboam and the centrality of Jerusalem to form a new northern kingdom: Israel. The two remaining tribes would from thereon be referred to as the southern kingdom: Judah. As we see from the passage, God had to step in to prevent a civil war over this split, although that would eventually happen later in the story. This was a very sad day for God's people. Remember, we are still just one generation removed from the height of God's united people under Solomon.

Full-blown idolatry. Sadly, Jeroboam was a far worse leader than even the foolish Rehoboam. Our passage ends with the people of Israel— the ten tribes who followed Jeroboam—being led into idolatry. They bowed down to golden calf statues instead of worshiping the one true God. Israel—the northern kingdom—would never again have a fully good king to rule over them. Judah would have a few more righteous kings, but even they began to head downhill into sin and idolatry. The kingdom had been divided, and the downward slope toward punishment and exile had already begun.

THE DOWNWARD SPIRAL OF THE KINGDOMS

We do not have time to learn about all of the many kings who ruled over God's people during the generations following David, Solomon, and Rehoboam. Instead, we will consider just two of the kings, who give us a good picture of the downward spiral of God's people during this time. Then we will talk more broadly about the recurring problem of idolatry in Israel. Next we will consider the prophets God sent to warn his people, with particular attention to the ministry of the great prophet Elijah in the time of the evil King Ahab in the northern kingdom. Finally, we have to think about how God punished his people by sending them into exile.

As we have mentioned, the time of the monarchy—after David and Solomon—was a slow, steady, and sad descent toward the exile. God was patient with his people, but he ultimately punished them for their sin, rebellion, and idolatry. Still, God's grace toward his people showed up again and again. He refused to completely abandon them at any point.

READ!

Read 1 Kings 15:9–16:6—an account of the reign of King Asa in Judah and King Nadab and King Baasha in Israel.

Here is a "snapshot" of what happened, generation by generation, in Israel and Judah in the years following Solomon and leading up to the exile.

The kings of Judah. The story was different in Judah, the southern kingdom. There were sinful kings, of course, and Judah eventually followed Israel into idolatry and then exile. Still, there were kings in Judah who followed the path of David and sought to restore right worship to God's people as they obeyed his word.

Asa was one of those kings, as you saw from the passage you read. He put into place some serious reforms, getting rid of sexual perversions and removing many of the idols that his father, King Abijam, had put into place. He did not take down the "high places"—places of idolatrous worship on mountaintops—which was a failure of many of the kings of Judah, even the good ones. Yet Asa was an example of a king of Judah who walked faithfully before God and sought to lead his people in righteousness and obedience. Asa was not the perfect and eternal King, but he reminds us that a good King was still coming for God's people!

The kings of Israel. In general, the kings who ruled over the northern kingdom—Israel—were evil, idolatrous, and disobedient to God. Even though some of them showed moments of goodness and repentance (even the wicked King Ahab seemed to repent at one point in his life), in general, the kings of Israel led God's people into depths of sin and idolatry that had never before been known in Israel. Both Nadab and Baasha—the two kings of Israel mentioned in the passage you just read —were good examples of this. Nadab "walked in the way of his father" (1 Kings 15:26), Jeroboam, and led Israel into more sin and idolatry. Baasha, after killing Nadab and taking the throne for himself, also did evil in God's eyes, and led all of Israel into sin.

The story of Baasha also shows us that the northern kingdom was a place of political unrest. This was not the only time that someone grabbed power through a rebellion that ended in the murder of the seated king. Evil abounded.

God's judgment and grace. As the story continues through the rise and fall of kings in both Israel and Judah, we continue to see the judgment and grace of the great God of Israel—and of the entire world. God was patient with his sinful people, keeping his promise and his plan moving forward despite sin and continual rebellion. God was not finished with this people, and he would keep his great promise to save them and to build a forever kingdom under the great Son of David! Yet God also would not ignore sin forever. The tension of the Old Testament is between the grace of this good God and his justice against sin that his holiness demands. During the reign of the kings, we are left waiting to see exactly how these attributes of God would be fully reconciled in his actions toward his obviously sinful people.

THE PERVASIVE PROBLEM OF IDOLATRY

We need to look more closely at a recurring temptation that seemed to plague God's people during the years of the monarchy: *idolatry*. Why were God's people so prone to this sin? Why did they find idolatry so appealing during this time?

READ!

Read 1 Kings 16:21–34—two accounts of very evil kings (Omri and Ahab) who both led God's people into terrible idolatry.

This passage gives us summary accounts of the reigns in Israel of King Omri and then his son, King Ahab. Central to the descriptions of both reigns is the sin of idolatry Both of these men practiced the worship of idols personally and led God's people into idol worship corporately. These were not good and faithful leaders for God's people by any means.

The chances are, though, that as you read these accounts about the temptation of God's people toward idolatry during the time of the kings, you struggle to understand how they could have been so drawn to something so silly and false. Probably few of us today feel an urge to bow down before a statue made of wood or metal! Our goal, then, is to understand idolatry during the days of the kings a bit more clearly, understand the people's "pull" toward it, and then think about how we are tempted to this sin today.

Understanding idolatry. We must begin by admitting that idolatry— the worship of false gods who supposedly ruled different parts of the earth and skies—was widespread in every one of the nations that surrounded Israel and Judah. They probably were the only nations in the world who worshiped one Creator God, who ruled every part of the earth and skies. To worship the Creator God, a God who was invisible (and not represented by a statue), set them apart as different from all the peoples around them.

163

We should also note that idolatry was bound up with many other parts of life. People did not simply enjoy bowing down to statues; they really thought that sacrifices and worship to the "god of fertility," for example, might help them have more children. Also, idolatry often was connected to sexual practices, so other sin sometimes was committed along with idol worship.

The pull toward idolatry. Why did the people of the one true God feel tempted toward this kind of idolatry? First, it would have been difficult for them to keep following an *invisible* God who ruled them by his *word.* All the surrounding nations had physical and visible gods that they could bow down to, but the Israelites' God was unseen. The temptation to worship something visible and tangible was very real for God's people.

Second, the pressure to be like the people around them had long been part of the temptations of God's people (remember their first request for a king during the days of Samuel). They would have been constantly tempted to fit in with other peoples, so they were drawn to their practices.

Third, some aspects of idolatry probably were pleasurable and simply fun. Much idol worship was accompanied by great parties and feasts, as well as (as we mentioned before) sexual practices that were outside the bounds of God-ordained marriage. These other aspects of idolatrous worship probably drew some of God's people in as well.

Idolatry today. Before we dismiss God's people as foolish and sinful (which, of course, they were at times), we should consider our own temptations and tendencies toward forms of idolatry today. We may not be tempted to prostrate ourselves before wooden statues, but we may be very tempted to almost "worship" money, relationships, or success more than God himself. We, too, still feel the tendency to attach our ultimate meaning and purpose to people or pursuits other than Jesus Christ. This is the *same* tendency that the people of God felt during those days so long ago. Like them, we struggle with idolatrous hearts that tend to worship things other than God alone. Like them, we need a great King and Savior who can forgive us for our sins and reign over us perfectly forever.

THE PROPHETS OF GOD

How did God respond to the sin of his people before the judgment of exile? He did not judge them without warning. Instead, he faithfully spoke to his people through prophets—men whom he began to raise up for his people during the time of the monarchy. We will examine the role of the prophets generally, then look in more detail at the powerful ministry of just one of them: Elijah.

READ!

Read Hosea 1–2—the fascinating opening chapters in this rich prophetic book.

As we have seen, very sad days for God's people followed the reign of King Solomon. The kingdom split under his son, Rehoboam, and the kings who followed him were not, in general, any better. There were some good and righteous kings in Judah, but none in Israel, the northern kingdom. In general, the people of God were headed in a dangerous direction during the days of these kings—toward sin, idolatry, and judgment by God.

But in this same time, God began to raise up prophets—men who spoke his word boldly to his people. What do we need to understand about the prophets and their role in the big story of the Bible?

Preexilic/postexilic. We are focused now especially on "preexilic" prophets—those who spoke to God's people before the exile. Some of the prophets, of course, ministered during and even after the exiles to Assyria (Israel, in 722 BC) and Babylon (Judah, in 586 BC). But given where we are in the story of the Bible, we are interested especially in those prophets who warned God's people and brought God's truth to them in the days before they were taken away in judgment.

The role of the prophets. God sent the preexilic prophets to call the people back from their sin, invite them to repentance, and warn them of God's coming judgment if they did not repent. More specifically, in Scripture, we find the prophets talking about:

- God's *law*—and the way the people had abandoned obedience to it
- God's *justice*—and the way the people had chosen injustice instead
- the sinfulness of *idolatry*, which is a turning away from worship of the one, true, invisible God
- the coming *judgment of exile* if the people would not repent and turn back to God
- the ultimate *grace* and promise of God, which would eternally never fail, even though God would judge his people

These topics are often mixed in the messages of the prophets. They were quite comfortable warning the people of God's coming judgment against their sin, and also comforting them with words of his eternal salvation.

The ministry of Hosea. You just read two chapters from the prophet Hosea, one of the preexilic prophets. Hosea spoke to the northern kingdom—Israel—and focused mainly on identifying and highlighting the adulterous and awful nature of their sin of idolatry. Specifically, Hosea went after the worship of Baal, which had become very prevalent in Israel during his time. God called Hosea, unlike many of the other prophets, to allow his life to speak as well as his words. Thus, Hosea took an adulterous woman to be his wife so that his grace toward an unfaithful spouse could model for the people of Israel God's faithfulness to a people who kept turning to other gods in worship. As you read, you surely saw the strong ways that Hosea identified the sin of

God's people, but also how he comforted them with words about God's final salvation.

Lessons about God. Ultimately, the very existence of the prophets during these days reminds us that God is gracious to his people; he does not leave them without communication and his good word, even during times of great sin. Through the prophets, God continued to confront his people with his word and continued to call them back toward right worship of him and a proper relationship with him. God would judge his people, but he was gracious and patient. One day he would provide a final sacrifice for this sinful people; he would find a way to deal with their sin and idolatry forever so that they could follow and serve him permanently.

THE PROPHET ELIJAH

Hosea is sometime called (along with Isaiah, Jeremiah, and others) a "writing" prophet because we have his words recorded in a book of the Bible. Elijah, whom we will learn about now, is sometimes called a "nonwriting" prophet because there is no book that is made up primarily of the prophecies that he spoke to God's people. Still, some of his powerful actions and words are recorded for us in the book of 1 Kings, showing us that Elijah had a powerful ministry for God to his people during the reign of one of Israel's most evil and brutal kings: Ahab.

READ!

Read 1 Kings 18—the account of the great confrontation between the prophet Elijah and the prophets of Baal on Mount Carmel.

Elijah was one of the greatest prophets in all of Scripture. In fact, John the Baptist was compared to—and identified with—Elijah when he came to bear witness to the coming of Jesus Christ as the New Testament began.

Life was not easy for a prophet of God during the time of Ahab. Glance back at 1 Kings 16:29–34 to remind yourself of the kind of king

Ahab was for God's people in Israel. The worship of Baal prevailed, evil was the norm, and God's prophets were banished from the land (although some of them hid in a cave and survived during this time).

A drought as punishment for idolatry. It was into this situation in Israel that God called his servant Elijah. He spoke God's word to a wicked king whose wife—Jezebel—was even more evil than he was. In 1 Kings 17, we see Elijah predicting a long drought in Israel, brought about by God as a judgment on his people for their sinful worship of Baal. After Elijah predicted the drought, he lived for a while in the wilderness, where he was sustained by God. He also was taken in for a time by a Gentile woman, whose son he raised from the dead.

The confrontation. After a while, though, God called Elijah back to Israel—it was time for a great confrontation with Ahab and the prophets of Baal. Elijah challenged Ahab to a kind of "prophets' duel" on Mount Carmel, and Ahab, who employed 450 prophets of Baal, accepted. The challenge was to see whose "god" would answer prayer to rain down fire from heaven to consume a sacrifice placed on an altar. First, the prophets of Baal went through their rituals, cutting themselves with knives and crying out to Baal to give fire to their offering. Nothing happened.

Then Elijah was up. He began by soaking the sacrificial offering in water—making it essentially impossible to burn. Then he prayed to God, who sent down miraculous fire from heaven that consumed the sacrifice *and* all the water! It was an amazing moment. The prophets of Baal were put to death, and it seemed that there was at least a partial return to God by some of the people of Israel.

What God was doing. What was God doing in this account? He was reminding his people, through the prophet Elijah, that he alone is God in Israel and all the world. Baal was a false god—a lifeless idol—that the people had foolishly chosen to worship instead of the one true and faithful Creator. God was claiming authority and power over his people in a way that could not be denied. Sadly, though, the people would not turn from their sin for long. Idolatry continued, and even Ahab—who saw Elijah's duel with the prophets of Baal firsthand—did not seem to change his evil ways.

A bigger battle. In the bigger picture of the Bible story, though, we need to see that this epic battle pointed forward to a far greater confrontation on a mountain. It was on the hill called Golgotha, where Jesus was crucified, that the epic confrontation between God and all the forces of evil, Satan, sin, and death took place. There, through Jesus's sacrificial death (and through his resurrection three days later), God conquered the forces of evil—and the sin of his people—forever. This was an eternal victory, far greater than the one on Mount Carmel!

THE EXILE

We've come to the end of this scene of the Bible story: "God's Kingdom—Rise and Fall." After many years of warning his people through his prophets, God finally brought the judgment of exile on both Israel and Judah because of their sin. This was the sad end of the monarchy—but it was not the end of the story!

READ!

Read 2 Chronicles 36—the sad account of the exile of Judah to Babylon, which took place around 586 BC.

Israel went into exile first—to Assyria—in around 722 BC (see 2 Kings 15:29). God brought the mighty Assyrian army against the northern kingdom, over which no truly righteous kings had reigned. The people went away into slavery and never really returned—at least not all at once—to a unified kingdom in Israel. The existence of the ten tribes that composed the kingdom of Israel (Judah and Benjamin made up the kingdom of Judah) was all but destroyed through this exile. God's judgment—about which many of his prophets had warned for many years—had finally come to the northern kingdom.

Judah held out longer; God was patient with the southern kingdom, as some faithful and righteous kings (such as Josiah and Hezekiah, just to name a couple) led God's people in reforms and in great returns to faithful worship. Still, Judah also declined steadily into more and more sin. Eventually, as you read in 2 Chronicles 36, its people also were conquered, captured, and taken away as slaves to Babylon (in roughly 586 BC).

The final days. Second Chronicles 36 focuses especially on the final rebellion of King Zedekiah. This king had the ministry of the prophet Jeremiah right in front of him; Jeremiah faithfully proclaimed the warnings and the calls of God to him. Still, Zedekiah rejected this word from God and turned his heart against Jeremiah, and therefore against God himself. As you saw, verses 15–16 of this passage are intended to be the sad summary of the continual ministry of the prophets and the continual rejection of God's word by the kings and by all the people of Israel and Judah.

The exile to Babylon. Finally, after many years of patience and many warnings, God sent his people into exile. He allowed Nebuchadnezzar, the king of Babylon, to conquer Jerusalem and all of its people. The temple and the great palace of the kings were destroyed. The survivors were taken away forcibly to serve the king of Babylon in his land. This was the sad end of the monarchy in Israel; it would never go back to what it once was. God's people went away as slaves to Babylon because of their continual sin, rebellion, and idolatry. God's judgment had come.

The return. The last little paragraph of 2 Chronicles (vv. 22–23) skips ahead seventy years—a very long time in Babylon—to the day when God's people returned home. The story was not yet over. God was not done working in the lives and hearts of his people. His salvation plan, promised in Genesis 3:15, was still "in play." His promise to Abraham was still active. The story would go on, even though the monarchy was long gone. A better King was coming, and the great salvation of God would soon be shown to all the world. The next scene of the story will pick up where this one leaves off—with the return of God's people to Israel.

REVIEW

David's failures amid a generally faithful reign gave way to Solomon's greater failures (despite his great God-given strength, wealth, and wisdom). The kingdom was divided, and God's people never again experienced the blessing of the days of David and Solomon. The northern kingdom of Israel spiraled into sin and idolatry (and went into exile first), and the southern kingdom of Judah (despite some good and faithful kings) soon followed. God's people became slaves in a foreign land—and yet, God still did not abandon his gracious saving promises to them.

PRAY!

As you close this chapter with prayer, ask God to remind you of his great faithfulness to his people—which includes you. Thank him for not quitting on his plan for his people, but for continuing to work graciously on their behalf and ultimately promising them a much greater King than Solomon: Jesus Christ himself!

Chapter 10

GOD'S PEOPLE—
CAPTIVE AND
COMING HOME
PART 1

The sin of the people of Israel and Judah, especially their idolatry, led God to allow them to be captured and deported to other countries, as we saw at the end of the last chapter. But there's much more that is important to know about this period in the big story of the Bible.

We're now moving into a new scene in the story of the Bible: "God's People—Captive and Coming Home." In this chapter and the next one, we will learn about the period of the exile, as well as the people's return from the exile back to Jerusalem and their "fresh start" as they came back to the land.

To get started, let's try to understand God's purpose for the exile, learn what books in the Bible record the return, think briefly about the role of the prophets during this time, and most importantly, consider how all of this points us forward in the story to the coming of Jesus Christ, God's Son.

The purpose of the exile. Our last chapter ended with God finally sending the people of Judah—the southern kingdom—into exile when the nation was conquered by King Nebuchadnezzar of Babylon in 586 BC. What was God's purpose in all of this? He had warned his people many times about their sin, and especially about the sin of idolatry, which their kings had led them to practice. Judah's King Zedekiah was the final ruler who rebelled against God; he rejected the word of God from Jeremiah, and God finally punished his people. So God's purpose for the exile was to punish his people. But even this seventy-year time of captivity was not the end of the story. God was not done with his people.

Books in this scene. The two central books in the Bible that tell us about the people's return from exile to Jerusalem are Ezra and Nehemiah—both of which are named for their central human figures. We will spend time looking at what these books record about these two faithful men who led God's people back into the right worship of him. The books of Daniel and Esther also give us glimpses of God's faithfulness to his people during the general period of the exile; we will study those stories very briefly, too.

The role of the prophets. Another major part of the biblical story during this scene is the role of God's prophets in the lives of his people. Their role became more pronounced during the exile and after the return to Jerusalem. God was constantly speaking to his people—even during the exile—through faithful men who continued to bring his word to his people. As the exile ended, the prophets began to turn the eyes of God's people toward the future coming of a better King, and a more permanent kingdom and salvation of God.

The path to Jesus Christ. As you know, the person of Jesus Christ is central to Scripture; it is all about him! So we will also study how this scene of the Bible story is meant to show us the role of Jesus Christ and the gospel (his death for sins and resurrection from the dead). The "path"

to Christ in this scene will mainly be one of longing and the lack of fulfillment. After the exile, God's people began to realize that the kingdom of
Israel would never again be like it was under King Solomon. They were
constantly ruled by foreign nations. They began to long for a day when
God would again rule over his people with power, glory, and blessing.

Remember!

Your suggested memory verses for this chapter come from the
account of Ezra's arrival in Israel along with many others from
God's people. Many years before Ezra's arrival, the first group of
exiles had returned from Babylon to Jerusalem and had rebuilt
the temple. Ezra came to reestablish the right worship of and obedience to God in the land, according to God's word (we will see
the problems that Ezra found in Jerusalem later in this chapter).

*And Ezra came to Jerusalem in the fifth month, which was in the
seventh year of the king. For on the first day of the first month
he began to go up from Babylonia, and on the first day of the
fifth month he came to Jerusalem, for the good hand of his God
was on him. For Ezra had set his heart to study the Law of the
Lord, and to do it and to teach his statutes and rules in Israel.
(Ezra 7:8–10)*

DANIEL IN EXILE

The Bible gives us several stories of people—and of God—during the
exile. First, we will look briefly at the account of Daniel. As you probably know, Daniel was a prophet of God. He was just a young man
when he was taken away into exile after Judah was conquered by King
Nebuchadnezzar of Babylon. His story reminds us that God was still
working during the seventy years of the exile, ruling over his people
and working by his own strength to bring his blessing to all nations.

📖 **READ!**

Read Daniel 1–2.

As Daniel approached Babylon as a captive, he was probably terrified, lonely, and missing his home. But God would be faithful to this young man. He would bless him richly during his people's time in Babylon.

Daniel's "stand." After a brief account of the Babylonian capture of Jerusalem (Dan. 1:1–2), the narrative quickly moves to the Babylonian court and palace, where Daniel and other promising young Jewish men were gathered for training in the service of King Nebuchadnezzar. It was a great honor for Daniel to be chosen for this service—an indication that God's work in his life was not finished. But Daniel and his friends chose to take a very dangerous position: they refused to eat the rich food of Babylon during their time of training. Instead, they asked their supervisors to let them eat simply, because they belonged to the God of Israel. Probably this was less about the food itself and more about taking a stand for God, declaring boldly that they were set apart as belonging to God. As you saw from the passage you read, God richly blessed this decision by Daniel and his friends, and he gave them favor with their supervisors and all the people of Babylon.

Daniel and the dream. God's work did not stop there. We find that, like Joseph, Daniel was given great wisdom from God to interpret dreams. Do you remember how God ultimately brought Joseph into the palace and service of Pharaoh so many years before this story? God did a very similar thing in the life of Daniel, who interpreted a dream of Nebuchadnezzar—something that the wisest men of Babylon had failed to do.

Daniel's power. By God's strength and hand, Daniel was exalted to an incredibly high position in Babylon. What an amazing rise to power! Daniel was a Jew who had come to Babylon as a captive, but he now was ruling over many people of a pagan nation. This could only be the work of God for his own glory and the good of his people—even in exile.

God's work. What do we learn from the account of Daniel in Babylon? It shows us that God's work in the lives of his people—and for his own glory in the nations—was not yet done. God was just as much the God of Babylon as the God of Israel, and he would make sure that his people not only survived but even *prospered* there. God would take care of his people and keep his great promise to Abraham moving along. The story was not over; God was still focused on using his people to bring his great blessing to all the world.

ESTHER IN PERSIA

The Bible gives us one other account from the time of the exile—this time in Persia, not Babylon. As you will see, the story of Esther, like that of Daniel, reminds us that God's faithful presence is with his people no matter where they go. He is always behind the scenes, preserving his people and continuing to work all things out according to his perfect plan.

READ!

Read Esther 5, 8, and 9—but also read as much of the rest of the book as you can.

The historical situation of the book of Esther is a bit more complicated than that of Daniel. Most likely, the Jews who were living in Persia during Esther's time were descendants of those who had been taken away as captives of the Babylonians. Years had passed, though, and the empire of Persia now ruled all the lands and nations that Babylon once controlled. It seems that the account of Esther took place after the Jews had been allowed to go back to Jerusalem, so it could be that the Jews in this story had chosen to stay in Persia rather than return to Israel. At any rate, it is safe to say that this story took place following the exile, as God's people had been "dispersed" among the nations that were ruled by Persia (Est. 3:8).

The book of Esther, very interestingly, is the only book in the Bible that does not mention God at all! While Esther and Mordecai—the book's main characters—act together to save and preserve the lives of the Jewish people, we are given no indication of their personal faith in God, love for his word, or holiness and obedience. We simply do not know too much about what motivated Esther in all her actions.

But while this book does not mention God by name, it contains a story that has his "fingerprints" all over it. God is very present, but he is behind the scenes, working all things out for the preservation of his people by his hidden yet powerful and sovereign hand.

What are the key points in this account?

The threat. During the days of King Ahasuerus in Susa, the Persian capital, a man named Haman hatched a plot to destroy all the Jewish people living in the kingdom of Persia. Obviously this man hated both God and his people. It seems likely that, had this plot actually come to pass, even the Jews who had gone back to Israel would have been in danger, as that land was technically under the control of the Persians during this time. So God's people were in a very real predicament; a sentence of death, from the king of Persia himself, hung over their heads.

The preservation. Amid this threat, Esther, a young Jewish woman (who had kept her ethnicity hidden), miraculously rose to the position of queen through a kind of ancient beauty contest. Esther's uncle, Mordecai, hearing of the threat against the Jewish people, urged Esther to confront the king—her husband—and beg him to spare the lives of the Jewish people. Esther finally agreed to do this, Haman was exposed as a villain, and the Jewish people gained a tremendous victory over all their enemies. They ended up much better off than before Haman hatched his plot.

The lesson. So what is the point of this book, which does not even mention God by name? Why is the story of Esther recorded for God's people in the Bible? It seems that God wanted his people to know that—even throughout the years of exile and dispersion—he was at work to preserve their lives as well as his great promise to Abraham. God had not abandoned his people forever; he would not allow them to be wiped out from the face of the earth. God would do what he needed to do to keep his plan safe—a plan that would one day involve his own Son entering the world as a *Jewish* baby boy.

EZRA AND THE RETURN FROM EXILE

Now let's shift our focus to the beginning of the book of Ezra, where we find an account of the first wave of returned exiles who came back from Babylon to Jerusalem. In the passage you will read next, you will be confronted with God's faithfulness to his people and will see how he began to restore them to their own land.

READ!

Read Ezra 1 and 2—the beginning of the account of the return of the Israelite exiles from Babylon to Jerusalem.

Ezra, the scribe after whom this book is named, does not actually show up until chapter 7—more than fifty years after the events recorded in the passage that you just read. In Ezra 1 and 2, we see God's great faithfulness to his people in the return from exile—faithfulness that emerged in several ways.

God's faithfulness to his people. It may have seemed a bit tedious to read all of Ezra 2; there are many difficult and unfamiliar names on that list. But hopefully the cumulative effect of that list struck you in a significant way as you saw the record of all the people whom God brought back to his place in Jerusalem. These people left slavery and captivity, and came back to the place that God had promised to his people.

It is difficult to not see God's great faithfulness to his people demonstrated in this passage. He had not abandoned them forever, even though he had punished and disciplined them for their sin through exile to Babylon. As he had promised, he faithfully brought them back to the land through the decree of a mighty pagan king.

God's faithfulness to his word. Did you notice how the book of Ezra begins? Ezra was careful to point out to his readers that everything that would happen in this account would be according to "the word of the LORD by the mouth of Jeremiah" (1:1). Jeremiah the prophet had spoken to King Zedekiah of Judah, calling him to repent of sin and turn back to God, threatening exile as the punishment for his sin (Jer. 38:17–18). He also had promised that God would bring his people out of exile after seventy years in Babylon (29:10). Now, according to Ezra, God was keeping this word he had given to his people more than seventy years earlier through Jeremiah. God is faithful to his word!

God's continuing work. Perhaps the most amazing part of this account was how God worked in the heart of a mighty pagan king—Cyrus— to decree this return to the land for God's people. Cyrus, the king of the known world during this time, was only a pawn in the hands of God, who was working out his good purposes in the lives of his people. God stirred up this pagan king's heart to do exactly what he wanted him to do for his people.

God was very obviously not done with his people; his work would continue in their lives, and in Israel and Jerusalem. The story was not over, even though we will soon see that the human monarchy was dead. Someday, a better King would come, and God would begin to reveal more of his great plan of redemption through a greater King—and kingdom—to come.

REBUILDING THE TEMPLE

When God's people returned to the land, they began to rebuild the temple, which had been destroyed seventy years earlier by King Nebuchadnezzar of Babylon during his invasion of Jerusalem. There was great hope in this rebuilding, as God's people sought to reestablish the right worship of God in his place in Jerusalem.

▌ READ!

Read Ezra 3—the account of the people laying the foundation for the rebuilt temple in Jerusalem. Then read 2 Chronicles 5—the account of the dedication of the original temple of Solomon.

Ezra 3 begins with a celebration—God's people kept the Feast of Booths as they gathered back in Israel. Most likely, they had not kept this feast in this way during the exile in Babylon; this was a fresh start for the Israelites back in the land.

But the heart of this chapter comes next—the beginning of the reconstruction of the temple, the most important activity of God's people when they returned to Jerusalem. First, the foundation was laid, then the people stopped to have a celebration with singing and praise to God. Let's dwell on this celebratory moment briefly.

The first dedication. You also read 2 Chronicles 5, which records the dedication of the temple of Solomon. Did you notice the similarities between that celebration and this one in Ezra? The people of Israel sang the same song: "For he is good, for his steadfast love endures forever" (2 Chron. 5:13; Ezra 3:11). The beginning of the new temple was another great moment of hope for God's people.

A moment of hope. The Israelites had been in captivity in Babylon for seventy years—a very long time. For at least two generations, God's people had had no temple, no place of worship, no opportunity to sacrifice, and no organized priestly system, such as had been established under the reign of King Solomon, to help them approach God. God was faithful to his people in exile, but this still was a huge moment for the Israelites. After many years, they were joyfully returning to their home as well as the worship of their good God.

Not there yet. Even though this was a moment of great hope for God's people, there were two very strong indications that much more was to come for God's people. What were those indications?

- First, the glory of the Lord descended on Solomon's temple right after the people finished their song of praise (2 Chron. 5:13). That does not seem to have happened in Ezra 3. It seems that God's presence may not have dwelt in the second temple in the same special way it did in the first temple many years before.
- Second, there was unexpected weeping amid the celebration of God's people. Who was weeping? It was the old men, who were old enough to remember the glories of the temple that Solomon had built. They realized that this new temple would never come close to matching the glories of the old temple; they could tell this just by looking at the foundation. So they wept as they realized that this was a sign that the kingdom of Israel would never return to its former glory.

So even though God's people returned to the land with great hope and rebuilt the temple of God, the book of Ezra leaves us with a sense of incompleteness. Things would not return to the state of glory and blessing experienced in the reign of Solomon. God's people began to understand that they were still waiting for a better temple; we know from the New Testament that this better temple would be the body of God's own Son, who would come to earth to be, in himself, the ultimate "meeting place" between the holy God and sinful humanity.

EZRA THE SCRIBE

We're now going to skip forward more than fifty years to the time when Ezra the scribe came to Jerusalem to teach God's word to God's people. We will look at Ezra's firm commitments as a "preacher," as well as the drastic effect that God's word had on God's people during those days.

READ!

Read Ezra 7, then Ezra 9–10.

In the passages you just read, you were finally introduced to the character of Ezra, for whom the biblical book is named. Ezra, we find, was probably the best model in the Old Testament for what a preacher should be for God's people. He was a man of God's word, who brought that word to bear powerfully in the lives of the Israelites who had returned from exile. Let's take a close look at this man's commitments and the impact of his word ministry on God's people during this time.

Ezra's commitments. Ezra 7:10—the final verse of the passage you are memorizing as you read and study this chapter—is a remarkable summary of Ezra's commitments as a word-centered leader of God's people. He had given himself to the careful study of God's word; his goal was to *know* it well. Ezra also had devoted himself to "do" the word of God; his goal was to *obey* everything that God had commanded. Finally, this verse tells us that Ezra had set his heart to make known the statutes of God to the people of Israel; his goal was to *teach* God's word faithfully to God's people.

Ezra, then, was a great gift from God to his people during these days. He entered the story of God's people as a faithful leader—a man who would call them back to right worship and obedience, according to the word of God. This was exactly what the people needed!

The people's situation. When Ezra arrived in Jerusalem more than fifty years after the new temple had been completed, he found that God's people were reestablished in the land but not necessarily reestablished under the rule of the word of God in every area. As you saw from Ezra 9 and 10, the main problem that plagued God's people was intermarriage. We need to be very careful as we seek to understand this issue, as well as the commitments that Ezra called God's people to make during this time.

It is important to see that the issue of intermarriage was not an issue of *race* but an issue of *worship*. For centuries, God had been accepting Gentile people into his community—people who had turned to him by faith and made him their God. Rahab, the prostitute from Jericho, had been accepted into the community of God. Ruth the Moabite had become the great-grandmother of King David himself! But in their return to the land, God's people had intermarried with others who had not accepted their God. Because of this, the Israelites were being led toward idolatry and sin. This situation was extremely dangerous; it affected the pure worship of God's people. This was why Ezra called the people to turn away from this kind of sin.

The impact of the word. So what was the outcome of the ministry of the word through Ezra during this time? We see that one huge impact of God's word, when it really rules over the lives and hearts of God's people, is that it brings conviction of sin and helps restore God's people to pure worship of him. Ezra did not just preach the word to God's people in an informative way but called them to respond to God's word with drastic repentance for their sin and changed lives of obedience. The impact of God's word in the lives of the people (Ezra 9–10), leading to confession and repentance, shows us the way in which that word demands that people respond with transformed hearts and lives. This also must be our response when we hear the message of the gospel today!

MEETING NEHEMIAH

During the time of the return from exile, another key figure played a major role in the lives of God's people: the great leader Nehemiah. Like Ezra, he was a man who had a passion for God's word, a love for God's people, and a concern for God's place. He came to Jerusalem with a focus on rebuilding its wall and repairing the damage that had been done to this great city.

READ!

Read Nehemiah 1–2—the record of Nehemiah's arrival in Jerusalem after serving for a time in the household of the king of Persia.

From what we know of the history of this period, it seems likely that Nehemiah came to Jerusalem from Susa, the capital city of the empire of Persia, about ten to fifteen years after Ezra had arrived. So these two men were contemporaries; they worked together in the leadership of God's people in the years after the return from exile. Nehemiah's specific focus was the city of Jerusalem itself.

The state of Jerusalem. You saw from the passage that you read that Nehemiah had a very good position in Susa; he served as the cupbearer to the king. Yet as Nehemiah was serving in Susa, he received word that the wall of Jerusalem—and the city in general—remained in ruins. Evidently God's people had not been firmly committed to rebuilding the wall of the city. They had gone about their lives and largely neglected the important work of repairs on the once-great city of God's people. Jerusalem lay desolate and in ruins—completely open to the attacks of any of the surrounding nations.

Nehemiah's heart. We get a glimpse into the heart of Nehemiah as we see his response to this news about Jerusalem. He "wept and mourned for days" (Neh. 1:4)! Nehemiah then took time to confess his sins and those of his people. Evidently he became so distraught over the state of Jerusalem that the king himself noticed and asked him what was wrong. By God's grace, when Nehemiah explained the reason for his misery, the king released him and allowed him to travel to Jerusalem to oversee the repairs of the city and its wall.

Nehemiah, as we see from this passage, had a burning passion for the people and the place of God. He was devoted to God's people and wanted them to live in security in Jerusalem. He loved God's city—the place where the kings had ruled and where God's people had worshiped in the temple for centuries.

God's faithfulness. Let us take a step back in order to remember where we are in the big story of the Bible. Nehemiah is just one more example of God's faithfulness to his people during the days following the exile. Along with many others of his people, he exalted Nehemiah to a position of power and influence. God then granted him favor before the king of Persia, who allowed him to go back to Jerusalem in order to continue the work begun by Ezra and many others—to restore God's people in God's place. God was showing his grace to his people; he was bringing them back into the land and even providing for Jerusalem to be rebuilt and fortified. He was reminding his people that his work in and through them was not done—even though his work moving forward would not involve a human monarchy, as it had before.

The lesson. What can we learn from this amazing man Nehemiah? We can see that God wanted his people to have a burning passion for the community of God and the place of God. In Nehemiah's day, the focus was on the city of Jerusalem and the people of Israel. Now, on this side of the cross, God's people are those who know and worship Jesus, and his place is the church. Like Nehemiah, we are called to love God's people and be devoted to the security and welfare of his church. Is this the case in your life and heart today?

NEHEMIAH'S FAITHFUL LEGACY

As we come to the end of the account of Nehemiah, we will see that, like Ezra, Nehemiah was passionate not just about God's place but also about God's people—their holiness and commitment to him, according to his word. We also will begin looking ahead to the four hundred years after Ezra and Nehemiah before Jesus entered the scene. We will begin to see that what God had planned for his people was much different—and bigger—than the kingdoms of David and Solomon.

◣ READ!

Read Nehemiah 12–13—the conclusion of the book of Nehemiah.

One word has repeatedly popped up in the story of Nehemiah: *restoration*. This word is a wonderful description of what God was doing for his people during the days of Ezra, Nehemiah, and the return from exile in Babylon to Israel. God was restoring his people—faithfully bringing them back to his place and showing them that his work in their lives would continue. Let's look back together at the restoration that God did through Ezra and Nehemiah, and then look forward to all that was still to come.

God's restoration of his people through Nehemiah. As you know, God stirred Nehemiah's heart to rebuild the wall of Jerusalem. Despite great opposition from some in Jerusalem, Nehemiah led this great project of building and repair to completion. He secured the wall of Jerusalem, and the rebuilt wall was dedicated with a great celebration, as you read in Nehemiah 12. God used this great leader to build Jerusalem back up and secure it against its enemies.

You also read about Nehemiah's role in restoring God's people under the word of God. Many people, under the leadership of Nehemiah, fell under the conviction of sin as they read from God's word, and began to put away the evil practices they had engaged in. Nehemiah, as you saw from chapter 12 of his book, was incensed at some of the sin of God's people, and even pulled out the hair of some of the leaders who should have known better. Under Nehemiah, God's people came to have not only new walls but also a new commitment to holiness and obedience to God's word.

God's restoration of his people through Ezra. Think back to the work of Ezra the scribe, who came to Jerusalem from Babylon to teach the word to God's people there. The temple had already been rebuilt when Ezra arrived, but obedience and holiness were not the norm during those days. Under Ezra, a new commitment to obedience was established, as many of the men of Israel put away the foreign wives that they had taken, who were leading many people into sin and idolatry.

So under both Ezra and Nehemiah, we find that restoration happened for God's people. They were back in the land; the exile was over. God was restoring the temple, the wall, and right worship of himself in Jerusalem.

What next? With all this restoration in Jerusalem, there were probably some Israelites during this time who thought to themselves, "All right! Now we are back. Soon, God will raise up a new king for us, and our kingdom will return to power, as in the days of David and Solomon." That never happened. In fact, during the four hundred years between Ezra/Nehemiah and the beginning of the New Testament, the nation of Israel became less and less significant in the world. God's people were constantly ruled by foreign powers; the area that included Israel changed hands several times, until finally the Romans took control of Jerusalem. These four hundred years were also a time of silence from God's prophets, who had spoken to God's people before, during, and after the exiles to Assyria and Babylon, concluding with the words of the prophet Malachi, whose prophecy pointed God's people ahead to a forerunner of the Messiah. God's people were left waiting—hoping that God would still do something huge through them.

In the next chapter, we will look more deeply at the words of God's prophets to see more clearly how God was telling his people to hope during this time. We will begin to see, as many of God's faithful people did, that God had something far greater planned than another physical kingdom with a human king on the throne.

REVIEW

We saw once again in this chapter that God did not abandon his people—even as they experienced his punishment and discipline through the years of exile. God raised up prophets to speak his word to his people, and he worked through his exiled people (such as Daniel) to bring his saving blessing to the nations. Ultimately, God faithfully brought his people back to the promised land to rebuild and begin again—but not like in the glory days of David and Solomon. His saving promises pointed to something greater than this return—something, and someone, still to come.

PRAY!

As you close this chapter with prayer, thank God for his faithfulness in raising up such leaders for his people as Ezra and Nehemiah. Thank him for his love and grace to continue his plan in his people—and through them to the world—even after the seventy years of exile. Thank him that he had something far greater planned than a return to the literal Davidic monarchy—that he was planning to bring his own Son into the world to be the true and eternal King!

Chapter 11

GOD'S PEOPLE— CAPTIVE AND COMING HOME
PART 2

We've walked together through the historical narratives that record for us what went on during the period of the exile and how men such as Ezra and Nehemiah led in the restoration of God's people in God's land—Israel. In this chapter, as we continue studying the scene of the Bible that we have titled "God's People—Captive and Coming Home," we will focus on the role of the prophets, who continually spoke to God's people before, during, and after the exile. You see, it was through these faithful men that God continued to communicate to his people, explaining his purposes to them and showing them how they should hope in the fulfillment of his great promises.

In the coming pages, we will look briefly at the historical situations of some of the prophets, the main themes of their messages, and the key contributions that they made to God's people during the days in which they lived. In other words, we will try to examine the important ways in which God used each of these prophets to give his people insights into his great saving plan and work in the world. All of them point to Jesus, but they all have slightly different ways of doing so.

First, however, let's try to gain a general understanding of the situation, role, and message of the prophets so that you will be ready to begin studying them individually.

The ministry of the prophets. We can define a prophet as one who spoke God's word to God's people. While some of the prophets (such as Jonah) also spoke God's word to pagan nations who were not part of God's people, the role of the prophets was especially for Israel during the days of the Old Testament. In those days of the monarchy, the exile, and the return from exile, God's people had his law in written form, but they obviously did not have the rest of the Old Testament, much less the New Testament. So God spoke to his people through prophets—men whom he called to bring his communication to his people. He raised up voices for them, men such as Isaiah, Jeremiah, Ezekiel, and Daniel, who faithfully told God's people what God wanted them to know. All throughout the days of the monarchy—and even throughout the exile—God spoke to his people in this way. As we will see, the ministry of God's prophets helped God's faithful people know what to look forward to in terms of God's saving work in the world.

The timing of the prophets. Scholars usually group the prophets into three main categories according to the time frames in which they ministered: preexilic prophets (before the exile), exilic prophets (during the exile), and postexilic prophets (after the exile). While some of them, such as Jeremiah, prophesied in two of those time frames, many had a role in just one of those periods.

You will probably also hear some prophets referred to as "major" prophets and some as "minor" prophets. Those designations are based on the length of their writings. Isaiah, Jeremiah, Ezekiel, and Daniel are the "major" prophets, and the men for whom the rest of the prophetic books are named are the "minor" prophets.

The message of the prophets. While the different prophets of course had slightly different emphases, according to their specific situations and the distinct call from God on each of their lives, they generally brought home the same points to God's people again and again. Those main points were as follows:

- They called God's people to *repentance* for specific sins that they had committed against God's word and law. Some of the major sins that they addressed were idolatry, injustice, and hypocrisy.
- They warned God's people of *judgment*, which ultimately took the form of the exile to Assyria and Babylon.
- They reminded God's people of God's ultimate *salvation*, which would come to them in an eternal way because of God's merciful and gracious character.
- They began to point God's people to the *Messiah*, who would accomplish all of God's saving purposes for his people in the world in a way that no merely human leader could do.

We will focus on this last point especially in this chapter as we begin to see the role of the prophets in pointing God's people forward—past the reigns of David and Solomon to a greater King and Savior, and to eternal answers to God's great promises to Adam and Eve, Abraham, and David.

Remember!

Your suggested memory verses for this chapter come from one of the prophets you will study soon: Isaiah. It is amazing, is it not, that these verses are in the Old Testament? Isaiah clearly pointed God's people forward to a Savior who would suffer and die in the place of God's sinful people. This would be the ultimate answer for the sin of God's people and would be the great way in which God would bring a lasting salvation to them.

> Surely he has borne our griefs
>   and carried our sorrows;
> yet we esteemed him stricken,
>   smitten by God, and afflicted.
> But he was pierced for our transgressions;
>   he was crushed for our iniquities;
> upon him was the chastisement that brought us peace,
>   and with his wounds we are healed.
> All we like sheep have gone astray;
>   we have turned—every one—to his own way;
> and the Lord has laid on him
>   the iniquity of us all. (Isa. 53:4–6)

DANIEL THE PROPHET

Let's begin this study of the prophets by looking at the ministry of Daniel—a prophet who spoke to God's people during their exile in Babylon. We are going to learn more about the vision that God gave to him. This vision was one of great hope for the future; it was intended to remind God's people of God's great eternal purposes for them through the great ruler who was to come.

READ!

Read Daniel 7—a vision that God gave to Daniel about all that would come later in the story of his world.

Daniel is somewhat unique among the prophets because we have so much information about his life during the exile to go along with his prophecies that were written down for us. In the last chapter, you studied the account of Daniel rising to power in Babylon and saw how God was faithful to him during the exile. But Daniel also spoke to God's people during the exile, as God gave him great visions of what was to come in the distant future.

The chapter you just read is a confusing and difficult one, and Daniel's other prophecies are not much simpler! We will simply seek to summarize this chapter of Daniel and show how God spoke through this prophet to his people during this time. What do we observe in Daniel 7?

The four beasts. In chapter 7 of Daniel's prophetic book, he recounts a vision of four beasts who rise out of the sea (a symbol of evil and chaos in the Jewish mindset). In verses 15–18, this part of the vision is explained to Daniel. The beasts represented great kingdoms that would come and reign on earth. While we do not know exactly which kingdoms were represented by these beasts (perhaps Rome was one of them), we do know that Daniel's vision pointed to the ultimate victory of God and his people over the reign, violence, and power of all earthly kingdoms at the end of time.

The "son of man." It is in Daniel that the title "son of man" is given to the Messiah—Jesus—who would bring God's great rule and salvation to earth forever and ever. In Daniel 7:13–14, God the Father (the "Ancient of Days") gives all power and authority to this "son of man," who will rule over an eternal kingdom that will never be destroyed. In the New Testament, Jesus picks up on this title from Daniel and applies it to himself. Clearly Daniel was pointing God's people ahead to the Son of God, Jesus, who would rule God's eternal kingdom and people forever.

The final judgment. Daniel also pictures the final judgment of the world in verses 6–12. The vision that God gives him helps him to see that God one day will judge the entire world from his throne; the books will be opened (probably symbolizing the stories of the lives of every human being) and the entire race of humanity will stand before the

Creator. God gave Daniel this great gift of a vision of the end—the final judgment—so he could pass it on to God's people.

Daniel and Revelation. If you read the book of Revelation for even a few minutes, it is easy to see that many of John's visions seem to line up very directly with what God showed Daniel in his visions. This makes sense, of course; the same God showed these visions to both men. For example, the final judgment of the earth that is described in Revelation 20:11–15 mirrors Daniel 7:9–12 very closely. Daniel's vision of the four beasts is mirrored in John's vision of the great beast in Revelation 13. Clearly God's purpose through the ministry of Daniel was to begin giving his people pictures of what would come. He wanted to use Daniel to point his people ahead to the times of evil near the end of the world, but also to the final judgment of God and the ultimate victory of the Son of Man—God's own Son, the great Messiah, Savior, and King.

Is that not a great gift from a gracious God? Even during the exile in Babylon, God was busy giving his word to his people through Daniel, showing them his eternal purposes for his people through the reign of his Son, and reminding them that all who put their faith in him would be saved eternally from his judgment!

ISAIAH THE PROPHET

It is not easy to spend just a few pages on the biblical prophets, for their witness and ministry was huge! One of the best examples is the next prophet we'll consider: Isaiah. The prophetic book he wrote contains sixty-six chapters! He brought God's word powerfully to God's people and pointed them ahead to Jesus with hopeful expectation, even amid the looming threat of judgment and exile because of their sin.

READ!

Read Isaiah 1:1–2:5—a passage that helps introduce you to the overall message of this prophecy. Then read Isaiah 52:13–53:12—the account of the "servant" of God, who would suffer on behalf of God's people.

What are some things we should know about the life and ministry of Isaiah?

Historical situation. Isaiah ministered during the reigns of four different kings of Judah before, during, and after the exile of the northern kingdom (Israel) to Assyria, but before the exile of the southern kingdom (Judah) to Babylon. Because of this, we can call Isaiah a "preexilic" (before the exile to Babylon) prophet. In the days of Isaiah, Assyria was a major threat not only to the northern kingdom but also to the southern kingdom. In the book of Isaiah, we see some accounts of how the powerful empire of Assyria posed serious problems for the kings of Judah.

Main themes. Isaiah covered a lot of ground with his prophecies; as I noted above, the book is sixty-six chapters in length! Still, we can summarize some of his main themes:

- Judgment. You read chapter 1 of Isaiah, which summarizes much of what God was going to say to his people through Isaiah in the rest of the book. God's judgment was about to fall on Judah because the people had largely turned away from the true and pure worship of him. This judgment would surely come against God's people, according to Isaiah, and it would take the form of exile to Babylon.
- Future salvation. However, you saw in Isaiah 2:1–5 that despite the threats of God's very real judgment, he also was promising to bring to his people a future salvation that would be global, total, and full of grace and mercy. The beginning of chapter 2—like other places in Isaiah—pictures a future day when the nations will gather in the pure worship of God. Isaiah consistently looks ahead—past the exile—to a future day of God's great salvation for his people.
- A need for repentance. The theme of "vain offerings" appears often in Isaiah's prophecy (as you saw in 1:11–13). God did not want more animals from his people; he wanted them to mourn for their

sin and turn back to him with hearts filled with true worship. This is what repentance must look like for the people of God.

Key contributions. Perhaps the most specific and unique contribution that Isaiah makes for God's people is the way in which he describes for them the *person* through whom God was going to accomplish his great purposes for eternal salvation. This person would be a great ruler—a King, according to Isaiah's prophetic words in chapter 9. Also, this person would be a "suffering servant," as you read in chapters 52–53. He would bear the sins of God's people and suffer in their place in order to bring them forgiveness, grace, and peace with God. Through Isaiah, God did much to help his people form a picture of what they should expect from the coming Messiah—the "anointed one" through whom God would bring final salvation and an eternal kingdom for his sinful people.

JEREMIAH THE PROPHET

The book of Isaiah has the most chapters of any prophetic book, but the book of Jeremiah has more words than any other book in the entire Bible! The prophet Jeremiah had a long and difficult ministry, as you will see from your reading for this section. Even so, God was faithful to give his people great words of truth regarding both judgment and future salvation through this faithful man for many years.

In this brief discussion of Jeremiah, as with Isaiah, I hope you will get a better understanding of the historical situation of this prophet and consider some of the main themes of his prophecies, as well as the specific ways that he contributed to God's people's understanding of the coming salvation of God.

READ!

Read Jeremiah 29:1–23—Jeremiah's "letter to the exiles" after Jerusalem was destroyed by the forces of King Nebuchadnezzar of Babylon. Then read Jeremiah 31—the entire chapter.

Unlike Isaiah, Jeremiah lived through and experienced the judgment of God that he prophesied about. This had a huge impact on him personally; he is sometimes called the "weeping prophet" because of the very personal laments he wrote over the fall of Jerusalem.

Historical situation. Jeremiah lived and ministered in Judah before and during the exile of God's people to Babylon. It is important to understand that Jeremiah lived in incredibly chaotic and violent times, including the terrible invasion of the Babylonians. He witnessed the destruction of the temple, the ravaging of Jerusalem, and the capture of God's people. He saw the terrible results of sin and the awful judgment of God against his people.

Jeremiah, then, was an "exilic" prophet, as he brought God's word to God's people both before and during the exile. His message was not well received by God's people, and he probably ended up dying in Egypt, where he was sent by those who were angry with him—even though he had faithfully spoken God's word to them.

Main themes. While Jeremiah spoke to many of the same big themes as the other prophets of God—judgment against sin, the need for repentance, and future salvation—he did so in some unique ways. For example, Jeremiah spoke of God's judgment on his people through Babylon, but he also looked ahead to the way that God would judge Babylon for its role in oppressing God's people (chaps. 50–51). He explained to the people that exile was God's judgment against their sin, but he also told them very specifically that after seventy years of exile, God would bring them back to Israel (chap. 29). Jeremiah also very specifically brought God's words of judgment and conviction to the kings of Judah, which was probably what made him an unpopular figure for much of his life. Powerful kings do not seem to enjoy hearing about their sin and the fact that they sit under the judgment of God! We know, for example, that Zedekiah—the final king in Judah before the exile to Babylon—simply refused to listen to Jeremiah's prophecy.

Key contributions. One of Jeremiah's key contributions to the hopes of God's people regarding the coming Messiah (and salvation through him) comes from one of the passages that you just read. Look again at Jeremiah 31:31–34 and notice the huge promises that Jeremiah made to God's people about the "new covenant" that God would make with them in the days to come. Jeremiah looked ahead to a day when God would remember the sin of his people no more. He pictured a time when everyone would know God personally in God's place, and his law would be written on their hearts.

Most gospel-centered readers of the Bible see this section of the prophecy as pointing forward to the great salvation that God was going to bring to his people in a new way—through the death of Jesus Christ on the cross as the final sacrifice for the sin of those people. In fact, when Jesus gave the bread and the wine to his disciples at the Last Supper as a way for them to celebrate and remember his death, he told them that the wine was the new covenant in his blood (Luke 22:20)! It seems clear that Jeremiah was pointing to a new and final way that God would deal with the sins of his people through the new covenant sign: the body and blood of his own Son.

EZEKIEL THE PROPHET

God also spoke to his people during the exile through Ezekiel. This prophet talked about the same God, of course, but his focus was slightly different than those of Isaiah and Jeremiah, as we will see.

📖 READ!

Read Ezekiel 36 and 37—two amazingly rich chapters of prophecy that pointed God's exiled people to a future and greater day of God's powerful salvation, which he would bring to them by the actions of his "spirit."

As we've done with other prophets, let's think about the prophet Ezekiel—his ministry to God's people, the main themes of his message to them, and some of his key contributions.

Historical situation. Ezekiel, like Jeremiah, ministered to God's people during the exile to Babylon. He spoke to a people who were enduring great suffering, having seen their holy city—and their temple—destroyed by the enemy Babylonians. Ezekiel was a bold and sometimes harsh prophet, who spoke to people who had once thought that Jerusalem and its temple would never be defeated. He reminded them of God's judgment, but also pointed them to a great future day of "spiritual resurrection" for God's people.

Main themes. Ezekiel focused on a few unique aspects of God's rule and salvation for his people. These included:

- The *holiness* of God. Ezekiel was very concerned with presenting God as ultimately holy and glorious before his people. He was careful to explain to them that God acts for his glory alone, and he is concerned with his own holiness and character. The sin of God's people is so terrible because it is done against this infinitely holy God.
- The *Spirit* of God. As you saw in the passages you read, as Ezekiel focused on the future salvation that God would bring to his people in a final way, he explained how the "Spirit" of God would have a central part in it. He described how God would put a new spirit in his people (Ezek. 36:26) and spoke of the role of God's Spirit in making the dead "come to life" (37:1–14), which is a picture of spiritual resurrection (more on this in a moment).
- The *sovereignty* of God. Finally, Ezekiel was concerned with presenting the ultimate sovereignty of God to his people—he is the Lord over all the nations of the earth. God is not a God who lives in a temple in Jerusalem (as Ezekiel reminded the people in his vision of the presence of God departing from the temple in Jerusalem; Ezek. 10). God is over all the earth, and he would judge Babylon for its harsh treatment of God's people.

Key contributions. Ezekiel's focus on the work of the Spirit of God is a special and unique way that this prophet points God's people ahead to Jesus. The vision of the valley of dry bones, which Ezekiel recounts in chapter 37, is a picture of conversion for God's people. In order to be saved, they needed to be "spiritually resurrected" through faith in God's Son, which could happen only through the power of God's Holy Spirit.

Jesus alluded to this vision of Ezekiel in his conversation with the Pharisee Nicodemus in John 3:1–15 (read that conversation right now, if you have time). Jesus told this religious leader about the need to be "born again," which was similar to the picture that Ezekiel presented in his vision. Jesus was explaining, to a man who knew God's word very well, that he needed to be converted. Without faith in Jesus and the gift of the Holy Spirit, human beings are like skeletons lying in a valley.

MICAH THE PROPHET

Many of the prophets seem to come back to certain themes again and again. There are proclamations of God's imminent judgment, which would come to his people because of their terrible sin against him. There are calls to heartfelt and genuine repentance, considering God's approaching judgment. Finally, there are prophetic pictures of great hope, as the prophets point God's people ahead to future glorious days of great and eternal salvation.

In many ways, the book of Micah expresses these central themes perfectly. You could almost summarize Micah by saying that it is all about *judgment* that will come soon, *salvation* that will come much later, and *repentance* that is demanded now. You will be reading the final three chapters of this powerful prophetic book, and there you will see how Micah called God's people to respond to him in repentance in light of the glorious future day of God's salvation that would be made evident to his people through a coming shepherd and King.

READ!

Read Micah 5–7—the final three chapters of this prophetic book.

Having read several chapters of Micah, you now have a bit more of a feel for the book and a better understanding of the calls that he made to God's people. With that understanding in place, we can now move through some basic descriptions and summaries of the ministry and work of this faithful prophet to God's people.

Historical situation. The prophet Micah ministered and spoke to God's people more than one hundred years before the fall of Judah to Babylon. Thus, he was a "preexilic" prophet. He warned the people of Judah about sin and told them of the judgment that would come if they did not turn in repentance to God.

We do not know much about Micah personally, other than where he was from, but he was clearly one through whom God spoke his powerful and truthful word to his people.

Main themes. While Micah touched on many of the same themes as his contemporary Isaiah (many scholars believe these two prophets knew each other personally), there were some distinct ways in which Micah talked about the familiar topics of judgment and salvation in his prophecy:

- Hypocrisy. While Micah, like other prophets, certainly called out the sin of God's people generally, he seemed to focus very specifically on the terrible sin of hypocrisy. Micah was very much against people who continued in religious rituals—sacrifices, public worship, prayers, and so on—while continuing with hearts and lives that were far from obedience to God's word. This comes out most strongly in Micah 6—part of your reading. The true "sacrifices" of God, according to the prophet Micah, are not animals, but lives and hearts that are given over to God in humble obedience and worship.
- The remnant. As Micah pointed to the future salvation of God that would follow judgment, he began to explain the concept of

a "remnant," which we hear about in other parts of the Bible as well. In chapter 4, for example, Micah describes God's gathering of a "remnant" for himself—a portion of the people of Israel that he would sustain, save, and make into a people who would serve and worship him. In other words, Micah was telling the people that God's judgment would not make a complete end of Israel; he would preserve some faithful people who would worship and serve him forever.

- Call to repentance. Micah, like other prophets, also issued very strong calls to repentance (calls that were ultimately unheeded by God's people over the next one hundred years). His book of prophecy ends—at the conclusion of chapter 7—with a reminder of the gracious character of God. Micah hoped in God's grace and mercy to pardon and forgive the sins of his people, and to one day remove evil from them in a final way.

Key contributions. The final words of this book—Micah 7:18–20—illustrate one important way in which Micah pointed God's people forward to a future and final salvation that God would bring to them. Micah speaks of a final end of sin that God would accomplish for his people. He would "cast" all his people's sins "into the depths of the sea." How would God do this in a final way for his people? Through the death of his Son.

In fact, Micah consistently pointed God's people to the person who would accomplish these great saving purposes for his people. He hints at the leadership of a great shepherd/King in chapter 5, and he announces that a ruler for God's people would come from the town of Bethlehem (5:2)—a prophecy that was directly fulfilled in the birth of Jesus!

ZECHARIAH THE PROPHET

We've now glanced over the work of several of the prophets who ministered before, during, and after the exile of God's people to Babylon. Clearly God never left his people without a witness to his word during this period; he was faithful to keep speaking to them through the prophets—reminding them of his identity, calling them to faith and obedience, and pointing them to the ultimate future hope of the Messiah who would come.

Another of the prophets, Zechariah, spoke to God's people during a time of discouragement and disillusionment. In his prophecy, Zechariah promised restoration for God's people and brought a great message of hope to them. But he also pointed them further into the future—toward a much greater restoration that was to come long after the rebuilding of the temple in Jerusalem.

READ!

Read Zechariah 12–14—the chapters in which Zechariah looks forward to the restoration of God's people under the leadership of a good "shepherd" and points to a day when all nations will gather in the place of God to give him worship and praise.

As we think about Zechariah's historical situation, we will begin to see the reason for the people's discouragement, which I mentioned above. Then we'll move on to consider some of Zechariah's main themes, as well as the specific ways that he helped God's people look forward to the great and final salvation of God through the work of his Messiah.

Historical situation. God's people had probably been back in Israel for thirty to forty years when Zechariah began speaking to them. They were out of captivity in Babylon; God had faithfully brought them back to their homeland. But life was hard. The temple had been rebuilt, but it was not anything like it had been before. The rebuilding of other parts of Jerusalem was taking a long time. It was probably a daily struggle for the people just to get by. They were discouraged—trying to hold on to hope amid extremely difficult lives.

Zechariah, then, was a "postexilic" prophet, one who spoke God's word to God's people who had returned from the exile but needed God's great hope and a picture of what he finally and ultimately would do in the world. They needed to be reminded that God's plan and promise are huge; he has something beautiful and glorious for his true people.

Main themes. As we look at the prophecy of Zechariah, three major themes seem to emerge from his messages to God's people after the exile:

- The warrior/shepherd. While it is true that Zechariah did not give a complete and detailed picture of everything about the life of Jesus, he did fill out for God's people, in remarkable ways, the ministry of the Messiah who would come to finally fulfill God's great promises to his people. This Messiah, according to Zechariah, would be a warrior, who would defeat all the enemies of the people of God (chap. 9). But he also would be a "shepherd" figure, who would be "struck" on behalf of God's people (chap. 13). This reminds us of the words of Isaiah, which you are memorizing as you read and study this chapter. Zechariah's prophecy helped God's people begin to expect this mighty figure, who would somehow be both a conquering warrior and a shepherding Savior. These words, as we now know, pointed to the roles of Jesus Christ as both the Savior and the Judge.
- The rule over the nations. While Zechariah clearly told God's people that the enemy Gentile nations would be judged for their evil deeds, he also pointed to a day when many from these nations would ultimately turn in worship to God. Chapter 14, which you read, is a great final picture of a multiethnic worship gathering in Jerusalem; it depicts people from all nations coming to praise and worship the God of Israel. Zechariah began to open the door for God's people to understand that God's final salvation would not be just a Jewish salvation. God's heart is for people from all nations of the earth to gather in worship to him.
- Repentance and renewal. The book of Zechariah also contains strong calls to repentance for God's people, as well as the promise of ultimate renewal. In both chapter 3 and chapter 5, Zechariah hints at the future reality of the permanent and complete removal

of the sins of God's people, and the full cleansing of the land of Israel. God's people of Zechariah's day were called to respond with continual repentance and faith in the God who could fully forgive and remove sin from his people.

Key contributions. As we have already mentioned, the prophet Zechariah filled out for God's people the picture of the coming Messiah, who would judge the nations, remove sin forever, suffer on behalf of the people, and rule forever over a multiethnic gathering of worshipers in God's place. Zechariah encouraged God's people in their immediate situation, but he also reminded them to keep their eyes on the big picture of what God ultimately was doing in the world.

As we think of the coming of Jesus Christ, and Zechariah's specific "pointers" to him, we cannot help but mention Zechariah 9:9—a verse that speaks of the King of God's people coming to them humbly, riding on the foal of a donkey. This glimpse of the Messiah in Zechariah was fulfilled by Jesus when he rode into Jerusalem before the Passover on a donkey's colt (Matt. 21:1–11). He is the humble King who entered the city to lay down his life for God's true people.

JONAH THE PROPHET

A while back, I gave you a definition of a prophet that went like this: "one who spoke God's word to God's people." God used prophets to bring his word to his people before, during, and after the exile. They brought words of conviction to people who persisted in sin, reminders to people who had forgotten the character of God, and words of hope to people who needed to remember God's ultimate goodness and grace.

But God also called some prophets to speak his word to people who were *not* part of the nation of Israel. Jonah, who is sometimes called the "reluctant prophet," was one of these. God commanded Jonah to do something that he did not want to do at all: bring God's word to the people of the Assyrian city of Nineveh—a place of violence, sin, and corruption. The Ninevites were enemies of God and his people. Clearly they needed God's word. But as we will see, Jonah himself had a few important things to learn about the heart of God as well.

📖 READ!

Read the entire book of Jonah; it is only four short chapters in length.

The book of Jonah is a different kind of prophetic book from many of the others that you have studied. It is a story—the account of a reluctant prophet who was called by God to bring a message of conviction and the need for repentance to an evil city. God obviously wanted to make clear to his people that his salvation and grace were available to anyone from any nation who would repent and turn to him in faith.

Historical situation. Jonah ministered in the ninth and eighth centuries BC—before the exiles of both Israel (the northern kingdom) and Judah (the southern kingdom). During his day, the kings ruled over the divided kingdom, and there were constant threats to God's people from enemy nations around them. One of these nations was Assyria, whose capital city was Nineveh. By all accounts, the Assyrians were a brutal, violent, and idolatrous people. Their sin was obviously opposed to all the teachings of God's word. It is no surprise that Jonah looked at these people as unclean and deserving of God's judgment.

This is why it was so surprising to Jonah when God called him to bring a word of warning to the people of Nineveh about the coming judgment of God against them. Jonah obviously did not want Nineveh to have a chance to repent, so he fled in the other direction, toward Tarshish.

You probably know the rest of the story already; God hurled a storm at the sea, and the sailors of the ship threw Jonah overboard to save their own lives. He was miraculously swallowed by a great fish, which God provided to save his life. Finally, after calling out to God for three days in the belly of the fish, Jonah was vomited out onto dry land and went to bring God's message to Nineveh. Amazingly, the Ninevites repented at the message of Jonah and turned to God in faith, so God spared the city from his great judgment. Jonah, though, was filled with anger that God had chosen to spare such a wicked people, and God had to remind him of his compassion and mercy.

Main themes. The book of Jonah reminds us of a few important points:

- God's grace is for *everyone* who repents and has faith in him—Jew or Gentile. Sinners everywhere can turn to God and find grace in him.
- The final salvation of God is for all *nations*; Jesus's death and resurrection made salvation and forgiveness available to all people.
- God's people should embrace God's *heart* for the nations. We do not know how Jonah responded after God confronted him; the book leaves us hanging, and the last we see of Jonah, he is sulking because God showed mercy to this pagan nation. Like Jonah, we need to let God extend his salvation wherever he chooses.

Key contributions. As we have already discussed, the book of Jonah reminds us that God's salvation is global in nature; it is not just for people who are ethnically Jewish. More broadly still, the account of the repentance of the people of Nineveh reminds us that salvation is a miracle from God. We should never think that some people are somehow beyond God's grace or salvation. God can reach down and save the most unlikely of people, and we need to trust him to do that and pray that he will!

Jesus picked up on the story of Jonah in the New Testament. He called Jonah's three-day stay in the belly of the fish a sign that pointed to his death, burial, and resurrection. Jonah's near-death experience, and then his "new life" afterward, pointed ahead to the death of the Son of God, who would be three days in the "heart" of the earth, only to rise again and begin to reign forever at the right hand of God (Matt. 12:39–40).

The message of Jonah, then, was a key one during the time of the monarchy in Israel. God was reminding his people even then that his salvation was bigger than them. Salvation and grace were global realities, and God's heart had always been about bringing people from all nations to repentance and faith in him.

MALACHI THE PROPHET

As we approach the prophet Malachi, we come back to God's people in Israel—and jump ahead again to the days after the return from the exile in Babylon. Malachi, who wrote the final prophetic book of the Old Testament, was probably the last prophet through whom God spoke before the coming of Jesus Christ. The Old Testament ends with the words and promises of God through Malachi hanging in the air—until the New Testament begins with another prophetic voice. God's people had the promises of all the prophets, of course, but after Malachi, God went "silent" for about four hundred years and no new word came to them until the arrival of Jesus Christ.

READ!

Read Malachi 3–4—the concluding chapters of this book of prophecy.

As we have done with the other prophets we have studied, we will examine Malachi's historical situation and some of the main themes of his message. We will also see how Malachi began to help God's people with some very specific expectations concerning the coming of God's Messiah someday.

Historical situation. Most biblical scholars agree that it is probably best to place Malachi during the time of Ezra and Nehemiah—in the years following the return of God's people to Jerusalem from Babylon. So he was a "postexilic" prophet, one who brought God's word to God's people after the exile.

Let's think about how Malachi shaped and guided the hopes of God's people during the years of divine silence and waiting.

Main themes. Like the other prophets of God, Malachi was not shy about calling God's people out. Their sin was especially bad because they had been specially chosen and loved by God. This leads to some central themes that Malachi focused on in his prophecy:

- God's love for his people. Malachi talked about the special nature of the love that God has for his people, which makes their sin even more disgusting. Malachi affirms that God loves his people dearly right at the start of his book (1:2). Furthermore, he says that God has served personally as the "father" to his people (v. 6). God's special and careful love for Israel made their rebellion and idolatry even worse. Malachi affirmed to God's people that the judgment that they had received from God because of their sin, was completely just. They deserved every bit of it.

- Evil and corrupt offerings. One specific area of sin that Malachi condemned was the people's failure to offer pure sacrifices and offerings to God. The sacrifices that the people offered to God (both literal and spiritual) were begrudging (chaps. 1–2). God's people had not served him with joyful and sincere hearts but had held back much of their worship and love for him. In chapter 3, Malachi reminds the people that many of them have not given to God as generously as they should have as part of their worship; the prophet describes this as "robbing" God (3:8). Clearly Malachi wanted the people to know that they owed God everything; their sacrifices, offerings, and giving needed to come from hearts that were completely given over to God in worship and obedience.

- A coming messenger. Finally, as Malachi concludes his words of prophecy to God's people, he points them to a "messenger" who would come in the future to "prepare the way" for God's coming to his people (3:1). Then, in chapter 4, Malachi points to the coming of "Elijah the prophet"—another way of describing the same messenger—who would come before the "great and awesome" day of God (4:5). While all of this may not have been completely understandable to God's people during Malachi's day, it was clear that he was telling them that a greater prophet would come, and that he would prepare the way for God to do something truly great in the world, and in the lives and hearts of his people.

Key contributions. So the Old Testament ended. It concluded with the words of Malachi hanging in the air—the prophecy of a "messenger" who would come for God's people to prepare the way for the coming of God. This messenger would be like Elijah the prophet, and he would restore relationships and point the people to the only hope for escaping the destructive and final judgment of God (4:6).

Four hundred years then passed—four centuries of silence. The words of Malachi—as well as those of the rest of the prophets—sat in the hearts and minds of God's people. Israel became less and less powerful as its territory changed hands again and again, the people constantly being ruled by other nations. Some faithful Jews held on to God's great promises of a coming Messiah and of a great salvation for Israel.

Then, finally, a voice began to cry out in the wilderness. "Elijah" had come, and he would begin to prepare the way for the coming of God in human flesh. This is where we will pick up the story in the next chapter.

REVIEW

The ministry of God's prophets had a powerful effect on God's people before, during, and after the years in exile to Assyria and Babylon. These prophets—mouthpieces for God—called his people to repentance, obedience, justice, and love while also beginning to point ahead to a kingly figure (the "Messiah" or "Christ") who would fulfill all of God's great and saving promises to his people.

⬆ PRAY!

As you close this chapter with prayer, give thanks to God for being a speaking God—one who has never left his people without a faithful witness to his salvation and to his ultimate good plan for them. Thank him that we can understand the ministry and work of Jesus Christ much more clearly because of the way the prophets pointed to him.

BETWEEN THE OLD AND NEW TESTAMENTS

You have finally made it into the New Testament portion of the Bible story. So far, you have examined how the big story of the Bible—of God's saving work in the world—developed, grew, and expanded over the years before Christ was born. You saw the fall of Adam and Eve, the call of Abraham, the deliverance of God's people from Egypt, and the rise and fall of the monarchy in Israel. Most recently, as you learned about the return of God's people from exile in Babylon, you examined the ministry of the prophets of God, who began to point God's people much more specifically to a greater King—and an eternal kingdom.

In the next scene of the biblical story—"God's Salvation"—we will finally discover, along with all of God's people, how God was going to bring this story together by revealing the central component of his saving plan and redemptive work in this world. It would be a work centered not on a mere human ruler in Jerusalem but on God's own Son come in human flesh, who would rule forever in a new heaven and new earth.

We will see how Jesus Christ broke onto the scene of God's story as God in human flesh. This would be God's way to keep his promises to his people so that they could live with him forever under his blessing.

But before we move into a study of the salvation of God through Jesus, we will look back at all of the big promises of God that were left hanging at the close of the Old Testament period. There were many of these, and it is important to remember that faithful Jews during the four hundred years after Malachi and before Jesus were holding onto these promises, watching for God to answer them, and looking for the Messiah who would bring them about. What were some of these promises that we have not yet seen finally fulfilled?

- Genesis 3—the crushing of Satan. Do you remember the very first "gospel" promise that God made to Adam and Eve even as he was preparing to banish them from the garden of Eden because of their sin? It was a promise that one day an "offspring" of Adam and Eve (a literal human descendant from them) would rise up to "bruise" (or "crush") the head of the serpent—Satan—forever (v. 15). We understood this to be God's first promise to his people of a final victory over sin and death. At the time of Jesus's birth, this promise was still waiting to be perfectly fulfilled.
- Genesis 12—the blessing to all nations. God's promise to Abraham, as you remember, was a promise of a people, a place, and great blessing to them and through them to the nations (vv. 1–3). We saw the partial fulfillment of this great promise during the days of David and Solomon, as God's people lived in the kingdom of Israel and began to bring God's blessing to the nations through the wisdom and reign of their great kings. This did not last long, though, and God's people continually demonstrated a tendency to be influenced by the sin and idolatry of the nations around them rather than to bring God's blessing to them. By the time of the birth of Jesus, God's faithful people were still wondering how God would perfectly fulfill his great promise to Abraham.

- Second Samuel 7—the forever king and kingdom. God had promised David something huge—that he would never lack a descendant who would rule over the kingdom of Israel, and that this rule would be eternal (vv. 12–16). As the kingdom of Israel crumbled, with no real king ever again ascending to the throne in Jerusalem after the exile, it seemed that this promise had all but vanished from the experience of God's people. Faithful believers, though, continued to look forward to a day when God would keep his promise; they looked ahead to a great "Son of David" who would rule as King over God's people forever.
- Isaiah 53—the suffering servant. There are numerous places in the Psalms and the prophets where a Savior is anticipated for God's people. Isaiah 53:4–7 is one of these. The prophet, by God's inspiration, began to help the people anticipate and hope for someone who would come to bear their sins and deal with their guilt in a final way. This person would be a servant of God and would sacrifice his own body for God's people. This promise, too, was still waiting to be fulfilled at the time that Jesus arrived on earth.
- Jeremiah 31—the new covenant. Finally, the prophet Jeremiah had pointed God's people to a day when the new covenant of God would be established on earth (vv. 31–34). This new way of God's work in the lives of his people would lead to his law being written "on their hearts." They would believe in him, follow him joyfully, and never depart from his leadership into sin or rebellion. God's people, by the time that Jesus arrived, were still waiting to see exactly how this new covenant would come into being.

So as you can see, many of God's promises were unfulfilled as the time for Jesus's arrival approached. Faithful Jews were expecting a King and Savior to come, although very few of them were expecting God to bring this Savior into the world in precisely the way he chose to do it.

Remember!

Your suggested memory verses for this intermission come from the words of the faithful man Simeon, who had been waiting his entire life to see the promise of God's salvation fulfilled; he finally saw it in the person of Jesus Christ. God's Holy Spirit revealed to him, as he saw the baby Jesus, that this child would grow up to be the great King and Savior that God's people had been awaiting for hundreds of years.

> *Lord, now you are letting your servant depart in peace,*
>   *according to your word;*
> *for my eyes have seen your salvation*
>   *that you have prepared in the presence of all peoples,*
> *a light for revelation to the Gentiles,*
>   *and for glory to your people Israel. (Luke 2:29–32)*

MALACHI AND MARK

As we discussed just above, the Old Testament ends with more questions than answers. The kingdom of Israel had risen to great heights under Solomon and experienced the partial fulfillment of God's great promises to Abraham. But then it had fallen to great depths because of sin and idolatry, and even the return from exile did not lead to a full return to its former glory. God's people were left with questions. How would God fulfill his great promises to his people? Would God find a way to finally deal with sinful and disobedient hearts? Would a perfect King ever come to rule God's people forever?

One of the unfulfilled promises of the Old Testament, as we will learn now, comes from the final prophet who spoke to God's people after their return from exile: Malachi. It is his voice that begins the Gospel of Mark, explaining to us how this book presents the continuing story of God's work in the world and in the lives of his people. We will see how Mark introduces John the Baptist—and Jesus—in this way.

READ!

Go back to the Old Testament—one more time—and reread Malachi 3 and 4.

Our last chapter ended where the Old Testament ended—with the prophet Malachi. After him, God's people waited in four hundred years of relative silence from God; they had the witness of many prophets, of course, but no new prophet brought a new word from God during that time. Thankfully, the final words of Malachi pointed them to a great prophet, whose coming would precede the coming of God himself to earth. This prophet would come to "prepare" the way for God; he would be as great as Elijah and would signal the beginning of God's great work in the world.

The continuing story. The fact that Mark begins his gospel with words from Isaiah and Malachi (he references Isaiah, since he was the more prominent prophet) is an indication that he sees the coming of John the Baptist—and Jesus—as part of the same story of God's work in the world that has been going on throughout all history. In other words, Mark is not claiming to be writing about something new—something disconnected from all that God previously was doing in the lives of his people. Mark quotes from the Old Testament prophets, telling God's people that what he is writing about is the fulfillment of everything God has spoken to them throughout history!

The great prophet. Specifically, as John the Baptist enters the scene at the beginning of this Gospel, Mark's point is to link him with the great prophet that Malachi had promised to God's people. He quotes prophecies from Isaiah and Malachi in verses 2–3 of chapter 1; then his next line is "John appeared" (v. 4). In other words, John the Baptist was the one whom God was sending to prepare the way for God himself, who was about to enter the world. John the Baptist was the great "Elijah," who was to come to declare God's judgment and salvation in all the earth. Finally, the day had come; God was about to do his great work of salvation in the world. The Lord of the universe was about to step down and enter the story.

The coming of God. The fact that John the Baptist is linked with this "Elijah" prophet in Malachi is an indication not only of who John was but also of who *Jesus* was. This prophet, according to Malachi, would come before God entered the world to bring salvation to those who repent and believe. What this meant, for Mark, is that the one to whom John pointed was not just another man—or even just a great king—but God himself. John the Baptist—the messenger of God—had arrived to point the way to God in human flesh.

So the story continued; God was ready to keep his biggest promises to his people in the coming of his own Son.

THE NEW TESTAMENT

Chapter 12

GOD'S SALVATION

Our journey through the big story of the Bible has showed us an inescapable truth: the coming of Jesus Christ to earth did not come out of nowhere. Again and again throughout the story God pointed his people ahead to the coming of the Messiah—the greatest work of God in the world he created. The apostle Paul affirms this truth again and again as he explains the gospel of Jesus Christ (see 1 Cor. 15:1-4 for just one example).

We come now to the next scene in the big story of the Bible: "God's Salvation." Here we will discover that the salvation from God, centered on the person and work of Jesus Christ, is the pinnacle and climax of the entire biblical story. The Old Testament pointed forward to Jesus; the New Testament presents Jesus—and then applies his work to the lives of believers as they seek to follow him as part of his church until he returns. We will see that Jesus himself is our model for reading the Old Testament this way.

Remember!

Your suggested memory verses for this chapter come from the very end of the Gospel of Matthew. As Jesus prepared to ascend into heaven, he "commissioned" his disciples for their work on earth in the years to come.

And Jesus came and said to them, "All authority in heaven and on earth has been given to me. Go therefore and make disciples of all nations, baptizing them in the name of the Father and of the Son and of the Holy Spirit, teaching them to observe all that I have commanded you. And behold, I am with you always, to the end of the age." (Matt. 28:18–20)

SIMEON AND ANNA

Before we get to the birth of Jesus Christ, it will be good to first examine the connections that the Bible story shows us between the Old Testament and the New Testament—that is, how the Gospel writers go out of their way to show us that the coming of Jesus was part of the continuing work of God in the world and in the lives of his people.

READ!

Read Luke 2:22–38—the account of Simeon and Anna, two faithful people who were waiting patiently for the coming of God's Messiah to earth.

We'll begin by exploring what the coming of Jesus Christ meant to two believers—Simeon and Anna—who were waiting on the fulfillment of God's promises, faithfully holding on to what they knew to be true from the Scriptures.

"Old Testament believers." In some ways, it is not very helpful to have a big division in our Bibles between the Old Testament and the New Testament. It is true that there were four hundred years between Malachi and the Gospel events, but there are similar spaces between other books of the Bible as well. Ultimately, the New Testament continues

the story of the Old Testament. People such as Simeon and Anna did not know they were "New Testament characters"; it is actually better to see them as "Old Testament believers"—people who had the words of the prophets and who were faithfully looking forward to the coming of God's Messiah. Simeon and Anna remind us that God's faithful people—even in the years before Jesus—were saved as they took God at his word and looked ahead in faith to the saving work that God would one day accomplish through a great Savior.

The work of the Spirit. The Gospel writer Luke tells us that God had revealed to the old man Simeon by his Holy Spirit that he would see—with his own eyes—the Messiah that God had promised to his people. When the baby Jesus was brought into the temple in Jerusalem, God obviously revealed to Simeon that this was that promised Messiah. We see his joyful response in the passage that you just read. He realized that God's salvation had come; God had sent his own Son into the world to be the Messiah and Savior of sinful people. Simeon, unlike all the believers before him, got to actually see the person of Jesus.

Anna, too, was a faithful believer in God's word who had been waiting for God's salvation to be fully revealed. No doubt she had pored over the words of the Old Testament prophets and knew that the Savior would be born in Bethlehem and would be a "suffering servant" who would die for the sins of God's people. When Anna realized that God's Savior really had come, she went out and began spreading the good news of God's fulfilled promise to everyone who would listen to her.

Faith, not sight, in every age. Luke's account of Simeon and Anna should remind us that, in every age and generation, God's faithful people have been called to take God at his word—to follow him by faith, not by sight. Simeon and Anna lived for years without the vision of the person of Jesus Christ, the Messiah. Yet they held on to God's word and God's promise by faith. Even if they had not seen Jesus as a baby, they would have been saved, for they had put their hope in what God would one day do through his Messiah.

This is an important lesson for us, even though we know the full story of the gospel of Jesus Christ. We, too, are called to hold on to the word and promises of God until we reach heaven. We are called to believe in a God whom we cannot see and a Savior whom we have not yet met face to face. One day, though, we will see Jesus. We will bow before him and rejoice that we can see with our eyes what we have believed in our hearts.

GABRIEL, ZECHARIAH, AND MARY

If you have been around the church or any Christian community for an extended period, you may already be very familiar with the story of the announcements of the births of John the Baptist and Jesus by the angel Gabriel. If not, these will be wonderfully new and exciting events for you to study! After all, Gabriel's announcements to Zechariah and Mary give us, in a way, "God's perspective" on all that is happening in this part of the Bible story. We not only learn about these births in this part of the story but also, through the words of God's angel, all that they would mean for God's people who were awaiting God's great salvation.

Let's look now at how both John the Baptist and Jesus were "announced" by Gabriel to God's people. We will also see how John's father and Jesus's mother responded to all that God was doing in the world, and what that means for us today.

READ!

Read Luke 1—a long chapter that records the announcements of the births of John the Baptist (to Zechariah) and Jesus Christ (to Mary).

The account of Jesus's birth is recorded for us; we will study it just below. But there is a sense in which the simple account of the birth of Jesus would not fully tell us all its significance. We need the explanation of his birth to really begin to apply its truth to our lives. Thankfully, Jesus's birth came with "announcements" that were sent by God himself through his angel Gabriel. Through these words of explanation that God gave to Zechariah and Mary, we can begin to see God's perspective on the birth of his Son and why we must understand just how significant this birth really was.

The announcement of John's birth. The angel Gabriel came to a priest named Zechariah in the temple to tell him that he was going to have a son, John, who would play a role in the ministry of Jesus Christ. John would be the prophet promised by Malachi, who would prepare the way for the coming of the Lord. Zechariah had trouble believing this, which reminds us that even a priest of God can struggle with doubts. Even so, God was faithful, and he promised to bring this great prophet into the world through Zechariah and his wife, Elizabeth.

As Gabriel announced the birth of John the Baptist to Zechariah, he told him something very significant about what would begin to happen in the lives and hearts of God's people—both through the ministry of John and then more fully through the ministry of Jesus. God would use this man to "turn" many of his people toward him. In other words, God would use John's ministry, which would point to Jesus Christ, to bring a great *repentance* among God's people as they looked to him in faith (Luke 1:16–17). This repentance would be one important way that John would help prepare God's people for the coming of Jesus.

The announcement of Jesus's birth. Unlike Zechariah, Mary is a wonderful example of childlike faith regarding the truth of God's word. When Gabriel approached her with the news of her coming pregnancy (which would happen by the power of the Holy Spirit) and the identity of the child she would bear, she responded with joyful faith and humble obedience (see Luke 1:38). This is amazing given Mary's youth, as well as the magnitude of what the angel promised her about her child.

According to Gabriel, Jesus would be the one who would bring the *eternal kingdom* to God's people. In other words, he would be the eternal King—the "Son of David"—whom God promised to King David

(Luke 1:32–33). God was telling Mary that she would bear the one who was going to fulfill his great promises to his people finally and perfectly for all time. He would be God in human flesh, the promised King who would reign over God's people into all eternity!

The songs of response. Mary and Zechariah both ultimately responded with songs of praise as they realized all that God was about to do in the world through the birth of Jesus and the preparation for his ministry through the work of John the Baptist. Mary sang out in praise to God (Luke 1:46–55), and Zechariah responded to the birth of John the Baptist with worship and prophecy (vv. 67–79). If you have time, read through those songs again and see the reason for Mary's and Zechariah's great praise to God.

Our response also should be praise when we remember the coming of Jesus Christ to this world. The gracious Creator of the universe chose to show eternal mercy to his people. He allowed some people to repent and find forgiveness and eternal salvation through the great King and Savior that he brought into the world—his own Son. The birth of Jesus was no ordinary birth, as Gabriel's announcements remind us.

JESUS'S INCARNATION

What exactly happened at the birth of Jesus Christ? To answer this question, we are going to carefully examine the reality and significance of what we refer to as the incarnation—the taking on of flesh by the second person of the Trinity. His incarnation is what Christians celebrate at Christmas, and it is what makes all the difference for God's people.

READ!

Read John 1:1–18—one of the most well-known descriptions of the incarnation of Jesus Christ in all of Scripture.

Unlike the other Gospel writers, John begins his Gospel with theology—an extended meditation on the wonderful reality of the incarnation of

Jesus Christ. He declares that God—specifically, the eternal second person of the Trinity—became incarnate to bring God's salvation to his people, who are lost in the darkness of sin. Let's examine what John teaches us about this amazing truth.

Jesus—eternally existent. First, John says that Jesus was active in ruling and reigning as God from the beginning of time. The term that John uses for Jesus—"the Word"—is a way to talk about the eternal wisdom that is beyond this world. John tells us that, with God the Father and God the Holy Spirit, God the Son was active in the creation of the world, and that "all things were made through him" (1:3).

This is an incredibly significant teaching. This passage tells us that the child born to Mary really was fully God. Jesus is not just a part of God. He is not merely like God. He really *is* God. The eternally existent second person of the Trinity took on human flesh and entered the world that he had been active in creating.

Jesus—really human. Second, though, John wants to be clear that this great God—God the Son—became fully and really human. Read John 1:14 one more time. John says that the word "became flesh." There is no way of getting around the truth that this simple phrase teaches. Jesus did not just take the form of a human being; he *became* a human being. John goes on to say that he "dwelt" among the people. The word that he uses for "dwelt" is one that also is used to describe what God did in the midst of his people back in the days of Moses: he "tabernacled" among them. God in human flesh (rather than a tent, like the tabernacle) came to earth to dwell with his people as one of them.

We need to hold on to this point, as well as the first one! Jesus is fully God; we must not affirm less than this, according to the Bible. But Jesus is fully and truly human; the Bible affirms this as well. This is the wonder of the incarnation, and it leads to the beauty of our final point about Jesus's incarnation.

Jesus—born to save. Ultimately, for John, the message of the incarnation is that sinners can now be fully forgiven and eternally saved by God. All who believe in the "name" of Jesus can become "children of God" (John 1:12)—people who are "born again" (3:3) through faith in him. Why is this the case? Because someone who is fully human lived a human life and represented all of humanity. But also because someone who is fully God paid the ultimate price that human sin deserves. Jesus, in his wonderful incarnation, finally provided the way for God's people to be fully forgiven and eternally saved. All who repent of sins and trust in the finished work of the God-man on the cross will be forever made right with God.

JESUS IS BORN

We have finally made it to the account of the birth of Jesus Christ in Bethlehem. As you will see from your reading in a moment, it was not the birth that many of God's people expected for the promised King of Israel. It was a humble birth, but it nevertheless came with a royal announcement from the angels of heaven.

◼ READ!

Read Luke 2:1–21—the account of the birth of Jesus in Bethlehem, the announcement of his birth by God's angels, and the visit of the shepherds to the place where he was born.

From all that you have studied in the Bible story so far, you know that God's prophets promised big things about what God would do one day in the world—and in the lives of his people. A great *ruler* would come. A *Son of David* would sit on the throne of Israel forever. A conquering *warrior* would rise to defeat God's enemies—even Satan, sin, and death—in a final way. You can imagine, then, that with all these prophetic hopes in their minds, God's people had certain expectations about the birth of the Messiah. But Jesus's birth differed from these expectations in many ways.

Jesus's birth fulfilled prophecy. First, though, we should notice the ways in which Jesus's birth really did fulfill Old Testament prophecy. Jesus was born in Bethlehem, fulfilling a specific prediction that had been made to God's people through the prophet Micah. Jesus came from the house and line of King David—through both Joseph's and Mary's lines, it seems. These fulfillments and many others show that, in every way, Jesus was clearly the King whom God had promised to his people.

Jesus's birth was announced by angels. Second, while Jesus's birth was humble, it was announced gloriously by a host of the angels of heaven. As the angels appeared to sing about the birth of Jesus, they shouted "glory to God in the highest" (Luke 2:14). The Messiah had been born, and God's salvation had come to earth.

The apostle Peter, writing long after this, tells us that the angels of heaven "long" to look into the salvation of God (1 Pet. 1:12). They want badly to see how God brings salvation and forgiveness to his people. They sang to announce the birth of Jesus, but also from sheer joy that God's salvation had arrived on earth.

Jesus's birth was humble. Jesus's actual birth, though, was not the kind you might have expected for a great King and Savior. It was announced by angels, yes, but they reported it to shepherds in the fields—the lowliest of workers during the time of Jesus. Also, Jesus was not born in a palace or even in a warm and comfortable house. He was born in a stable—a place where animals were kept. By all accounts, Jesus entered this world in almost the humblest way possible. He was born not with royal fanfare but in the quiet of the night with animals in a stable.

Since his time on earth, the Son of God—Jesus—has taken up his reign in heaven, and he will reign forever as King. His birth, though, reminds us that the first time he came to earth, it was as a humble servant of God's people. The Lord of all humbled himself to become human, and ultimately to serve God's sinful people in the greatest way: by dying for their sins on a cross.

JESUS—TRULY HUMAN

Clearly Jesus was not going to reign over God's people—at least not immediately—in the way that they might have expected from the great Son of David. He was going to identify with the people of God, as we will see from the passage you will read next. He would be the King, but he also would be the Savior who would link himself to the people of God in every way. Let's see how Jesus did this through his baptism and his time in the wilderness.

READ!

Read Matthew 3:1–4:11—the account of the baptism of Jesus by John, and then of his temptation by Satan in the wilderness.

It seems that for thirty years after his birth, Jesus grew up quietly into manhood. He was no ordinary man, of course; he was the perfect Son of God in human flesh. But he did not demonstrate his divinity powerfully during those thirty years. Most likely, Jesus was trained by Joseph as a carpenter, and lived in obedience and humble service to his parents during this time. It was not until he reached the age of thirty that his public ministry to God's people began.

As Matthew 3 begins, we see John the Baptist speaking boldly to the Pharisees and Sadducees (the religious leaders of the day) about their hypocrisy and their need for repentance. He also began to speak about the great Messiah who was coming—the one to whom he would directly point people. As promised by Malachi, John was preparing the way for Jesus to enter the scene for God's people, and to be the King and Savior that they needed.

Jesus's baptism. When we consider the fact that John was baptizing people as they repented of their sins, Jesus's baptism can be a bit confusing. Jesus was not sinful, of course; so why did he choose to be baptized by John? John saw this as well—and said that it would be better for Jesus to baptize him! Yet Jesus insisted. Why?

It seems that, in his baptism, Jesus was intentionally identifying himself with God's sinful people, placing himself in the shoes of sinful humanity. Jesus was not sinful, but he was showing God's people that he would one day be "made . . . to be sin" (2 Cor. 5:21) for them on a cross to bring them lasting forgiveness and eternal life.

Jesus's temptation. Jesus's temptation in the wilderness, which Matthew records at the beginning of chapter 4 of his Gospel, is yet another way that Jesus identified himself with God's people. The Israelites spent forty years wandering in the desert, being tempted toward sin and failing miserably to walk in obedience to God and his word. Jesus suffered temptation for forty days in the desert, but he consistently and faithfully stood up to the temptation of Satan and refused to give in. He was true Israel—that is, the perfect representative for God's people, who passed every test that they, throughout history, had failed. The New Testament will later explain that Jesus was tempted in every way as we are, yet he did not sin (Heb. 4:15).

God was showing his people, through the suffering and temptation of Jesus in the desert, that their great representative leader had finally come. He would be tempted and tried, yet he would remain perfect. God one day would accept the sacrifice that this perfect human being—who is also fully God—would offer to him on a cross for the sins of God's people.

JESUS CALLS DISCIPLES

Not only was Jesus the true Israel, but he also set out to call for himself a new people of God. As Jesus prepared to enter the public phase of his ministry, he began to gather people to follow him, and he led them as the Savior whom God had promised to his people many times throughout history.

READ!

Read Matthew 4:18–22 and 10:1–4.

The accounts of Jesus's calling of his disciples—both in Matthew and in other Gospels—are amazing to us. These men, many of whom had jobs and families, immediately responded to the call of Jesus and followed him. This does not necessarily mean that they abandoned their families, but it may mean that they took significant time away from their work in order to follow Jesus and participate in his work and ministry.

These men evidently saw something about Jesus that intrigued them—and even fascinated them. They saw him as a great leader, and perhaps they sensed that he was engaged in a special work that God was about to do for his people in the world. They eventually would come to understand more and more about the nature of this work, although it would take them some time to fully grasp how Jesus would accomplish God's salvation for his people.

What was Jesus doing in the calling of these men? What was his purpose for gathering these twelve disciples together at the outset of his ministry?

Reflecting Israel. Jesus's gathering of twelve disciples to follow him was an intentional reflection of the way in which God had "organized" his work in the nation of Israel. You remember that God's people were divided into twelve tribes, based on the families of the twelve sons of Jacob (who was later called Israel). These tribes served as the basis for the organization of God's people well into the days of the monarchy in Israel. Now Jesus was gathering twelve disciples to follow him. Jesus was showing people that he was the "true Israel"—he would lead a new people for God, which would involve the continuous saving work of God in the world—a work now being perfectly fulfilled through him.

Training a few. Jesus would go on to give very intentional and special time and training to the twelve disciples whom he called to follow him. He would focus especially on them, as they would be present for the bulk of his magnificent teaching about God and his life-changing work in the world. Jesus often would speak to the crowds, who surrounded him during many parts of his public ministry, in parables, but would then explain the parables more clearly to his disciples. Jesus's goal, it seems, was to help these twelve men understand exactly what he was all about.

Preparing for the future. Since we know what happens later in the Bible story, we can explain Jesus's commitment to these men as preparation for the future, when he would ascend to heaven and no longer would be on earth to personally and bodily lead his people. Jesus's gathering of the twelve disciples was his way of preparing them to take the good news of his salvation to all the world. These would be the men whom Jesus would one day call to lead and grow his church—the institution Jesus founded to carry the gospel into all the nations.

JESUS IN HIS HOMETOWN

Jesus went back to his hometown of Nazareth when it was time for him to begin his public ministry. Let's consider a passage from the Gospel of Luke that shows us how it went there and why this was not the great start for the Messiah's ministry that we might have expected.

READ!

Read Luke 4:16–30—the account of Jesus in the synagogue in Nazareth, his hometown.

Jesus grew up in the town of Nazareth. There he likely was trained as a carpenter under the leadership of Joseph, his father. People knew him there and had watched him grow from a boy to a man.

The passage that you read records Jesus going into the synagogue—the local place of worship for the Jewish people—and reading from the prophet Isaiah in the presence of the people who were gathered for worship. Jesus then made a very bold statement; he told the people that the passage that he read was "fulfilled" in their hearing through him (Luke 4:21). In that passage, Isaiah spoke about one who would be "anointed" by God—a Messiah—and would help deliver captives and poor people (referring to those especially who are spiritually poor and bound by sin). Jesus was saying that *he* was that anointed one—the Messiah for God's people.

The people of Nazareth obviously had some trouble accepting what Jesus was saying, and they began to make comments about him being the son of Joseph, the carpenter, whom they knew well. Jesus responded by directing them to Elijah and Elisha, and describing the grace of God that came to people through both of those Old Testament prophets. When the people realized the implications of what Jesus was saying to them, they revolted against him and tried (unsuccessfully) to kill him.

This is a sad story, because it shows us the hardness of heart many of the Jewish people displayed toward Jesus. But there are two important lessons that we need to take away from this account.

Difficult to believe. First, we need to understand that, for many in Jesus's day, it was genuinely difficult to believe that Jesus could really be God in human flesh. Sometimes we have the idea that it would have been easy for us to believe if we had just been there to see Jesus. But the Gospel accounts tell us—again and again—that many people who saw and heard Jesus in his days on earth refused to believe that he was the Messiah and the Son of God. This was especially difficult for the people of Nazareth. They had watched Jesus grow up; to them, he was a normal boy from their town. It would be only through the gift of God—faith—that anyone (then or now) would be able to believe that Jesus was the promised Messiah—the Son of God.

Salvation to all. Second, though, this passage reminds us of an important aspect of Jesus's ministry, which he revealed clearly through the two Old Testament stories that he referenced in response to the rejection that he received from the people of Nazareth. Jesus mentioned two Gentiles—the widow who helped Elijah and the Syrian general Naaman, who was cleansed by God from his leprosy through the help of Elisha. These two Gentiles put their faith in God—in Old Testament days—and received God's grace and favor. Jesus was telling the people that in his day—and even from the beginning—God's gifts of grace and faith were available to all people who repent and turn to him in faith. The salvation that he had come to earth to offer was not for Jews only, but for all people. This idea of Gentile inclusion in God's plan of salvation was what made the people of Nazareth incredibly angry—so angry that they tried to drive Jesus out and kill him!

JESUS'S PARABLES

I hope you can sense that you are growing in your understanding of how God continued the story of his saving work in the world, keeping his great promises to his people through the coming, life, death, and resurrection of his own Son: Jesus, God in human flesh. Having considered some of the early events in Jesus's life and ministry, we now need to wrestle with his teaching, which he often delivered to people of his day in the form of parables. We will see how Jesus himself explained his use of parables, and what this meant for the role of his disciples—both during his life on earth and after his ascension into heaven.

This discussion is the first of several in this chapter that focus on specific categories of Jesus's life and ministry. This fits our goal of gaining a broad picture of all that Jesus did and accomplished through his incarnation and his earthly mission.

READ!

Read Matthew 13:1–23—the account of Jesus's parable about the sower of the seed, as well as his explanation of the parable to his disciples.

We cannot study every one of the parables Jesus tells in the Gospels. Instead, we will examine the role of the parables in his teaching ministry, which was central to what he came to do on earth. The fact is that Jesus spoke often in parables, choosing to teach about the truths of the kingdom of God in this "hidden" and mysterious way. The parable that you have already read is a wonderful example of Jesus's teaching in this way; it helps, too, that it is accompanied by an explanation from Jesus about the parable itself, as well as his explanation of his general purpose for parables.

The meaning of this parable. The parable that you read is about the ministry of the word—the gospel—that would soon go out into all the world. Jesus took time to explain this to his disciples privately after the crowd had gone away. He wanted his disciples to know that as they one day spread the good news about forgiveness of sins through his death and eternal life through his resurrection, they would see many different responses to this message. Some people would reject it right away (the hard ground). Some people would accept it for a while but choose the pleasures of the world instead (the ground with thorns). Some people would seem to accept it, but the message would not go deep into their hearts (the rocky ground). But as they shared the good news of Jesus with the world, his disciples would find that some people would accept the gospel by faith and bear amazing fruit as they followed the Savior (the good ground).

The purpose of the parables. Sometimes we have the idea that Jesus told stories in order to make the truths of God clearer to people. While Jesus did speak God's truth to those who would listen, the purpose of parables, according to Jesus, was quite the opposite. The passage that you read tells us that Jesus spoke in parables not to make the truth of God clearer, but actually to hide it, in some ways, from people. The passage from Isaiah that Jesus quoted refers to people who are blind and deaf; they are kept from understanding and believing God's word because of hard hearts and closed minds. In fulfillment of this prophecy, Jesus spoke in parables so that those with hard hearts and closed minds would continue to reject the message of salvation that he brought!

There also seems to have been a practical reason for Jesus's use of parables. We know that, from very early on in his public ministry, the Pharisees and other religious leaders were out to kill him. The use of parables was a way for Jesus to speak the truth that he wanted to speak but in a hidden and almost "coded" way, so as to avoid arrest and execution before the perfect time that God the Father had ordained for his death.

The role of the disciples. While Jesus spoke in parables to guard the message that he was bringing from God to God's people, there would come a day when his disciples would proclaim the truth of the gospel boldly, loudly, and clearly in all the world. In other words, the use of parables would be over after Jesus's resurrection and ascension; the disciples would preach the gospel of Jesus Christ without any riddles or mystery.

This is why Jesus took time (as we see in this passage) to explain the parables to his disciples—even when he left the crowds slightly confused at some points. To his disciples, he spoke clearly. He was explaining the gospel to them and helping them gradually come to understand the meaning of his life, death, and resurrection. He was preparing them to shout out the message of salvation through him in no uncertain or hidden terms one day.

JESUS'S MIRACLES

Another important aspect of Jesus's earthly ministry was his miraculous works. As you probably already know, Jesus worked wonders during his time on earth. He healed people, multiplied food, and even raised people from the dead! As we will see, Jesus had a very specific purpose for the miracles that he performed. They were not ends in themselves; they were part of something greater that he was seeking to reveal to the world.

READ!

Read Matthew 9:1–8—the account of Jesus's healing of a paralyzed man.

In the short passage you read, you saw the record of just one of the many miracles that Jesus performed during his ministry on earth. He did many such miracles. You probably already know about the feeding of the five thousand, the raising of Lazarus from the dead, the calming of the storm, and others.

We do not have space to discuss all of his miracles, so we will focus on the purpose behind them. What part did miracles play in the public ministry of Jesus Christ in the world?

Miracles—not the point. This may seem like a strong statement, but it is true: Jesus's miracles—such as the healings and exorcisms that he performed during his time on earth—were not the ultimate point of his coming and his ministry. If they had been the point, then Jesus would have healed everyone in Israel—and perhaps even the world—who was sick or dying; he was and is God, and he was capable of doing that! But Jesus did not heal everyone in Israel. He did not miraculously solve every sickness, problem, and issue in the world. So miracles were not the main point of his coming; they pointed to something far greater.

What was the point? So what was the point of the miracles and healings of Jesus in the world? They were all part of Jesus's greatest concern: helping people see his identity as the Son of God so that they could come to saving faith in him. We see this very clearly in the account that you read from Matthew 9. Jesus told the scribes (who were very critical of him) that he was going to heal the paralyzed man in order that they might "know that the Son of Man has authority on earth to forgive sins" (v. 6). Jesus performed this miraculous healing as a sign to show the people who he is. He is the "Son of Man"—the great ruler, King, and Savior of God's people, who is promised throughout the story of the Bible. He was now on earth, and he could do something far greater than make people physically well; he could forgive their sins with the authority of God, making people spiritually and eternally well!

The right response. Some people did not experience physical healing from Jesus but received the eternal healing that he was pointing to through the physical healing. Look again at the conclusion of the passage that you read. Some people "glorified God" as they saw the authority and power of Jesus (Matt. 9:8). It seems that some of those who were there, seeing the healings that Jesus performed, responded in the way that he intended all people to respond to his miracles—with faith in him as the one who had truly come from God.

This idea—that Jesus's miracles are indications of his identity—is developed strongly by the Gospel writer John. In fact, John did not call Jesus's healings miracles—he called them signs. For John, they were not just random miracles or tricks that Jesus enjoyed performing for people. They were intentional signs that pointed to his identity as the Son of God. They were intended not to be ends in themselves but to point people to saving faith in the Savior of the world who had come for God's people. The miracles were not the point; belief in Jesus was the point! And belief in Jesus will lead, one day, to resurrected life—a reality to which Jesus's miracles also pointed.

JESUS AND THE RELIGIOUS LEADERS

As you probably know, Jesus had frequent confrontations with the strict religious leaders of the Jewish people—men such as the scribes, Pharisees, and Sadducees. They were furious that he called them out for hypocrisy and pointed God's people to a better way to follow God and love others. We need to examine this important aspect of Jesus's earthly ministry.

READ!

Read Matthew 15:1–20—an account of just one of the occasions when Jesus identified the serious hypocrisy of some of the religious leaders of his day.

The Pharisees and scribes, two sets of strict Jewish religious leaders, approached him to condemn him and his disciples for not keeping the "tradition of the elders" with regard to hand washing (Matt. 15:2). It is important to note that what they were describing was *not* an official part of God's law; it was an added tradition—something that their forefathers had called God's people to do as an "extra" part of Jewish ritual.

Jesus responded to the criticism of the religious leaders by telling them that they had made a habit of making God's word "void" by relying on their traditions more than keeping the heart of what God's word taught (Matt. 15:6). He gave an example of the way in which the religious leaders had twisted the commandment about honoring one's father and mother and had made an exception to it. This exception seemed "spiritual," as it released people from honoring their parents if they were devoting themselves to God. But Jesus said that this actually denied God's law and therefore was wrong.

Jesus ended this confrontation with some very strong words to the Pharisees and scribes. He linked them with the hypocrites that Isaiah prophesied about—people who praised God with their lips but had hearts that were far from giving genuine worship to him. He went on to explain to his disciples that religious hand washing had nothing to do with truly clean hearts, which can be given only by God!

What does this passage teach us about the pattern of Jesus's interactions with these religious leaders during his life? In what ways can we summarize the issues that he saw with their leadership of God's people?

The religious leaders. Again and again during Jesus's ministry, he confronted—and was confronted by—three main groups of religious leaders who had problems with what they took to be his relaxing of the strictness of God's law. These three groups were:

- The *Pharisees.* They probably were the strictest and most respected group of Jewish leaders during Jesus's day.
- The *Sadducees.* They were a group of religious leaders like the Pharisees, but they did not believe in a resurrection.
- The *scribes.* Another group of religious leaders who were responsible for copying and interpreting God's law.

All these men knew the Scriptures extremely well. Unfortunately, many of them had become corrupt. They had come to rely on outward rituals as the substance of their religion. This leads to the next part of our discussion.

The problem. In a word, Jesus often called out these religious leaders for their *hypocrisy*. Hypocrisy is, essentially, saying one thing and doing another. The religious leaders were putting extremely heavy burdens on God's people regarding their keeping of the law of God—and many extra laws that the leaders had added to that law! Many of them, though, had hearts that were far from God. They were selfish, greedy, and full of pride. Jesus confronted them on all these issues, telling them that they had missed the entire point of God's law: love and worship for God himself. The law had never simply been about keeping rules; it had always been about faith, obedience, and love for God and others.

Jesus's response. As you saw in the passage you read, Jesus's response to these men was not gentle. In fact, some of Jesus's strongest and harshest words were reserved for them. He said they were like "white-washed tombs" (Matt. 23:27)—people who look good on the outside but are completely dead on the inside. He said they were "vipers" (v. 33)—snakes that were full of venom. He told them that their father was not Abraham (as they claimed) but Satan (John 8:44)!

Jesus's point with all these harsh words was to wake people up to the reality that a saving relationship with God does not come from an ethnic heritage or from keeping a bunch of rituals and laws. A saving relationship with God has always come through true faith in God, which results in heartfelt obedience to him. Jesus also would show God's people that forgiveness for sins would come through what he would soon do on the cross.

JESUS AND THE LAW OF GOD

The previous section showed you how Jesus confronted and engaged with the Jewish religious leaders of his day. He boldly condemned the hypocritical practices of many of them—practices that had exalted human traditions and rituals over heartfelt and humble worship of God and love for other people. Jesus was directing people to true faith in God rather than hypocritical outward signs and rituals.

It is obvious, though, that Jesus was not somehow against the law of God. This fact is nowhere clearer than in his famous "Sermon on the Mount," as the teaching in Matthew 5–7 has come to be called. In this beautiful sermon, Jesus explained to the crowds that he had come to "fulfill" the law of God in every way (Matt. 5:17). His goal was to show them what true life and faith in him really look like; it actually leads to *more* holiness than the scribes and Pharisees possessed!

READ!

Read Matthew 5–7—an account of Jesus's Sermon on the Mount.

The Sermon on the Mount, at first glance, can seem like an incredibly intimidating message from Jesus. It is true, of course, that Jesus was calling God's people to a very high level of obedience and holiness. Consider just a few of the statements that he made in this sermon:

- Jesus said that the righteousness of God's people must exceed the righteousness of the scribes and the Pharisees (Matt. 5:20), which would have been striking to people who saw those men as the great religious leaders of the day—the most holy people.
- Jesus said that God's people must be "perfect," just as God the Father is perfect (Matt. 5:48).
- Jesus went far beyond the letter of the law in many ways. For example, he told the people that not only is adultery wrong, but simply looking at a woman with lust is the same—in God's eyes—as committing adultery (Matt. 5:27–28).

So what do we make of this sermon? How can we, as God's people today, learn from these intense words of Jesus to the people?

Start with Jesus. In some ways, it is good to start with the very end of the record of Jesus's Sermon on the Mount—the last verses of chapter 7. Did you notice how Matthew concludes this account? He tells us that all of the people who heard the sermon were amazed—not only at the teaching itself, but at the "authority" of Jesus, the one who taught (vv. 28–29). He taught in a different way than the scribes and Pharisees; he taught as if he were the one who had written the law (in a way, he had). This is very important for us to see. Jesus was interpreting the law of God authoritatively through himself. To respond to the teaching of the Sermon on the Mount, people first need to respond to Jesus. The first response is not to say, "How must I do this?" but, "Whom must I trust and put faith in so that I can do this?" The answer is Jesus—God's Son.

See the fulfillment. After we have taken that important first step, we need to see how Jesus was clearly saying that he was fulfilling, not abolishing, the Law and the Prophets of the Old Testament (Matt. 5:17). Jesus came not to bring a completely new "order" for God's people but to fulfill all of God's commands and promises in himself. This is incredibly important, and it reminds us that the Bible—and God's saving work in the world—is really one grand story. Jesus was affirming the beauty and truth of the law of God, and showing how, through faith in him, God's people can fulfill and obey God's law in *greater* ways than the people of the Old Testament.

Follow him and obey! We cannot avoid the strong moral calls that Jesus began to make to people who wanted to follow him and worship God with their lives. His overwhelming point through this sermon was to show that God's true people, who follow him by faith, are even *more* righteous and holy than the outwardly religious scribes and Pharisees. Jesus called his people to a higher obedience, a more complete purity of mind and heart, and lives of even more love and humility. The first step, as we have said, is to respond to Jesus in faith. Then the call is to follow him into this kind of holiness and godliness as he gives us strength to do it.

JESUS ENTERS JERUSALEM

We're now going to move ahead in the story to the final days of Jesus's life. In your next reading, you will see him entering Jerusalem amid the shouts of crowds of people. You will see him being betrayed by one of his closest friends. And you will see him giving his disciples a new "meal" to help his people celebrate and remember his death until he returns to earth.

■ **READ!**

Read Luke 19:28–40—Luke's account of Jesus's triumphal entry into Jerusalem just a few days before his crucifixion. Then read Luke 22:1–23—the account of the plot to kill Jesus and his institution of the Lord's Supper during the Passover meal with his disciples.

By his last week on earth—at least in his pre-resurrection body—Jesus had taught, healed, and led his disciples for about three years during his public ministry in Israel. Finally, he actively and intentionally set his face and his heart toward Jerusalem, where he would go to a cross to die for the sins of God's people. His time had come.

The passages you just read reveal a few important points that we need to consider about the days before Jesus's death.

The triumphal entry. Do you remember our brief study of the prophet Zechariah? Zechariah is the second to last book of the Old Testament, and it contains some beautiful words of prophecy that point forward to Jesus's coming to earth as the King of God's people. In Zechariah 9:9, the prophet speaks about the King coming to his people while riding on a donkey's colt. This prophecy was very specifically fulfilled when Jesus entered Jerusalem. The King of God's people had come, and the people cheered for him and welcomed him with open arms. This was probably the absolute height of Jesus's public popularity, and there was no doubt that many people would have made him their king at this time. Jesus, though, was not there to reign—at least not in the way that many people thought. He had come to Jerusalem to "reign" from a cross, where he would die, and then to rise again to break the power of sin and death forever. Just days after the people shouted out to Jesus as the Son of David, they would cry out for Pontius Pilate to crucify him.

The betrayal of Jesus. As Luke 22 begins, we see the tragic fall of one of Jesus's twelve disciples, Judas Iscariot. We know from other Gospel accounts that he had already begun to fall into sin; he was greedy, and sometimes took money for himself from the disciples' money bag. Judas became possessed by Satan, and he set out to betray Jesus to the religious leaders of the Jews. In exchange, they gave him money, and the plot to kill Jesus began. While Judas was obviously guilty and sinful, we will see that even this was part of God's great plan. Jesus had to go to the cross and be killed if God's people were really going to be saved and forgiven.

The Last Supper. Jesus and his disciples were in Jerusalem for the Passover meal—the one instituted to celebrate and commemorate God's faithfulness to his people hundreds of years before in Egypt, before he delivered them from slavery to Pharaoh. During this celebration, Jesus instituted a new "meal" for his people—one that we still practice today in churches that worship Jesus Christ as Savior and Lord. Jesus gave this meal—now called the Lord's Supper or Communion—to his disciples to point to the meaning of his death, which was quickly approaching. He broke bread, explaining that his body would be broken for them. Also, he poured out wine and spoke of the new covenant made in his blood. In this, Jesus was telling them that the prophecy of Jeremiah (31:31–34) was being fulfilled in what he was about to do on the cross. God was bringing eternal salvation to his people—to all who would trust in the blood of Jesus, which can finally take away sins.

After these events unfolded, Jesus approached the cross. We will look deeply at his death there—and its meaning—next.

JESUS'S CRUCIFIXION

The death of Jesus Christ on a cross is the climax of the Gospels, and of the entire Bible as well. Everything in the story so far has been leading up to the moment when the Son of God would die for God's people. With this event, God's salvation had finally been accomplished, even though the significance of his death on the cross would need to be fully explained to his disciples.

📖 READ!

Read John 19—the account of the end of the trial of Jesus, and then his crucifixion, death, and burial.

As we read a chapter of the Bible like John 19, we should be filled with a sense of "heaviness." This chapter records the ultimate sinful act in all of history—human beings putting to death the Son of God. No sin has ever been more terrifying and wretched. God's Son came to earth to show the way to salvation, and the very leaders of God's people led the way in putting Jesus on a cross to die.

Yet we know that even this evil was part of the wonderful plan of God to save and forgive sinners. Jesus's death was no accident; it was God's surprising and merciful way of providing the final sacrifice for the sins of his people—for they could never provide a sacrifice great enough to cover their sin and reconcile them to God.

As we consider the suffering and death of Jesus, we should think through the following realities that John records for us.

The physical suffering of Jesus. First, we need to see the real—and terrible—physical suffering that Jesus endured at the hands of human beings. He was whipped, beaten, mocked, and tormented with a crown of thorns. Then he was literally nailed to a cross—hung on a wooden structure with pointed metal nails that were driven through his hands and feet. The physical suffering that Jesus endured was torturous, and he endured it purely out of love for God's people and out of hope for what he was going to accomplish for them.

The spiritual suffering of Jesus. Second, though, we need to understand that the physical suffering of Jesus did not nearly equal the spiritual suffering that he endured in his sacrifice. On the cross, God the Father turned his back on his Son in wrath; the guilt of God's people was counted as Jesus's own. As a result, he endured all of the bitterness and utter agony of guilt, shame, and the unrestrained anger of God against every sin of God's people for all time. This is why, in another Gospel account, Jesus is recorded to have cried out the words of Psalm 22:1: "My God, my God, why have you forsaken me?" (see Matt. 27:46). This was eternal suffering, the full experience of the horrors of hell.

The real death of Jesus. Third, the Gospel of John is clear that Jesus really died. We cannot skip over this quickly. The sacrifice for all the sins of all of God's people for all time was complete because the perfect Son of God really died. Jesus's lifeless body was removed from the cross and buried in a tomb; the text of John says this very clearly. We must recognize that Jesus's death was real. The sacrifice was completed. A perfect life had been given in the place of the lives of all of God's people.

The meaning of Jesus's death. Finally, we should remember all that Jesus's death means for sinful people who put their faith in him as Lord and Savior and give their lives and hearts to him. It means that full payment has been made for the sins of all who believe in him. Jesus is fully human, so he was able to fully represent humanity before God. But he is also fully God, so he was able to pay the full price and receive the punishment that sin against the holy God truly deserves. This was the final sacrifice—the finished work of salvation and substitution for all who will accept it. It was the fulfillment of all the prophecies that pointed to a final salvation for God's people. This is why, as Jesus hung his head to die, he cried out, "It is finished" (John 19:30).

JESUS'S RESURRECTION

We've been thinking deeply about the reality and significance of the death of Jesus Christ on the cross. We considered Jesus's physical and spiritual sufferings, and saw how Scripture was fulfilled as he laid down his life as the final sacrifice for the sins of God's people. Before we move on, take a moment to think about all the promises from God to his people that were fulfilled in the sacrificial death of Jesus, and then give thanks for the Savior who fulfilled those promises.

Of course, while Jesus really died, he did not remain dead! Let's now consider the wonderful miracle of the resurrection of Jesus Christ—its reality and its great significance for all who choose to repent of sin and follow him as Lord and Savior!

📖 READ!

Read John 20—an account of the resurrection of Jesus, as well as several different appearances that he made to his followers after he rose again.

As we consider this amazing chapter of Scripture, we will focus on the reality, the proof, and the meaning of the resurrection of Jesus Christ.

The reality of the resurrection. None of the Gospels record the actual event of the resurrection; we do not know what it looked like when Jesus rose from the dead. All of them are unified, though, in their simple and clear affirmation that Jesus really did rise bodily from the dead. Jesus really did die on the cross; everyone around him during his death saw this without a doubt. Likewise, Jesus really did rise from the dead; he appeared to hundreds of people who became witnesses of this amazing miracle to all the world.

Jesus rose with an obviously physical body. In the passage you just read, you saw that he allowed Thomas to literally touch the wounds he had received on the cross. Another passage records him eating fish with his disciples (Luke 24:42–43). Jesus's body was physical, but it was also a special resurrection body. His disciples were kept from recognizing him at various points, and he was able to appear suddenly, and even enter a room that had locked doors.

The witness of John 20—and the other Gospel accounts—is that Jesus really rose bodily from the dead. He appeared to his disciples bodily and showed them that he was alive.

The proof of the resurrection. Many of the Gospel accounts—especially Mark—show us very strongly that the disciples struggled to fully believe in Jesus and to fully understand the significance of his death and resurrection. Until the crucifixion, and even in the days following it, as Jesus was in the tomb, it seems that his disciples remained confused. They simply could not understand why their Messiah and King had to die.

Given this slowness of the disciples to believe, it is clear why Jesus sought to prove to them that he really had risen from the dead. He showed himself to Mary Magdalene, outside of the tomb (John 20:14). He showed his disciples his hands and his side (v. 20). He even allowed the "doubting Thomas" to physically touch him, since Thomas had been so unsure that Jesus really was alive (v. 27). Jesus kindly, patiently, and graciously showed his disciples, beyond a shadow of a doubt, that he really had risen from the dead.

As we look back at the years that followed the resurrection, we should see the witness of the disciples of Jesus as a wonderful sign of its reality. Many of the men who saw the risen Christ were put to death for their faith in the years following Jesus's ascension. They died affirming the reality and truth of the resurrection. It is difficult to believe that these men would have died for something that they did not know to be absolutely true.

The meaning and significance of the resurrection. It is in the rest of the Bible that the meaning and significance of the resurrection of Jesus Christ is really explained, so we will just summarize here. Jesus's rise from the dead means, first, that God accepted his sacrifice for sins on behalf of God's people. If the sacrifice had not been sufficient, Jesus would have stayed dead! Jesus rose because, after he had paid for sins, there was no more death to be died. Sin had been completely paid for, and God had put his stamp of approval on the sacrifice of Jesus for his people.

Second, though, Jesus's resurrection from the dead means that all who trust in him, repent of sins, and follow him also have the hope of resurrection and eternal life. The Bible goes on to explain that while Jesus was the first to take on a resurrection body, all his people, too, will rise again and experience the glorified bodies that come with the resurrection of the dead. Jesus's resurrection gives hope to God's people that sin has been forgiven and that death does not have the final victory over them; Jesus has conquered sin *and* death for God's people. The victory has been won!

AFTER JESUS'S RESURRECTION

Jesus's ministry continued briefly after his resurrection. He was with his people for just forty more days, and he spent that time teaching them more about his work and about the way it fulfilled all of God's word. You see, the disciples, even after Jesus's death and resurrection, still did not completely understand how everything that he had done for the world was in fulfillment of the great promises God had revealed to his people in all of Scripture. Jesus essentially needed to show them how the great story of God's saving work in the world was all connected. We will learn about this topic now as we consider Luke 24.

READ!

Read Luke 24:13–49—the account of Jesus on the road to Emmaus, when he spoke with two disciples about the connection of his death and resurrection to all the promises of God throughout the Old Testament Scriptures, and then his appearance to all of his disciples.

What are some conclusions and observations we can make about this account of Jesus's postresurrection lessons for his disciples?

Slow of heart. The men on the road to Emmaus, and even Jesus's closest disciples, were "slow of heart" to truly understand and believe all that Jesus's death meant in terms of God's promises and prophecies to his people (Luke 24:25). They also had failed to see that the resurrection of Jesus was a sure thing, according to the Scriptures. These disciples had been with Jesus, but they still needed to be taught about how his life, death, and resurrection were *the* great answer to all the Old Testament promises of God.

We should not be too hard on these people, however; we, too, probably would have struggled to believe and understand. We, too, would have needed the careful and loving explanation of Jesus, who opened the Scriptures to the two men on the road and showed them how he had become the great answer for the deepest issues and problems of God's people.

Jesus's "Bible story" sermon. Jesus essentially gave the same message both to the men on the road and to all his disciples: unfolding the entire story of the Bible, with himself as the main character and the climax! Look again at what Jesus told the men on the road to Emmaus as they struggled to connect God's story from the past with the coming of Jesus into the world. He said it was "necessary" for the Messiah to suffer, die, and be raised from the dead, for the Old Testament demanded it (Luke 24:26–27)! Verse 27 also gives a summary of the message that Jesus gave to these men: he explained to them, from all the Old Testament, the things "concerning himself." It seems that he went through the entire Bible (Old Testament) and showed them how all of the story was moving toward and pointing to *him*. He did the same thing for all of his disciples, showing them that everything that was written in the Old Testament needed to be fulfilled in his work (v. 44). Jesus retold the whole story of the Bible to his disciples and showed them how he was its main character.

Implications for us today. What does all of this mean for us as we begin to wrap up this scene of the Bible story? It means that we need to understand that Jesus saw *himself* as the main character in the Bible—the ultimate King, Savior, and Messiah who would fulfill all of God's promises to his people for all time. In short, Jesus is the center of the Bible.

This means that if we are to read and understand the Bible in the way that Jesus himself did, we need to be orienting our study around the relation of every part of it to his life, death, and resurrection. This is precisely what we are trying to do as we study the Bible as one big story from Genesis to Revelation.

JESUS'S FINAL DAYS ON EARTH

We are now coming to the end of our study in this scene of the Bible story: "God's Salvation." Before we get there, we need to focus on the very end of Jesus's time on earth. As Jesus prepared to return to heaven with God the Father, he gave his disciples a very important charge; they would be the ones who would begin to carry the message of his salvation to every part of the world. Let's think together about the Great Commission of Jesus, found in Matthew 28.

READ!

Read Matthew 28—the final chapter in Matthew's Gospel.

Interestingly, the different Gospel writers focus on very different aspects of Jesus's postresurrection work and teaching of his disciples. Luke, as you saw earlier, focuses on Jesus's explanation of the entire Bible to his disciples—with himself as the central character. John focuses on Jesus's proof of his resurrection to his followers. Mark's Gospel focuses on the continued disbelief and confusion of the disciples, even after Jesus's resurrection. Matthew records for us the Great Commission that Jesus gave to his disciples just before his ascension. Matthew wants to show us the "sending call" of Jesus. What can we learn from this ending to Matthew's Gospel?

Jesus and YHWH. One thing that people often miss in this passage is that Jesus very intentionally claimed to be the God of the universe.

God—Yahweh—had said to his people, through the prophet Isaiah that they would be his "witnesses" throughout all the world (Isa. 43:10). Jesus was claiming full authority as God and calling his followers to make disciples of all nations and bear witness to *him* in all the earth (see also Acts 1:8, which includes Jesus's specific use of the word *witnesses*). This was a hugely significant statement from Jesus, one that tells us who he is!

The call to make disciples. The specific call of Jesus is to "make disciples of all nations" (Matt. 28:19). The disciples, who had given everything to follow Jesus, were now instructed to multiply themselves by sharing the gospel and "teaching" (v. 20) others everything that Jesus had taught them. Finally, this disciple-making process was to be accompanied by the covenant sign of baptism, which was to be done in the name of the Father, Son, and Holy Spirit (v. 19).

Jesus, fully God and fully man, was calling his disciples to make more followers of him as they boldly proclaimed his message in all the world. Because of the depth and significance of the gospel message—that God truly saves sinners through his Son—this message needed to be shared in every corner of the earth. Jesus wants all people everywhere to hear about him and worship him.

The success and the continuing call. As we look around our world today, we cannot help but see the amazing success of this Great Commission through the witness of the disciples. The gospel of Jesus Christ has truly gone global—there are churches of people who love and worship him all over the world. The gospel has spread from his first twelve followers to essentially every corner of the earth.

Yet there is still more work to be done. It is important for followers of Jesus to understand that the Great Commission is for every disciple of Jesus. The call—today as much as then—is to continue to "make disciples" of Jesus, teaching his gospel and the word of God to everyone everywhere. If you want to follow Jesus as Lord and Savior, then this is your commission as well. Will you accept this call?

REVIEW

We have come to the climax of the story of God's redeeming work in the world for his people: the coming, life, death, and resurrection of Jesus Christ. He is the Son of God, who took on flesh to serve as the perfect representative for God's sinful people. Jesus obeyed God's word perfectly in the place of God's people, then died on the cross in their place to bear the punishment for their disobedience. He rose from the dead, giving assurance that all who repent and put their faith in him will live forever under his perfect reign.

⬤ PRAY!

As you close this chapter with prayer, give praise to God for bringing his salvation to his people through the person and work of his Son, Jesus Christ. Thank him that he kept his big promises to his people. Thank him that he offers forgiveness of sins to all who will believe in his Son. Thank him for the promise of resurrection and eternal life for all who love Jesus.

GOD'S CHURCH
PART 1

Now that we have explored "God's Salvation" by exploring the coming, life, death, and resurrection of Jesus Christ, we're going to move into a new scene of the Bible story: "God's Church." Here we'll begin to see how the gospel of Jesus transformed his disciples, and then more and more of the world in which they lived. God's salvation had come to earth with power, grace, and glory in the person of Jesus Christ. Now it was time for the message of this great salvation to go to the ends of the earth.

We will spend this chapter in the book of Acts, as we see the beginning of the formation of the church—something that had never really existed before, at least not in the way that it began to exist after Jesus's ascension. We will see how God began to powerfully use his people to spread the message of salvation through his Son throughout all the world.

Remember!

Your suggested memory verses for this chapter come from Peter's wonderful sermon at Pentecost, in which he traced the history of the story of the Bible and showed how Jesus Christ fulfilled the great promises of God to his people.

Brothers, I may say to you with confidence about the patriarch David that he both died and was buried, and his tomb is with us to this day. Being therefore a prophet, and knowing that God had sworn with an oath to him that he would set one of his descendants on his throne, he foresaw and spoke about the resurrection of the Christ, that he was not abandoned to Hades, nor did his flesh see corruption. This Jesus God raised up, and of that we all are witnesses. (Acts 2:29–32)

JESUS'S PLAN

How exactly did Jesus envision his gospel going out into the world? The book of Acts gives us the answer.

READ!

Read Acts 1:1–11—the account of Jesus's postresurrection time with his disciples, and of his promise to them before his ascension. Compare this passage to the end of Matthew 28 and consider the careful instructions Jesus gave to his disciples.

As the disciples gathered around Jesus during the forty days that he was with them after his resurrection, they did so privately and quietly. Jesus taught them about the meaning of his work and gave them "proofs" of his resurrection simply by being with them in his physical resurrection body. Jesus had done something incredible: the Son of God had died for the sins of God's people and had risen from the dead to conquer death forever for all who would believe in him!

But as Jesus prepared to return to heaven, his disciples still seemed to not quite understand what his work in the world would look like in the coming years before his return to earth. They even asked him if he was going to "restore the kingdom to Israel" (Acts 1:6), probably asking him if it was time for God to bring the glory and the power back to his people on earth. Jesus, though, has a very different plan for his people—and the message of his gospel—until he comes again.

Witness. Jesus gently corrected the misguided view of his disciples and told them what their key role would be in the coming years after he returned to God the Father in heaven: *witness.* They would be witnesses to him—his life, death, and resurrection, which is the full message of the salvation of God that has come to earth. Jesus told the disciples that their witness would go from Jerusalem to Judea to Samaria, and then to all the ends of the earth. In other words, God's promise to Abraham was about to be fulfilled in the greatest way yet—God's great message of salvation would finally begin to bless the peoples of the earth as the disciples spread the good news of Jesus Christ everywhere.

Church. As we study the book of Acts and then the Epistles of the New Testament in the next chapter, we will become more acquainted with the surprising way that God chose to do his work in the world during this time. It was God's plan to work through his *church.* He would not gather a great army for himself or raise up a great political leader like David or Solomon. God would entrust his glorious gospel to his people, who collectively would make up the church—which would be built and grown through the proclamation of the message that Jesus entrusted to his disciples. The church would become God's great way of building his eternal kingdom.

Holy Spirit. In order to carry out this plan, Jesus commanded his disciples to wait in Jerusalem for a special baptism of the Holy Spirit, the powerful gift that God would give them as they began the important work of witnessing to all the people in Jerusalem, Judea, Samaria, and beyond. In the next section, we will learn about the very beginning of this witness, as God's Holy Spirit empowered these once-frightened disciples to boldly bear witness to Jesus.

We are about to see the church grow from a huddled group of just a few disciples of Jesus in the days following his resurrection to a body of people from all nations of the world who loved and worshiped the risen Savior. The next step of God's work in the world was beginning as the apostles prepared to bear witness to all that they had seen and heard.

These apostles—men who had seen the risen Lord and been commissioned by him to proclaim the gospel, write inspired Scripture, and lead the first generation of the church—would rise up to spread the good news of Jesus from Jerusalem to Judea to Samaria and even to the ends of the earth.

THE DAY OF PENTECOST

In obedience to Jesus's command, his disciples waited in Jerusalem for God to "baptize" them with the gift of the Holy Spirit. In this section, we will see what happened as the Spirit came with power to begin the work of witness through the disciples. We will see the miracle that happened at Pentecost and the great conversion of many people that occurred when Peter powerfully preached about Jesus Christ. And we will see the beginning of the church of Jesus Christ, as new believers in him began to gather to worship him in fellowship with one another. This is the next scene of God's great work in the world—a scene that *we* are a part of!

READ!

Read Acts 2—the account of the miracle at Pentecost, Peter's sermon, the conversion of many people, and the beginning of the church of Jesus Christ in Jerusalem, which would become God's primary means of accomplishing his purposes for the gospel in the world.

The passage you just read is foundational for understanding the beginning of God's work in the world through his people, the church, so let's take some time to discuss the important events recorded for us here.

The miracle. Jesus, as you remember, had told his disciples to wait in Jerusalem to be "baptized" by the Holy Spirit. They had already put their faith in Jesus; this baptism was to be a special gift for them from God. It would be a special empowering to help them begin the important work of bearing witness to the death and resurrection of Jesus Christ as the centerpiece of the saving work of God in the world.

Finally, the day came. At the celebration of the Jewish feast of Pentecost in Jerusalem, many people were gathered from all over the world. God's Holy Spirit descended on the disciples, and something amazing happened: they started proclaiming the gospel of God's salvation through Jesus in different languages—languages that they had previously not known! Thanks to this "gift of tongues," everyone gathered in this place began to hear the message of Jesus Christ. The Holy Spirit had come with power, and something big was about to happen.

Yet amid the confusion, some people simply accused the disciples of being drunk with wine. So Peter stood up to speak to the crowd.

The sermon. Peter's sermon had a very simple message: Jesus is the fulfillment of God's promises and prophecies to his people throughout all of Scripture and all of history. Peter first quoted from the prophet Joel to explain what was happening around them as the disciples were filled with the Holy Spirit. Joel had pointed God's people to a day when the Spirit of God would be poured out; Peter told the crowd that this was happening in their midst. Then Peter quoted from Psalm 16—a psalm of David that points to an eternal King who will never die. Peter calmly reminded the people that King David died. According to Peter, David was prophetically pointing to an eternal King and Savior who would be far greater than him—Jesus Christ, the risen Savior and King of God's people.

Peter ended his message by telling the people the bad news: they had put this great King to death. They were guilty of sin, and they needed to repent and put their faith in the risen and reigning Son of God.

The beginning. God used the gift of tongues and the sermon of Peter to bring three thousand people to faith in Jesus Christ. This was the amazing first "explosion" of faith and the seed of the church of Jesus Christ, which God has been using in the world ever since. In Acts 2:42–47, you read the beginning description of this church in Jerusalem, which was formed by people who believed the apostles' message about Jesus Christ. They began to meet regularly, share together, and learn more about Christ through the teaching of the apostles. The church was beginning, and this was the start of the gospel of Jesus Christ being spread to the ends of the earth.

PETER'S PREACHING

The preaching of Peter was greatly used by God during the early days of the church. In this section, we're going to see two powerful examples of the way in which he pointed people to Jesus through the witness of the Old Testament Scriptures. In Peter's teaching, we'll see yet another affirmation of the truth that the Bible is one great story of God's saving work in the world.

READ!

Read Acts 3:1–4:22—the account of the powerful witness, in both preaching and healing, of Peter and John in the early days of their proclamation of the gospel of Jesus Christ.

As you read from Acts 3 and 4, you saw the boldness of Peter and John as they began to speak about the salvation of God through Jesus Christ. God used them to heal people miraculously from time to time, although their focus seemed to be on the proclamation of the message of the gospel of Christ—his death and resurrection. To see what we can learn about the preaching of the apostles during this time, we will simply look at the two messages of Peter that are recorded for us in these chapters of Acts. How did he use the Old Testament to explain all that Jesus had accomplished for God's people?

Jesus as fulfillment of promises. First, Peter saw Jesus as the fulfillment of all of God's great promises to his people. He linked God's work in Jesus Christ to his work through the great patriarchs of his people (Acts 3:13). Then he told the people that God had promised throughout the ministry of the prophets that his Christ would "suffer" (v. 18). Peter even told the Jewish people that "all" of the prophets of God pointed forward to the time when Jesus would accomplish salvation on earth for God's people and be exalted as the Messiah and the eternal King (v. 24). All of this made the people even more guilty. They had crucified this Messiah, who had come as the great fulfillment of all of God's promises to his people.

Jesus as the only way of salvation. In Acts 4:12, we find a wonderful summary of all that Peter said the fulfillment of promises through Jesus meant for God's people. What did it mean that Jesus was the promised Messiah? What did it mean that the Son of God had come to earth to fulfill all of God's promises to his people? It meant that salvation could be found nowhere else—there was no other Savior for God's people than the one whom God had so wonderfully provided for them. Peter, in other words, showed the people the implications of the coming of Jesus Christ. He was clearly the only way to salvation, and all who rejected him would be rejecting the God of all history. This was the God who had sent his Son to fulfill his work of salvation in the world; all people must accept this Savior!

The continuing story. Peter's preaching should remind us of an important application: the Bible really is God's one story of his saving work in the world and in the lives of his people. This is certainly how Peter read and interpreted the Bible and preached it to the people of his day. He looked at the promises of God to Abraham and to his people through the prophets, and saw all of them coming together gloriously in the person and work of God's Son, Jesus Christ. On this basis, Peter proclaimed Jesus to the people of his day. He told them that God had continued and fulfilled his work in the world through his own Son. This amazing gift was the basis of Peter's call for repentance and belief. The Messiah had come, and all people everywhere should worship and believe in him.

THE STONING OF STEPHEN

The gospel was exploding in Jerusalem; you saw this from the account of the miracle at Pentecost, when three thousand people were converted to faith in Jesus Christ in just one day! God was powerfully using the witness of the disciples to tell others about the salvation of Jesus Christ, and the message was beginning to go out with great success.

The gospel witness of God's people, though, was not without opposition; you can see this in the story of Stephen. As God's people continued to grow, those who hated Jesus and his gospel became more and more violent in their opposition to it. But many of God's people stood firm in their witness even as they faced persecution and death.

READ!

Read Acts 6:8–7:60—the account of Stephen's witness, his arrest and false accusation, his great speech before the Jewish council, and his murder by those who hated Jesus and the gospel.

In the passage that you read, you saw the account of the first martyr— someone who is killed for faith in Jesus Christ as Lord and Savior. Stephen, a faithful follower of Jesus, was put to death brutally by the leaders of the Jews, who were violently opposed to the gospel.

Stephen's ministry. Stephen was not one of the twelve apostles, but he obviously had come to faith in Jesus Christ by the time of the events recorded in Acts 6. The text tells us that he was "doing great wonders and signs" and speaking to people about Jesus with great wisdom, according to the Spirit of God (vv. 8, 10). Some Jews, however, became extremely angry about the ministry of Stephen; he was evidently showing people the error of their legalistic ways and pointing them to salvation, which comes by faith in Jesus Christ alone. These enemies of the gospel stirred up people to make false accusations against Stephen; as a result, he was arrested and brought before the Jewish council to make his defense.

Stephen's sermon. Stephen's defense before the council turned out to be one of the richest and most beautiful biblical sermons that is recorded for us in all of Scripture. As he defended the message that he preached about Jesus Christ, he explained:

- The promise of God to Abraham, and how it was the beginning of a promise that would point to Jesus
- The story of Joseph, and God's hand amid the details of that account
- The ministry of Moses, whom God used to lead his people out of slavery
- The great leadership of David, whose son Solomon built a glorious house for the worship of God

Stephen mentioned the temple of God as a direct "path" to Jesus. He reminded the people that the God of the universe does not live in man-made temples, for he cannot be contained. He then told the Jewish leaders that they were responsible for killing the prophets in the past and, most recently, for killing the Messiah from God: Jesus Christ himself!

Stephen's death. As you can imagine, the Jewish leaders reacted extremely viciously to the biblical indictment that Stephen brought against them. In a crazed fit of anger and rage, they dragged him outside the city and stoned him to death. This was a terrible murder committed by people who could not accept the fact that they had missed the point of the Old Testament Scriptures, which was to direct them to Jesus Christ—the very man whom some of them had helped crucify.

Thus, Stephen became the first martyr as he was put to death for his faith. He was the first of many faithful men and women of the church who would stand strong by faith in Christ, even until death.

As Acts 7 closes, we see a hint of someone else who would soon come to the fore in the story of Acts: a young man named Saul was there as Stephen was killed, giving approval to his death. Let's now begin to think about his role in God's plan.

SAUL'S CONVERSION

Saul—a young and very bright Pharisee—began to lead a charge against God's people during this time. He did not believe that Jesus was God's Son, the Messiah, and he hated the gospel that was being spread about Jesus with every fiber of his being.

Yet in the passage we will discuss in a moment, you will see how even a murderer like Saul is not beyond the reach of the grace of God through Jesus Christ. The account shows Saul being confronted on the road to Damascus by Jesus Christ himself. This confrontation would change the course of Saul's life forever—and would be God's way of raising up a great and powerful leader for his early church.

READ!

Read Acts 9—the account of the conversion of Saul. Also, glance back at Acts 8:1–3, which describes the persecution of Christians that Saul had been leading.

What do we learn in these dramatic accounts from the book of Acts?

The persecution of Saul. In Acts 8:1–3, you get a vivid description of the persecution that Saul was leading against God's people during the days recorded in the early chapters of Acts. Saul, a Pharisee (a strict Jewish religious leader), was opposed to Jesus and his followers in every way. He probably regarded the gospel as a way for people to get out from under obedience to the law; he saw no room for the free grace of the cross or the teaching of Jesus's resurrection from the dead. So Saul led the way in trying to snuff out the witness of the gospel in his world. He put Christians in prison and did all that he could to eliminate followers of Jesus completely.

The confrontation of Saul. Acts 9 records one of the most unlikely conversion stories in all of history. While traveling to Damascus to persecute followers of Jesus there, Saul was confronted by Jesus himself! He was struck to the ground by a blinding light and heard the voice of Jesus speaking directly to him. Saul was confronted by the risen Lord Jesus Christ, who declared to Saul that he had been persecuting *him.* Saul, who was left temporarily blind by this encounter, obeyed Jesus's command to go into Damascus and wait to be told what to do.

The conversion and call of Saul. Next, Jesus appeared in a vision to a Damascus disciple named Ananias, telling him to go to Saul. Now, if you were Ananias, just imagine how you would have felt about going anywhere near this terrible persecutor of the church. You certainly would not have trusted him in any way. Yet Jesus brought a very interesting message to Ananias, who was struggling to believe that God could truly change the heart of a man like Saul. He told Ananias this about Saul: "He is a chosen instrument of mine to carry my name before the Gentiles and kings and the children of Israel. For I will show him how much he must suffer for the sake of my name" (Acts 9:15–16).

Saul's conversion, it seems, was inextricably linked with his *call* from God. God was humbling this man to his knees and giving him a new purpose for his life. Saul would now be God's special tool for bringing the gospel of Jesus Christ to Jews and Gentiles alike—and this task would include suffering for Jesus.

God was showing his people then—and us today—that he can transform the life of literally anyone. Saul went from murderer of Christians to God's chosen instrument to proclaim Christ in the world. His conversion reminds us that no one is beyond the reach of God's grace.

The beginning of ministry. Saul immediately began to do exactly what God had called him to do: proclaim Christ to those around him (Acts 9:20). He began in the Jewish synagogues, where he proved to people from Scripture that Jesus is the "Christ" (v. 22), the one God had promised to his people in the Old Testament. Even though Saul right away started to face persecution, God protected him and began to use him to keep the gospel witness growing; thus, the church continued to be built up. This Saul, whose name was soon changed to Paul, would play a key part in building the church of Jesus Christ during this time.

PETER AND CORNELIUS

Another key development happened soon after Saul's conversion—God made it clear that Gentiles were now included in his saving work in the world. Even Peter, it seems, had not yet fully grasped this important reality. So God decided to show him in two ways—through a vision and through a direct experience with Gentile faith in Jesus.

READ!

Read Acts 10—the account of Peter's vision from God and his visit to the house of the Gentile centurion Cornelius.

As you know, Peter had been faithfully bearing witness to Jesus Christ to the Jewish people in Jerusalem; many had been converted. But as we see from Acts 10, God had an important lesson for Peter to learn.

The vision. It all began with Peter on a roof, waiting for dinner. He fell into a kind of "trance" (Acts 10:10), and God put a vision before him. A sheet came down from heaven, full of animals that were "unclean" by the standards of the law of Moses. Peter heard a voice telling him to "kill and eat" these unclean animals (v. 13). Peter refused, but the voice continued to tell him that God had made these things clean. Peter did not understand the vision, but he soon would.

The lesson. As Peter was pondering the meaning of this vision, some men arrived from Cornelius—a Roman centurion—asking Peter to go with them to their master's house. Cornelius was a Gentile, but he was a faithful and godly man who wanted to know more about the gospel of Jesus Christ because of a vision he had seen. Peter went with these men, in obedience to the urging of God.

When he arrived, Peter finally realized the meaning of his vision. Cornelius, a Gentile, was not part of the covenant family of Abraham by blood, but he nevertheless wanted to be saved through faith in Jesus Christ. Peter began to understand that God was teaching him a foundational lesson about the gospel: faith in Jesus is available to all people as a gift of God's Holy Spirit. It is not only for the Jews; Jesus truly came to save *all* people who repent of their sins and trust him as Lord and Savior. This would change everything for Peter.

The faith of Cornelius. In the presence of Peter, Cornelius and the people of his house received the Holy Spirit and came to full faith in Jesus Christ (Acts 10:44). By this faith, these Gentiles were fully included in the people of God. Peter went away with a powerful and important message to share with the Jewish believers in Jesus: even Gentiles could now be accepted into God's family if they would follow and believe in Jesus.

We do not have a difficult time accepting this, but the Jews in Peter's day certainly did. You see, Cornelius was not a follower of the law of Moses. He was not from the Jewish context; he was an "outsider." Jewish believers would have been amazed to be told that Cornelius did not need to become Jewish to be saved, and that the Holy Spirit would come to him simply as he put his faith in Jesus Christ—the Lord of all people.

The blessing to the nations. In this moment, we see most clearly (so far) how God's great promise to Abraham from hundreds of years earlier was going to be fulfilled. God had promised Abraham that his descendants would bring his blessing to all the peoples of the earth. Finally, through the gospel of God's own Son, the Gentiles were receiving the blessing of faith that comes through the Jewish Messiah, Jesus Christ.

PAUL IN ATHENS

Not long after God taught Peter about the availability of his salvation to all people—including Gentiles—we see the apostle Paul (whom Jesus had identified as his "instrument" for gospel proclamation to the *Gentiles*, Acts 9:15) sharing the gospel and preaching the message of Jesus Christ clearly in a very Gentile context. As you read about his message to the people of Athens in Acts 17, you will see the strategy that Paul used as he spoke about Jesus in a very different context than Jerusalem.

📖 READ!

Read Acts 17:16–34—the account of Paul in the "Areopagus" in the great ancient city of Athens.

Athens was full of many kinds of peoples and religions. In Acts 17, we see how the gospel went forward—with mixed results—in such a place.

The Areopagus. First, we should understand the context into which Paul was speaking in this passage. The Areopagus was an ancient gathering place in the great global city of Athens, Greece. It was a place where new religious, political, and ethical ideas were exchanged. Philosophers, poets, and religious leaders spent endless hours debating one another in this context, and it was probably a great source of entertainment for the people of the city (in a day before movies, computers, and other modern forms of entertainment). The apostle Paul stepped into this context to tell the message of the gospel of Jesus Christ.

The audience. Paul's audience in Athens was a largely Gentile one. The city was full of idols to many different gods, and the people there very likely had no real connection with—or knowledge of—the story of the Old Testament and of God's work in the lives of the Jewish people. They were religious, but not regarding the God of the Bible—the true God of the universe.

Paul's approach. Considering Paul's context and audience, it is not surprising that he started in a slightly different place than Stephen and Peter did in their sermons to the Jewish people. In this, Paul is a wonderful example to us of a bold witness for Jesus in a context that is very far from faith in Jesus Christ and even acquaintance with the Bible. What did he do?

- First, Paul began where the people were. He looked around the city and saw many different gods and idols that the people worshiped. One of these idols was a statue to "the unknown god" (Acts 17:23). Paul used this as a launching point to tell his hearers about the great Creator God, whom they had not yet come to know.
- Second, Paul started with creation to establish the fact that the God he proclaimed has all power and authority over the human beings he has made. He did not talk about Old Testament prophecies and promises because he was speaking to people who were not familiar with the stories of Abraham, Isaac, Jacob, and David.
- Third, Paul landed on Jesus as the *Judge* of the world (Acts 17:31)—a fact that Paul said was proved by his powerful resurrection from the dead. Paul wanted to establish for the people of Athens that God would no longer overlook their ignorance and their worship of idols. He had sent his own Son into the world, and now he commanded all people to respond to him in faith.

As you can see, Paul made his way to Jesus in this message in Athens. But he got there in a different way than Peter did at Pentecost (Acts 2). Unlike Peter, Paul was speaking to Gentiles. Still, they too could turn to Jesus in faith, even though they did not have the history of the Jewish people or information about the prophets of the Old Testament.

Mixed results. It is instructive for us that even the great apostle Paul met with mixed results in Athens. Acts 17 tells us that some people joined him and believed the message of Jesus that he was proclaiming;

that shows us that God did his work of conversion in the hearts of a few. But many laughed at Paul when he spoke of the resurrection of Jesus Christ. Some were willing to hear him talk more about this subject, but they were not yet at the point of personally believing in Jesus Christ. Such mixed results often seem to be the outcome when the gospel is proclaimed because God gives the gift of faith as he chooses.

THE LOCAL CHURCH

Now we need to take a step back and focus a bit more broadly on how this gospel explosion led to the formation of local churches in towns and cities. We will also explore what this meant for God's plan in the world—even down to our own time—and how this should help us understand our place in God's continuing story even now.

READ!

Read Acts 20:17–38—the account of Paul's final speech to the elders of the church in Ephesus.

Paul was moving closer to some of the trials and legal troubles that would bring him, finally, to imprisonment for the gospel in Rome. As he headed for Jerusalem, though, he called the elders of the church in Ephesus to come to him so that he could give them a farewell address. This was the last time that he would see these leaders, and it is a great gift that this speech is recorded for us in Scripture. Let's think through what this passage teaches us about the church of God, as well as our upcoming study on the New Testament Epistles.

Local churches. From the simple fact that Paul could call together a group of elders from the "church" at Ephesus, we can gather that the immediate effect of the spread of the gospel and the conversion of many people across Asia Minor was the formation of local churches in every city and/or town where there were believers in Jesus. The result of the ministry of the apostles was that local gatherings—probably meeting in homes—sprang up in places like Ephesus, Corinth, Thessalonica, and Philippi. People in these towns began to gather regularly for corporate worship—the teaching of God's word, the singing of praise, the celebration of the Lord's Supper, and times of prayer to God. By the time of Acts 20, we see—just as the apostles had directed—that these churches were ruled by elders who could govern well.

God's surprising plan. As we consider the reality of local churches springing up in the towns that had been reached by the apostles, we begin to see God's surprising plan for the growth and health of his gospel in the world. How would God make the message of salvation through Jesus go forward in his world? How would he protect and guard this gospel, and pass it on from generation to generation? God would do it through his church! Yes, this means the universal church—the gathering of all believers. But this plan is worked out practically in local churches in imperfect places such as Ephesus. It was God's plan to make his gospel go forward in the world through his people, gathered locally for worship and proclaiming the glories of Jesus Christ to all the nations. Even now, God is focused on doing his saving work in the world through the ministry and worship of his church.

Paul and the Epistles. In Paul's farewell address to the Ephesian elders in Acts 20, we begin to see a hint of what would make up most of the rest of the New Testament. Paul's words to the leaders of this young local church focused on the ways that he had faithfully led and served God's people, and the call to them to lead God's people well in the same way. He used his ministry as an example for the leaders of the Ephesus church to follow; spoke of his plans for gospel proclamation and witness; warned them about false teaching that might damage the witness of the gospel; and told them to be concerned with the gospel, not material possessions. All of these themes are further developed by Paul and other apostles in the Epistles to the churches. We will study several of these Epistles in the next chapter.

CHAPTER 13

THE END OF PAUL'S LIFE AND MINISTRY

Paul came to the end of his life and ministry in the great city of Rome, where he was a prisoner for the gospel. But even though Paul's life was over, the vibrant life and influence of the church of Jesus Christ in the world was just beginning.

READ!

Read Acts 27–28—the account of Paul's journey to Rome and house arrest there, and his faithful gospel witness through every part of his journey and imprisonment.

In the passages you just read, Paul was headed to Rome. The great apostle eventually would die there while under house arrest. We do not have a record of Paul's death in the Bible, but tradition has it that he was killed during a great persecution against Christians—probably while he was still a prisoner for the gospel. So ended the life of one of God's great servants—a man who was responsible, by God's grace and power, for the spread of the gospel in marvelous ways across the ancient world. Let's make a few observations about Paul's final days and then think about how we will continue to see his influence on Christ's church through his writings as we continue to work our way through God's big story.

Paul's final days. Even as Paul journeyed toward Rome as a prisoner, God used him to work in remarkable ways for his glory and honor. Paul was involved in a shipwreck, and the men of the ship were stranded on an island called Malta. While there, Paul survived a deadly snakebite and was enabled by God to heal a leading man from the town where they stayed. God used Paul in powerful ways even during his imprisonment.

While in Rome, Paul was guarded, but he had a certain amount of freedom; for example, he stayed by himself—something that was not allowed for all prisoners (Acts 28:16). He lived at his own expense, talked with many people, and continued to share the gospel of Jesus Christ "with all boldness and without hindrance" (v. 31).

Paul's faithful witness. The final verse of Acts shows us the faithful witness of the apostle Paul—even to the very end of his life. Here was a man who had been powerfully converted through a confrontation with the risen Lord Jesus, and had received a call to proclaim the gospel in all the world. Paul was not a perfect man, of course, but he was a faithful man; he never strayed from the gospel call that Jesus Christ had committed to him. Our final glimpses of Paul show him teaching about Jesus to the local Jewish leaders in Rome and welcoming people to his house (or prison cell) as he continued to bear bold witness to the salvation that comes only through the Lord Jesus Christ. We can only assume that Paul continued in these patterns and behaviors until he was finally put to death in Rome.

Paul's continuing influence. Even as Paul's life ended, the life of the church of Jesus Christ was only beginning. The church would continue to grow and flourish, even amid persecution, which was sometimes extremely intense and brutal under the rule of the Roman Empire. Christians were imprisoned, executed, and even thrown to the lions and killed for sport in the great Roman Colosseum. Throughout this persecution, though, God was faithful to his growing church and allowed his gospel to go forth in great power.

Even after his death, Paul continued to have great influence in the life of the church of Jesus Christ through the many epistles that he wrote under the inspiration of the Holy Spirit. In the next chapter, we will turn to some general summaries of a few of these epistles written by Paul, as well as some written by other apostles who were called and commissioned by God.

REVIEW

After Jesus's ascension to heaven, the Holy Spirit worked powerfully in gathering believers together, empowering the apostles to preach the gospel, and causing the message of Jesus to go forward and spread with power—from Jerusalem to Judea, Samaria, and the ends of the earth!

Believers in Jesus began to gather together in their local communities to worship, hear God's word, and proclaim the gospel. The New Testament church had begun.

▲ PRAY!

As you end this chapter with prayer, give praise to God for what he did in the life of the early church. Thank him for making his salvation available to all people—Jews and Gentiles—so that it has now even come to you. Thank him that you, through repentance of sin and faith in his Son, Jesus Christ, can now be a part of his people and his saving work in the world.

Chapter 14

GOD'S CHURCH
PART 2

The historical accounts of the early days of the church of Jesus Christ, recorded for us in the book of Acts, are a truly thrilling chronicle of the way in which Jesus began to use his disciples as witnesses to his life, death, and resurrection—the full message of the salvation of God. Led by apostles such as Peter and Paul, the disciples spread the gospel outward from Jerusalem to Judea, Samaria, and "the end of the earth" (Acts 1:8), establishing local churches wherever they went.

We explored this explosive growth of the good news in the last chapter as we began to consider a new scene of the Bible story: "God's Church." In this chapter, we will continue to study this scene by focusing on the Epistles—the letters that the apostles sent to the churches they established to instruct God's people more fully in the gospel of Jesus Christ and give guidance to the church leaders as they shepherded the people during those early days. These Epistles, as we know and believe, were written by men, but they were inspired by the Holy Spirit of God. They are therefore authoritative and powerful for our lives today as we also follow Jesus as part of God's church.

Remember!

Your suggested memory verses for this chapter come from the book of Romans—a passage that some have called the very center of the entire Bible.

But now the righteousness of God has been manifested apart from the law, although the Law and the Prophets bear witness to it—the righteousness of God through faith in Jesus Christ for all who believe. For there is no distinction: for all have sinned and fall short of the glory of God, and are justified by his grace as a gift, through the redemption that is in Christ Jesus, whom God put forward as a propitiation by his blood, to be received by faith. This was to show God's righteousness, because in his divine forbearance he had passed over former sins. It was to show his righteousness at the present time, so that he might be just and the justifier of the one who has faith in Jesus. (Rom. 3:21–26)

GALATIANS

As we study the Epistles, we will cover one entire letter at a time. Obviously this quick pace will not allow us to study every chapter and verse of every New Testament Epistle; you can get that level of detail in a Bible study or church sermon series. My goal is simply to give you a general sense of the main themes and purposes of some of the letters that God inspired the apostles to write to the early church. We will begin with Paul's epistle to the Galatians.

READ!

Read Galatians 1 and 3—two chapters that will give you a good overall feel for the main point that Paul is making to the Galatian church in this epistle.

Galatians is a short but powerful book. What are the key points we should know about it?

Context. It does not take long (as you saw from Gal. 1:6–9) to identify the problem in the Galatian church that Paul writes to address. It seems that some people—probably legalistic Jews—had come into the church and were preaching a "different gospel" (v. 6) than Paul had preached to these people. They were telling them that, while their faith in Jesus was good, they needed to follow Jewish laws and customs to really be in good favor and a good relationship with God. It seems that this kind of teaching was having a powerful effect on the Galatian believers—many of whom were probably Gentiles.

Paul was obviously filled with righteous anger at this kind of teaching. He uses strong language to denounce these false teachers (see Gal. 1:8–9), but also goes after the Galatian believers for falling prey to this false teaching (3:1–6). His entire letter is focused on correcting the false teaching that had permeated this church and bringing the people back to the true gospel of Jesus Christ.

Main theme. What is the true gospel of Jesus Christ ultimately about, according to Paul? It is certainly not about faith in Jesus Christ *plus* careful adherence to all the laws and customs of Judaism! Paul calls the Galatian believers back to the simplicity of the gospel message that he had preached to them: salvation comes by the grace of God through faith in Jesus *alone.* That means salvation is apart from human works.

Paul argues this from the Old Testament. In Galatians 3, which you read, he references Abraham, whom he calls "the man of faith" (v. 9). Paul reminds the Galatian believers that Abraham was justified not by works but by his belief in God; this was "counted to him as righteousness" (v. 6). His main point is to help the Galatian believers see the true nature of faith and the true message of the gospel of grace in Jesus Christ. He does not want them to be deceived and to fall back into a legalistic, "earning" view of their salvation.

Importance for the church. This message of the book of Galatians was important in Paul's day, as some Jewish leaders had infiltrated the church and filled the Gentile believers with false guilt for not keeping all the customs of the Jews. Paul needed to correct this thinking and bring the deceived people back to the core of the gospel.

This message is important for the church today as well. There is a temptation in every age to make salvation a matter of faith in Jesus *plus* something else. We human beings are naturally prone to want to earn our salvation with God, so we easily fall into the idea that we can somehow "work" to earn his favor. In every age of the church, Paul's message in the book of Galatians has helpfully reminded sinners that they can be justified before the holy God only by faith in his Son Jesus, and through the grace that comes through that faith. No one can earn his or her way into favor with God; that favor is provided to people who have faith in the one who died on a cross to save sinners.

PHILIPPIANS

The epistle to the Philippians is another letter that was written by the apostle Paul. He wrote to the church at Philippi to encourage the Christians there and to challenge them to keep growing in their faith in Jesus Christ.

READ!

Read Philippians 1–2—the first two chapters of this beautiful epistle.

The church at Philippi was fairly healthy—at least as far as we can tell. Paul begins his letter to this church by encouraging the believers, and even thanking them for their "partnership in the gospel" with him (Phil. 1:5). It seems that one of Paul's purposes in writing is to thank the Philippians for a generous gift (probably financial) that they had given him to help him in gospel ministry. The church at Philippi was a church that believed the gospel and had chosen to support Paul as a minister of Jesus Christ.

Yet despite the health of the church at Philippi, Paul saw a few specific areas for growth. These emerge from some of the calls that he gave to the Philippians in this letter. Let's consider some of the ways in which Paul pushed this healthy church to keep on growing.

Joy. If you were to read the entire book of Philippians, you might notice that, again and again, Paul calls the Philippian believers to "rejoice" in the Lord. It seems that they needed to be reminded to choose gospel joy. This, it seems, is part of the reason for Paul's explanation to them of how his imprisonment has served the purpose of the advance of the gospel in the world. They have been discouraged by the fact that Paul has been imprisoned, but Paul wants them to keep their joy, so he tells them that his imprisonment has actually helped him share the gospel with even more power and boldness (Phil. 1:12–14). Paul needs to remind the Philippian believers not to attach their joy to changing circumstances, but to find it in Jesus Christ and the advance of his gospel in their world.

Unity. Read Philippians 2:1–4 one more time and think about why Paul might have needed to offer these words to the church at Philippi. Then look ahead to 4:2–3, where you can see a specific example of the problem that Paul has identified in this church. What is the problem? There seems to be, at least in some pockets of the church, a lack of full gospel unity between believers. Paul goes as far as to call out two women by name in order to encourage them to "agree" in the Lord (4:2). This is why Paul spends time, in 2:1–11, calling for unity in Christ and then reminding the people about the humble example of Jesus Christ. He ultimately put his interests behind those of God's people as he laid down his life in sacrifice for them. God's people should not engage in petty fights and arguments with one another but should seek to think of others as "more significant" (2:3) than themselves, agreeing in the Lord and seeking unity in the gospel of Jesus Christ. The Philippians seem to have had some room for growth in this area.

Growth. Finally, glance over Philippians 3:12–17 and consider why Paul might have spent time explaining to this church his own continual pursuit of Jesus Christ. Paul, the great apostle, says in this passage that *he* is not done growing; instead, he is constantly straining onward and seeking to become more like Jesus and know him more and more. Why might Paul need to encourage the Philippian believers in this way? Perhaps it is because, while they are healthy, they have lost their desire and drive toward spiritual growth. Paul longs to remind this healthy church to not "rest" spiritually but to keep pressing forward to know Jesus more and to make him known in the world. Sometimes even the healthiest churches and Christians need to be reminded that they must keep on growing in their faith.

ROMANS

The book of Romans has been called the greatest theological "treatise" that Paul ever wrote. It is true that this epistle is Paul's most extensive meditation on the meaning of the death of Jesus Christ, the relation of God's salvation to the promises of the Old Testament, and the meaning of the gospel for the faith of both Jews and Gentiles. All of that means that Romans contains the most systematic explanation of the full gospel of Jesus Christ that we have in the Bible.

Yet as we will see, this epistle was written to a specific group of people—believers in Rome. Paul was not writing a theology book (although Romans contains rich and beautiful theology) but a letter to people in a local church as he continued to pursue his gospel ministry as a servant of Jesus Christ.

READ!

Read Romans 1–3, which will give you a sense of the way in which Paul begins this grand epistle. These chapters include one of the most beautiful and clear summaries of the gospel in all of Scripture (Rom. 3:21–26).

As I mentioned above, the letter to the Romans was not meant as a theology book. It was a real letter from Paul to Christians in Rome with a specific purpose. Let's try to get a basic picture of the context for this amazing letter, as well as its purposes and its main themes.

Context. At the time Paul wrote this epistle, the church at Rome may have been more like a collection of house churches meeting all over the city for the worship of Jesus Christ. Most likely, this was a mixed church, made up of Jewish and Gentile believers. It would not have been surprising if there had been some occasional struggles between the Jews and Gentiles, and Paul carefully addresses relations between these two groups in parts of his letter.

Purposes. One of Paul's purposes for writing this letter seems to have been to clearly explain the gospel. But there was a more practical reason he wrote it. He says he wants to come to see the Christians in Rome (Rom. 1:11–15) and use the city as a kind of launchpad for his continuing gospel ministry to Spain (15:24, 28). So Paul writes to encourage them with the truth of the gospel, but also to tell them to get ready for his coming and to support him as he moves on from there into other nations of the world with the gospel message.

That points us to what seems to be a related purpose for this letter. Some common themes and phrases show up in Paul's introduction to Romans (1:1–5) and his conclusion (16:25–27). One of the themes that Paul uses to "bookend" this epistle is the idea of the gospel of Jesus Christ bringing about the "obedience of faith" for "all nations" (1:5; 16:26). Paul is making the argument that because of the truth of the gospel of Jesus Christ, it must be taken to all nations. Paul wants the Romans to understand the importance of people everywhere hearing about Jesus and "obeying" the gospel by putting their faith in him and following him completely. In other words, Romans can be understood as a defense or explanation of Paul's global gospel ministry—to Gentiles as well as Jews.

Themes. In the chapters that you read, you saw one of the major themes of the epistle to the Romans. In Romans 1:1–3:20, Paul very carefully makes the point that all human beings are under the just and righteous wrath of God because of sin. Everyone deserves hell and judgment, and no one can stand as righteous before God—even by an attempt to keep God's law. Because of this, God also has a kind of "problem." How can he remain perfectly *just* to punish sin and also show *grace* to sinners, who cannot be saved by their own works? The beautiful answer, as you saw so clearly in Romans 3:21–26 (your memory verses for this chapter), is the cross of Jesus Christ. At the cross, God poured out his righteous and just wrath against sin by putting it on his own Son. That means that God also showed grace to helpless and hopeless sinners at the cross. The *cross* is the answer to how God can be both "just and the justifier" (3:26). In other words, one of Paul's central themes is the utter *righteousness* of God—in both judgment and salvation.

Paul discusses many other topics in this grand epistle; it is a long one. You should study this letter on your own in more detail than we are able to do now. If you do, you will find Paul also discussing the themes of:

- Being led by the law of the *Spirit* as Christians
- God's purpose for the *Jewish* people and the grafting in of *Gentiles*
- The *groaning* of the earth and of God's people as they wait for his final victory and salvation
- A Christian approach to *government*

This is an epistle that can be studied for a lifetime. It was a gift to the early Christians at Rome, and it is a great gift to God's people today as they continue to seek to follow Jesus Christ in everything.

1 CORINTHIANS

Do you remember how we characterized the church at Philippi when we considered it earlier in this chapter? We said it was a church that was fairly healthy. The Philippians were not perfect; they had areas for growth, as identified by the apostle Paul. But Paul seemed pleased with the life and faith of the church at Philippi, and he was especially grateful for the people's very tangible partnership with him in the gospel.

The church at Corinth, sadly, was a very different story. As you study the epistle of 1 Corinthians now, you are going to learn what Paul wrote to a church that could not be rightly described as healthy. The church at Corinth was full of problems, and Paul had his work cut out for him as he called the Corinthian believers to repentance, growth, and maturity.

READ!

Read 1 Corinthians 1–3 and 5–6.

We will start by considering the context of Paul's letter to this early church of Jesus Christ, then look at the many issues that troubled this church. Paul had a lot of things to address, which is part of the reason why this is such a long letter.

Context. The ancient city of Corinth was, by all accounts, a deeply sinful place—full of partying and all kinds of perversion and corruption. In fact, there is evidence that the term *Corinthian* came to be used almost as a synonym for a person who was sexually immoral and sinful! Considering this kind of context, it is perhaps not surprising that God's people in the church at Corinth seemed to struggle to stay separate from the world in which they lived. We will see in some detail what this struggle looked like.

A gifted, yet immature, church. Paul begins his letter by commending the Corinthians for their amazing spiritual gifts, which had come graciously from God. Paul even goes so far as to say that the Corinthians are "not lacking" in any spiritual gift (1 Cor. 1:7). They spoke in tongues, had great knowledge about the things of God, and had many skilled teachers and leaders for the people. This was truly a gifted church.

Sadly, while the church at Corinth was richly gifted, it was far from being a mature church. In just the chapters you read earlier, you were exposed to some of the glaring issues and problems in this early church:

- Divisions. It seems that one major problem in the church body was the existence of factions. The people had begun to line up behind different Christian leaders with whom they identified most closely (see 1 Cor. 3:4). These divisions were causing fights and quarrels as people began to identify more with their favorite leaders than unite behind Jesus Christ himself.
- Sexual immorality. First Corinthians 5 tells us of a disgusting sexual relationship that existed in the church between a man and his stepmother. The worst part about this was that the church body had done nothing about this. In fact, the Corinthian believers were "arrogant" about it (v. 2)! Perhaps they saw this acceptance as a mark of being "progressive" or "tolerant." Either way, Paul was furious that the church was allowing this kind of blatant sexual sin to go on without any confrontation or call to repentance.
- Lawsuits. Paul even mentions instances of believers in the church taking one another to court (1 Cor. 6:1–8). This, according to Paul, was not how followers of Jesus Christ should handle disputes. It hurt their witness to Jesus Christ and put secular rulers over them when they should have been able to find a path toward agreement in the Lord.

All in all, Paul saw this congregation as incredibly immature. In 1 Corinthians 13 (which you can read if you have extra time), he references several of the problems for which he has rebuked the Corinthians and shows them how they are not fulfilling the greatest gift and greatest sign of maturity: *loving* one another!

Paul's solution. Paul's ultimate solution for the church at Corinth was to remember the centrality of the gospel of Jesus Christ. It is Jesus who brings true unity, so Jesus would help the Corinthians love one another with mature love (and not simply gifts). In 1 Corinthians 2, which you read, Paul reminds the Corinthians of the centrality and simplicity of the message that he brought to them. He preached "Christ and him crucified" (v. 2), and he did it without an appearance of wisdom or a desire to look impressive in the eyes of the world. True maturity for this gifted and troubled congregation would come when the people returned to the power of the gospel. Unity, holiness, and love would come from submitting in repentance and humility to the rule of Jesus Christ.

PAUL AND TIMOTHY

Let's now look together at one more letter that was written by the apostle Paul. The book of 2 Timothy was written not to a church but to a person—to young Timothy, a pastor. This makes it a very different kind of epistle; it is one of the so-called "Pastoral Epistles."

As you read Paul's final charge and appeal to this young pastor, think about how Paul's legacy and training of this young man has had ripple effects even down to our present day. It will become obvious very quickly that Paul wanted to ensure that the gospel of Jesus Christ was faithfully communicated and passed on from generation to generation. So he decided to entrust this glorious gospel to Timothy, among others.

READ!

Read 2 Timothy—the entire book.

Second Timothy is the only one of the Pastoral Epistles that we'll discuss in this book. *Pastoral Epistles*, as you can probably guess, is a term for epistles that were written to pastors (two epistles to Timothy and one to Titus). Paul wrote these letters to young leaders of the emerging churches to instruct them in leadership of the church and to remind them how to be faithful to the gospel of Jesus Christ. These letters touch on many things—from church government to the role of women in the church to the constant battles with false teachers and heretical doctrines. However, in our study of 2 Timothy, our focus will be on the big picture—the purpose of this epistle from Paul to Timothy. To put it quite simply, this letter is all about gospel "legacy."

Timothy's situation. Timothy most likely was serving as what we would now call the pastor of the ancient church at Ephesus. He was young, and he seems to have been prone, at least in some ways, to timidity and shyness (in his other letter to Timothy, Paul tells him to not let anyone look down on him because he is young; 1 Tim. 4:12). Timothy had been by Paul's side; Paul mentions him as a faithful friend and colaborer in the gospel with him. He had learned from the aging apostle and gathered everything he could from his example as a faithful preacher of God's word.

Now, though, Paul had come to the end of his life. The words that we have in 2 Timothy are probably some of the final words that Paul ever wrote. His goal, in this epistle, was to pass on to Timothy the most important things for his future years of gospel ministry. What did he choose to focus on in this letter to the young man whom he had loved and trained so well?

Paul's focus. Paul's focus, not surprisingly, is on the gospel of Jesus Christ. In 2 Timothy 1:14, which you read, Paul calls Timothy to "guard the good deposit entrusted to you"—the gospel word that had been given to him. As Timothy carried on the work of God in the world— even long after Paul was gone—he needed to teach and defend the true gospel of Jesus Christ.

How would Timothy do this? How would he "guard the good deposit" as a faithful pastor to God's people, the church? He would do it by committing to faithfully and consistently teaching them the Bible— repeatedly. This is Paul's final and famous call as he closes this epistle: "Preach the word" (2 Tim. 4:2). The apostle wants his young protégée to stay faithful in explaining God's word to God's people so that many more people will know and believe the gospel.

A gospel legacy. It is important that we have this letter because it is really all about Paul's legacy. You see, there were a limited number of apostles—people who had seen the risen Christ and who had been specifically commissioned by Jesus to lead and establish his early church. Timothy was not an apostle like Paul.

Even so, the apostles left a legacy of teaching the word and proclaiming the gospel to the generations of faithful men and women who followed them. Timothy may not have been an apostle, but he carried on the tradition of the apostolic teaching—the message of the good news of the death and resurrection of Jesus Christ.

Even today, every time the Bible is preached and Jesus is proclaimed in Christian churches, the apostolic legacy continues in the world. What Paul passed on to Timothy has been passed on from generation to generation. Today, you are hearing about the good news of Jesus Christ because men like Timothy faithfully carried on the proclamation of the gospel that Paul and the other apostles shared so boldly—and died for.

JOHN'S EPISTLES

I hope you can see that the apostle Paul had an incredible impact and influence on the church of Jesus Christ through the letters that God inspired him to write to his people. Paul's letters began to circulate through the early churches, and it quickly became evident that they were part of the inspired word of God—part of God's great story, which had begun in the Old Testament and was continuing in the life of the church of Jesus Christ. As always, God had not left his people in the dark. Instead, he had given them his good word to guide them as they followed his Son.

But Paul was not the only apostle whom God inspired to write letters to his people. There were other men whom God used to give his good word to his church during the early days of the church. One of these men was the apostle John—the disciple of Jesus who also wrote the Gospel of John. He wrote three letters that are now part of our New Testament. We will do a general overview of the first of these letters in order to see what role it had in the early church.

READ!

Read 1 John 1–2, which will give you a good general feel for this epistle.

As you were probably able to tell from your reading, John had a different writing style than the apostle Paul. Of course, he also wrote with different concerns. It is a gift of God that we have letters from both John and Paul—as well as Peter (whose letters we will discuss next).

So what can we gather from this first epistle that the apostle John wrote to God's people during the early church days?

Audience. First, it seems as if John was writing to people who were quite familiar with Jesus Christ and the message of the gospel. John often refers to his audience as "my little children" and "beloved"—terms of affection and endearment that imply that he knew them well and was confident of their faith. John, then, was writing to people who were part of the community of the church and were seeking to live out vibrant faith in Jesus in real life.

Purpose. While John was confident of the faith of his audience, his writing does have an "edge." He seems to have a concern for even believers in Jesus Christ to be actively "testing" and examining themselves to see whether they really belong to Jesus Christ. John is extremely concerned with true and genuine faith, and he is not afraid to boldly challenge those who claim to be Christians regarding the genuineness of their love for God and their faith in Jesus Christ. First John is, in fact, a very good book to read to do self-examination regarding one's salvation! So how does John call believers to test themselves?

Tests. The first test that John offers to believers takes up much of the two chapters that you read. John makes the simple point that believers in Jesus who truly love him will not continue in *sin*. John does not mean, of course, that believers in Jesus will never commit sins again; we know that because he points to the forgiveness and grace of Jesus Christ (see 1 John 2:1–2). But John is firm in calling believers in Jesus to understand that to continue to "walk" in the darkness of sin while claiming the name of Jesus Christ simply does not work! A changed heart will lead to a changed life.

Second, John offers the *doctrine* test especially to help the believers to whom he writes deal with heresies, false teaching, and even deceitful spirits. How does John instruct Christians to test the doctrine that they hear—and their own faith? He tells them that anyone who "denies that Jesus is the Christ" is not from God (1 John 2:22). Later, in chapter 4, John will also discuss the importance of confessing that Jesus Christ has truly come in the flesh; this is part of the essential doctrine of the Christian church.

Finally, there is the *love* test. John says that people who have believed in God and claim to follow Jesus must bear fruit by really loving one another deeply. John says it about as clearly as he can in 1 John 2:9— that whoever claims to be in the "light" of belief in Jesus yet hates his brother is still in the "darkness" of sin. Christian love is, for John, a huge proof of genuine Christian faith.

So John offers Christians in his time—and now—these tests to check the genuineness of their faith. This is a rich epistle, one that is worth studying in much more detail than we can do here.

PETER'S EPISTLES

Just like John, the apostle Peter had a different way of writing (and some different points of emphasis) than the apostle Paul. God graciously used Peter, too, to bring his good word to his people as the church was growing all over the ancient world.

READ!

Read 1 Peter 1–2.

The very fact that we have two epistles inspired by God's Holy Spirit and written by the apostle Peter is quite amazing. Do you remember what Peter did on the night when Jesus was betrayed and tried by the Jewish leaders? He denied Jesus vehemently three times! He then ran away—weeping with shame because he had betrayed his Lord.

Yet that was not the end for Peter, by the grace of God. Jesus restored him and made him a great leader and pillar in his growing church.

He even used him to give God's powerful word to the church through the two letters that he wrote. What an amazing story and reminder of God's grace. God forgave Peter, restored him, and used him in mighty ways for the glorious gospel of Jesus Christ.

What are the most important points about Peter's first epistle?

Elect exiles. Did you notice how Peter begins his epistle? He addresses it to the "elect exiles" of the dispersion in Asia Minor (1 Pet. 1:1). What does Peter mean by this?

Some biblical scholars have assumed that Peter was referring to literal exiles—people who had been forcibly removed from their homes and taken to live as captives in other places. But the simple fact is that many of the Christians living in the areas that Peter mentions were not "exiles" in this way. Many of them were living in places where they had grown up. There had been a "dispersion" of the Jewish people because of persecution, but many of the places to which Peter wrote were fairly peaceful during his day. So what was Peter talking about?

It is probably best to understand Peter's phrase as referring to people who were, because of faith in Jesus Christ, "spiritual" exiles in the world. In other words, Peter was writing to people who did not really "belong." They no longer fit into the world; it was no longer their home.

It seems, too, that these elect exiles of Jesus Christ—all over Asia Minor—were facing various levels of persecution (this is a big theme in 1 Peter). Mainly, though, this persecution seems to have consisted of verbal abuse and social alienation. There may have been some people to whom Peter wrote who were literally being beaten or imprisoned for their faith, but most likely, most people in his audience were facing just insult and mockery. Peter's words, then, were to "spiritual" exiles who were being mocked and ridiculed in their towns and cities because of their faith in Jesus.

Holiness. One of Peter's central challenges to people living in this kind of situation is the call to *holiness.* Look again at 1 Peter 1:13–17;

Peter's call to holiness for exiles is unmistakable. Peter is not shy about calling believers to honor the Lord Jesus Christ by holy and obedient conduct during the period of "exile," as believers wait for their heavenly home with God.

At first glance, this call may seem to be a bit harsh—especially for people who are suffering as "exiles" and being insulted by friends and neighbors for following Jesus. Yet this is exactly how Peter calls even suffering people to act. He urges them to press on in obedience to God's word—the holy calling they have received. In other words, the fact that they are suffering does not exempt them from the call to holiness; if anything, it causes Peter to issue this call with even more urgency.

Witness. What is the purpose of the holiness of believers in Jesus, according to Peter? Surely it is about obedience to the Savior who has redeemed us from our sins. But for Peter, holy conduct is also all about *witness* to unbelievers. Look again at 1 Peter 2:9–12. Here we see another powerful call to holiness and obedience, this one specifically motivated by the witness such conduct can bring to the Gentiles. God's people are redeemed from sin so that they can proclaim his "excellencies" in the world (v. 9). They pursue holiness and obedience so that those who might be tempted to revile them will be led to "glorify God" when they see their lives of holiness (v. 12).

So Peter writes his letter to God's suffering people, spread out across the ancient world, trying to hold on to faith in Jesus Christ amid mockery and social alienation. He calls them to hold on to their faith, keep pursuing holiness and obedience, and continue shining brightly as witnesses for Jesus in the world.

THE BOOK OF HEBREWS

As we work our way through this brief survey of the New Testament Epistles, I hope you are seeing God's grace to his people during the early days of the church. He did not leave them without instructions; he was not silent as his people learned to follow Jesus and obey his word. God spoke through his apostles—men like Paul, John, and Peter—to give his good word to his people in order to teach them how to be his church in this world.

Now let's do a quick overview of the book of Hebrews. Again, this epistle will have a slightly different feel from the ones we have studied up to this point. You will see the purpose and focal points of this beautiful book, and will also consider what a great gift it is, as we continue to learn to piece together the different parts of the big story of God's saving work in this world.

READ!

Read Hebrews 3–5—just one beautiful section of this epistle that puts forward Jesus as the much better "Moses" and the great high priest whom God's people have always ultimately needed.

The book of Hebrews is a wonderful literary work—one that would reward months, and even years, of diligent study. For our purposes, we will simply seek to identify its overall theme, purpose, and value for God's people today.

General Epistles. Hebrews has been grouped with the letters of James, Peter, John, and Jude as one of the "General Epistles." This simply means that it was written for God's people in general rather than to a specific church or person (such as 2 Timothy, a pastoral epistle from Paul to Timothy). No one knows who wrote the book of Hebrews, but the author was steeped in knowledge of the Old Testament and was passionate about making clear that Jesus Christ was the fulfillment of all of God's promises and prophecies to his people throughout history.

Hebrews and the Old Testament. The book of Hebrews, perhaps more than any other book in the New Testament, gives us an expansive look at how not only prophecies but also events and practices from the Old Testament are ultimately fulfilled in the person and work of Jesus

Christ. In fact, some biblical scholars have even described the book of Hebrews as several extended sermons on passages of the Old Testament, sermons designed to show how these passages are perfectly and wonderfully fulfilled in Jesus. Hebrews helps us see many connections between God's work in the past and his work in the present (through his Son) that we might otherwise miss.

The theme of Hebrews. On this note, we probably can summarize the theme of the book of Hebrews as "Jesus is *better*!" That is the declaration of the book's author as he considers many practices, customs, laws, and pictures of the Old Testament. He sees Jesus, God's Son, and all that he did for the salvation of God's people as the infinitely better completion of all the "shadows" of the Old Testament that pointed forward to him. Here are just some of the points that Hebrews makes in relation to this main point:

- Jesus is better than *angels* (chap. 1) because Jesus is not just a "ministering spirit" (v. 14) but the actual Son of God who came to earth in human flesh.
- Jesus is better than *Moses* (chap. 3) because Jesus is a more faithful leader than Moses and has infinitely more glory than he did.
- Jesus is better than the *high priests* of God's people in the Old Testament (chap. 4) because he made a once-for-all sacrifice for the sins of God's people.
- Jesus is better than the *sacrifices* of the Old Testament (chap. 10) because the blood of bulls and goats could never actually take away the sins of God's people.

So as you can see, the author of the book of Hebrews is joyfully proclaiming the perfection and beauty of Jesus Christ. He is the one through whom God is fulfilling his great promises to his people. He is the high priest and the final sacrifice that sinners have always ultimately needed.

The value of Hebrews today. Hebrews, then, is a very important book for us today. Along with Romans, it is probably the best book for helping us "put our Bibles together" as we come to understand how God intended Old Testament practices, laws, and customs to point his people toward the final work of his Son. As Christian churches continue to read and study this epistle today, they can see the fullness of God's work for his people through his Son, and how the entire story of the Bible is really and truly all about him.

THE BOOK OF JUDE

The final New Testament Epistle we will consider is the little letter of Jude—the second to last book in the Bible. You may not be very familiar with this letter, but it is one of the most beautiful and powerful words to God's people in the New Testament. Our goal will be to capture Jude's purpose and main point in writing this letter to the Christians of his day.

READ!

Read Jude—the entire letter (it is just one short chapter).

The little letter from Jude is often overlooked. But it should not be! Jude offered an important call to the Christians of his day—and to followers of Jesus today.

Author. Many people do not realize that Jude, the author of this letter, was the brother of Jesus. He does not overtly identify himself in this way as he writes (probably from humility), but he probably grew up knowing Jesus personally. By the time he wrote this letter, he had come to see himself as a "servant" (Jude 1) of Jesus, recognizing him as the Son of God and the Savior of the world.

Purpose. Jude clearly tells his purpose for writing this letter. You probably noticed that Jude's purpose statement comes in verse 3; he says that he wanted to write about the common salvation that he shares with his audience, but he felt compelled to write instead about the need to "contend" for the gospel.

Jude quickly goes on to explain the reason for this call. Certain people, he says, have crept into the community of God and are enticing others to abandon their faith and pursue sin instead of holiness (v. 4). Considering this, the true gospel of Jesus Christ, and the life of obedience that accompanies it, must be defended and protected (v. 3).

Much of the body of Jude's letter, after this purpose statement, is made up of examples from history of people who turned away from faith in God toward sin, false belief, and the deception of God's people. Jude mentions Cain, Korah, and the cities of Sodom and Gomorrah (among others). His point is to remind God's people that there is a danger—in every age—of turning away from true faith in God into sin and wrong belief. Jude is calling his readers to be on their guard and to hold on to the true gospel of Jesus.

Theme. But there is another theme that pops up in this little letter. Did you notice it? Jude mentions forms of the word *keep* several times. At the beginning, he writes to people who are "kept" for Jesus Christ (v. 1). At the very end of his letter, his benediction is to the God who is able to "keep" his people blameless and without stumbling until the end (v. 24). What do we make of this?

It seems that even as Jude wants to call God's people to "contend" for the faith, he also wants to remind them that, if they really belong to God through faith in Jesus Christ, they are "kept" securely by the God of their salvation. He will never let them go! Jude wants God's people to be ready to fight for the gospel and defend it against sinful attacks. But he also wants Christians to be confident in the God who will contend for them—by keeping their hearts and souls secure until they see him face-to-face.

Jude's letter is a wonderful word of challenge for the church today— we must defend the gospel and contend for the faith that has been passed down to us. But it is also a word of encouragement—the God who has saved us by the grace of his Son will be faithful to keep us from stumbling until the end.

REVIEW

God speaks to his people by divinely inspired letters (epistles) written by the apostles to the early churches. These letters explain and apply the gospel to the lives of God's people, calling them to believe, obey, love one another, bear witness to Jesus, and resist false teaching and heresy. These letters still guide us today as members of churches who follow in the apostolic tradition.

▲ PRAY!

As you close this chapter with prayer, ask God to help you listen better to the epistles as you serve him as a member of Christ's church today. Pray that he would help you to heed the words of his apostles, which he inspired, so that you can grow in the knowledge of him and his grace.

GOD'S ETERNITY
PART 1

We are now ready to explore the final scene of our study of the Bible as one grand story of God's saving work in the world—a work that culminated in the death and resurrection of Jesus Christ, his Son. We can call this scene "God's Eternity." As we dig into this part of the story, we will take some time to remember that we are to see ourselves as a significant part of this story. This is the key to applying all that you are learning about God to your life.

Your place in this story. Throughout this book, we have looked back on God's great work in the world in past generations. We've seen that God was faithful to Abraham, to Moses, to David, and to his people during the days of his Son.

But something happened after the resurrection and ascension of Jesus Christ, and the beginning of the age of the church—*we* entered the story of God's work in the world. With the return of Jesus Christ to heaven, nothing else needed to be accomplished (at a big-picture level) in order for God to bring an end to all things and to start the eternal reign of Jesus with his people. Salvation had been accomplished through his death for sins on the cross and his resurrection from the dead. The gospel was spreading all over the world. We are still in that scene—the scene I called "God's Church"— today!

This means that *you* are a character in the great story of God's work in the world. You are either a follower of Jesus through faith in him or an enemy of God, who has chosen to reject his Son and live in sin and rebellion. There is no middle ground; there are only two kinds of human beings in this story.

Hopefully you have come to see the beauty, love, and wonder of the gospel of Jesus Christ during our study of God's word in this book. I hope you have given your heart to Jesus in faith and that you are living your life as a part of his church, waiting for the final scene of the story to be revealed. This final scene will be our focus in this chapter and the next one.

The final scene of this story. You see, all of God's plan for this world has been accomplished except for one part: the return of Jesus Christ and the final judgment of the world. Jesus has come, sin has been paid for, and Satan has been dealt a death blow (even though he has not yet been finally destroyed). Now God is simply waiting for his perfect time to send his Son back to earth to signal the end of history.

We do not know exactly why God waits or how long he will wait. Peter tells us that God is patient; he waits, in some sense, to give people on earth more time to repent and turn in faith to Jesus Christ (2 Pet. 3:9). The gospel is still spreading, and we know that God desires the message of Jesus to go all over the world (Acts 1:8). So faithful Christians seek to remain faithful to Jesus during these years as we await the final return of the King and Savior, and the end of all things.

In this chapter, we will look back at the way in which many Old Testament passages point forward—even past the first coming of Jesus—to the end of all things. We will see how the prophets gave God's people glimpses of all that would come. We will also see how some of the New Testament Epistles, and even Jesus himself, began to teach God's people about the conclusion of God's story. Then, in the next chapter, we will turn to the book of Revelation, which gives us the fullest picture of the ending of history.

As we live for God in this present age of the church, we look forward to all that he will still do in the future—in the final judgment of the world when Jesus returns, and in the perfect and eternal dwelling where he will reign forever over his people.

Remember!

Your suggested memory verses for this chapter come from the prophet Isaiah, who looked ahead toward a future day of glory for God's people that would come with the victory of God's Messiah.

> *Arise, shine, for your light has come,*
> *and the glory of the LORD has risen upon you.*
> *For behold, darkness shall cover the earth,*
> *and thick darkness the peoples;*
> *but the LORD will arise upon you,*
> *and his glory will be seen upon you.*
> *And nations shall come to your light,*
> *and kings to the brightness of your rising. (Isa. 60:1–3)*

ISAIAH: LOOKING AHEAD

As we begin our survey of what the Bible's prophets and apostles say about the conclusion of God's work in the world, the first passage that we will look at is Isaiah 60—a chapter that looks far beyond the first coming of Jesus Christ to the final glory of God's people into eternity. As you read this passage, you will begin to see how, even in the Old Testament, God was helping his people tune their hearts to hope for his final and perfect work on their behalf, which would last forever and ever.

CHAPTER 15

📖 READ!

Read Isaiah 60—the whole chapter.

As Isaiah looks ahead to the end of the Bible story, what does he show us about what will happen then?

The nations will come. First, Isaiah tells us repeatedly in this chapter that the nations of the world will come in a united way to the worship of the one true God. In Isaiah 60:3, he describes nations coming to the light of God. In verse 5, he describes the "wealth" of the nations flowing into God's place. In verses 10–11, he speaks of the kings of the nations ministering to God's place in a significant way. Finally, in verse 14, Isaiah looks forward to a day when the descendants of the enemies of God's people (those who would take the Israelites into exile) will bow down before God and worship him along with God's people.

Isaiah is telling God's people that, for all eternity, there will be a multiethnic gathering of people that will sing God's praises. His final plan involves bringing all kinds of people to faith in his Son. The eternal experience in heaven will be a great congregation of people from every nation in the world—people who truly acknowledge and worship Jesus Christ the Lord!

Wealth and beauty. Isaiah 60 also deals powerfully with the themes of wealth and beauty, which dominate his description of God's perfect and eternal place for his people. The city and place of God is built up with the "wealth of the nations" (vv. 5, 11) that comes to it. Then, in verse 7, God says that he will "beautify" his house, where he will dwell with his people and they will worship him. What is the point of all these descriptions of wealth, abundance, and beauty as Isaiah looks ahead to this final day?

Isaiah is showing that, long after this earth is destroyed, God will maintain the beauty of a place for his people that is far more glorious than the greatest palace or temple that this world has ever seen. The glory and splendor of the dwelling place of God with his people—heaven—will be great beyond our imagination. Isaiah is again turning the hopes of God's people toward what is to come in the last days.

The presence of God. Finally, Isaiah focuses squarely on the powerful presence of God with his people at the conclusion of the story. Like never before, God will dwell in the midst of his people in all his glory and splendor. The prophet says that the glory of the Lord will be "seen" upon his people (Isa. 60:2). No sun will be needed in this perfect place for God's people because the brilliance of God will shine among them to give them all the light they need (this is a theme that John picks up on as he describes his vision in the book of Revelation). Read verses 19–20 again and notice the amazing descriptions of the brilliance of God dwelling with his people.

As Isaiah describes this brilliant and close dwelling of God with people, he looks forward to a day that we still anticipate. We can be saved and forgiven through Jesus Christ, but we still live in a fallen world. We are still waiting for sin and death to be finally destroyed when Jesus returns so that we can live with God in this kind of closeness, splendor, and glory. That will be a great day!

ZECHARIAH: LOOKING INTO THE FUTURE

Like Isaiah, the prophet Zechariah points God's people forward to the conclusion of God's story, but with a slightly different emphasis. In your reading from Zechariah's prophetic book, you will see him speaking to the postexilic community of God's people in Israel, seeking to encourage the people by looking far ahead to a future day of God's final salvation, judgment, and restoration of his people.

READ!

Read Zechariah 14—the final chapter of this postexilic prophetic book.

You may remember that the prophet Zechariah spoke to people who had returned from the exile and were seeking to rebuild life and worship in Jerusalem after it had been destroyed and the people living there had been forcibly dragged out of their land years before as captives and exiles. The people were discouraged; life was not like it had been under the monarchy, and rebuilding physical structures—and customs and practices of worship—was slow and difficult work.

As Zechariah's prophecy comes to an end, then, he seeks to encourage the people with God's great promise of a day of perfect worship and perfect salvation to come—even though it is still a long way off from his perspective. We read about this promise in Zechariah 14. Here are just a few key observations about the specific hope that Zechariah offers with his words from God.

God's perfect judgment. The first piece of final and eternal hope that Zechariah offers to God's people in this passage is the promise of perfect divine judgment. Zechariah 14:3 describes God going out as a warrior to fight and defeat the nations who have opposed him and attacked and oppressed his people in the world. The promise from God through Zechariah, in other words, is that one day all wrong will truly be set right. Evil people and nations will be judged, and God will bring his perfect justice to all the earth.

God's perfect peace. The next piece of final and eternal hope for God's people that Zechariah offers is the promise of God's perfect peace and security, which will one day come in a lasting way. Zechariah 14:11 shows us the promise that, one day, the great city of God will never again be destroyed, and that Jerusalem (the place for God's people) will dwell in perfect security. This is a promise that God will finally bring lasting peace and safety to his people. They will dwell secure, with him as their God, forever and ever.

God's perfect worship. The final piece of Zechariah's future-looking hope for God's people is the promise of perfect worship. The closing verses of Zechariah 14 point ahead to a glorious future day when the nations of the world will go upward toward Jerusalem (just as living waters have flowed out from Jerusalem; v. 8), where they will go to make sacrifices to God and worship him joyfully and willingly. There will be no more corruption connected to the worship of God (no more traders in the house of the Lord), and every part of the city will be "holy" to God, as all people begin to turn their hearts to worship him with joy and obedience (v. 21). Zechariah looks ahead to a day when God's people will finally experience utterly pure and true worship of God.

Still waiting. As we look at all these great promises of hope that Zechariah offered to God's people, we realize that we are still waiting for the final fulfillment of all of them. God has yet to finally judge evil and set things ultimately right. We are still waiting for him to bring lasting peace and security to his people, who continue to face persecution in many parts of the world today. We are still longing for God to bring perfect worship that will continue unabated for all eternity in his holy place. Zechariah reminded the people in his day what we too need to remember. We are still waiting for these wonderful blessings that will come at the conclusion of God's story!

DANIEL AND THE FUTURE

Isaiah gave God's people a hopeful vision for the future *place* of God's people. This place will be one of glory, splendor, and beauty—a place where God himself will shine as the great light for his people.

Zechariah offered God's people a hopeful vision for the future *worship* of God by his people after God finally judges their enemies and brings peace and security to them.

As you read the words of the prophet Daniel, you will see how he points God's people to another day, far ahead in the future of God's story—the day of God's eternal *judgment* of all the earth.

READ!

Read Daniel 7—a chapter that has many similarities with the final chapters of John's Revelation.

When we look into John's Revelation in the next chapter, you will discover that much of what Daniel sees in the chapter you just read is echoed by John as he records his own vision of the end. This makes sense, as the same God gave both of these visions to these men.

Daniel records all that God showed him about the violence and chaos that will come in the final days of the earth—and about the final judgment of God and the reign of his Son forever. Let's summarize some of the main contributions that Daniel makes to our understanding of the conclusion of the Bible story, to which we still look forward today.

Final struggles. As the chapter begins (Dan. 7:1–8), Daniel records a vision of four beasts that come out of the sea (the sea was often used in Jewish literature as a symbol of sinfulness, violence, and chaos). These beasts, as we discover, are great national powers that wage war on the earth, motivated by a desire for domination and conquest. In the book of Revelation, these beasts are all rolled into one final great beast at the end—one whom we often refer to as the "antichrist." This part of Daniel's vision is showing God's people that, during the last days before Christ's return, we should expect times of great violence, conflict, and sinfully motivated conquest and chaos. World powers will never stop competing and battling until the very end of time.

Final judgment. Ultimately, though, all earthly powers will be silenced. Daniel's next vision is of God himself—the "Ancient of Days"—taking his seat on his throne to judge every human being who has ever lived (Dan. 7:9–12). Here is a picture of the final judgment of the world. "Books" are opened, which probably refers to the exposure of all the deeds that have been done on earth throughout all the ages. God himself—in all his terrifying holiness and glory—judges all humanity in a final way and establishes his judgment and salvation in all the earth forever.

Final reign. After this, Daniel sees something amazing. God himself sets up his Son—the "son of man"—to reign forever with all power, dominion, and authority in all creation (Dan. 7:13–14). This title, Son of Man, becomes linked with the concept of the Messiah—the "anointed one" whom God would send to his people to be their final King and Savior. It is a title that Jesus took up and used to describe himself when he came to earth as God's Son and the Savior of God's people.

Final hope. So what do Daniel's words—spoken from within the time of the exile—tell us today as we continue to wait for the return of Jesus and the end of all things? They remind us to soberly expect times of trouble and conflict in the days and years ahead as world powers continue to compete with one another and battle for control. But they also remind us that we have a hope that looks far past these conflicts, to the day when God himself will judge the earth with perfect justice and holiness. They remind us to look forward to a time when Jesus Christ—the perfect Son of Man—will be lifted up to reign over his true people forever. All who belong to him will rejoice at that day and will reign with him for all eternity.

THE OLD TESTAMENT AND THE RESURRECTION

The Old Testament also points us ahead to another important aspect of the conclusion of God's story, an aspect that is explained much more clearly in the New Testament: *resurrection*. It is true that there is little material in the Old Testament that explicitly lays out how the final resurrection will work. But as you will see in your next reading, there are hints of this reality there.

READ!

Read Psalm 16. Then read Job 19:25–27 and consider Job's words about what seems to be his hope for a future bodily resurrection long after his physical death.

As we have mentioned before, the New Testament is much more explicit in its explanations of the future resurrection of believers than the Old Testament. Passages that we will cover soon will go on to explain how the resurrection will happen and what we should expect and believe about it. However, it is important to recognize that resurrection hope—both for the Messiah and for God's people—was very much alive even in the days of the Old Testament. This is why you just read passages from the Psalms and Job. What can we observe and learn from these passages as we continue to think about how the Old Testament points us to the realities at the end of God's big story?

The hope of Jesus's resurrection. First, Psalm 16 points us strongly to the reality of the resurrection of the Messiah—God's "holy one" (Ps. 16:10), as David calls him. Peter, preaching on this psalm in Jerusalem many years later, pointed the Jewish people to the grave of David, reminding them that he could not have been talking about himself when he said that God's Holy One would not see "corruption" (Acts 2:29–31). David, speaking prophetically, was pointing in this psalm to the eternal resurrected life of God's Messiah—Jesus. Jesus would truly die, but he would rise again from the dead. He would never see corruption because he would rise after three days and live forever as God's great King over his people.

The hope of people's resurrection. In Job, we see the future hope of the resurrection of God's people more specifically. Amid his lament and cries to God, Job stops and remembers his ultimate future hope. He looks far ahead into the future, to a day when his "Redeemer" will stand on the earth (Job 19:25). He believes that long after his "skin has been . . . destroyed," he will nevertheless somehow see God in his "flesh" (v. 26). Job's hope is in the fact that one day God's people also will be raised from the dead. He pictures a day when the great divine King will stand on the earth, and God's people will rise from the dead to see him with their eyes. This is clearly resurrection hope—hope for the renewal of life for God's people at the very end of the great story of redemption.

Real bodily resurrection life. Finally, and more specifically, we should see that both of these passages are referring to true bodily and physical resurrection from the dead. David speaks of a Messiah who will truly not see corruption; the physical life of this Holy One will never end after his resurrection! Job, too, is extremely explicit in his language: his "skin" will one day be destroyed, but he will be raised up to see God in his "flesh." The Old Testament, then, hints at what the New Testament tells us explicitly—God's people have hope that, at the close of history, God will raise them up physically with resurrected bodies. The resurrection will be very real, very tangible, and very physical. This is the Christian hope for the last days, and it is clearly demonstrated for us—at least in glimpses—in the Old Testament Scriptures.

THE NEW TESTAMENT AND ETERNITY

Now let's turn to the witness of the New Testament regarding "God's Eternity"—the conclusion of God's story. We will not dig into the book of Revelation until the next chapter, but there are several other places in the New Testament that have much to tell us about all that will come as this world moves closer to its end.

READ!

Read Matthew 24–25—two chapters, recounting what sometimes is called the "Olivet Discourse," that contain the greatest concentrated amount of teaching from Jesus about the end times.

In his Gospel, Matthew gives us the longest "chunk" of teaching from Jesus about the final chapter of the Bible story. The Gospels tell us that Jesus spoke about heaven, judgment, and eternal life on many occasions, but it was in his Olivet Discourse that he talked about the final days in the most detail.

Jesus obviously wanted his disciples—including us—to be prepared for all that will come as the final days of the world approach. He wanted his people to be ready for his return and to understand that the final judgment is coming. So what can we learn about God's eternity from Jesus's words to his disciples in Matthew 24–25?

Suffering will come. The first theme that strikes us is the great "tribulation" (suffering) that Jesus describes as he looks ahead to the final days of the world. Matthew 24:9–14 details this tribulation of God's people, during which some of them will even be put to death. This time will be full of such intense suffering that some people will even fall away from their faith because of it. Yet through it all, the gospel of the "kingdom" will continue to be proclaimed in all the world, according to the perfect plan of God (v. 14).

Jesus's words connect and agree with what Daniel looked forward to in the passage that we read earlier. They also agree with what John prophesies about as he records his vision in the book of Revelation. Before the end comes, it seems there will be times of suffering, persecution, and hardship on earth. We do not know how extensive this tribulation will be or exactly how long it will last. We should assume, though, that things will get worse in the world before Jesus returns, but that his gospel will continue to go forward with power.

Jesus will return. Twice in the chapters that you read from Matthew, Jesus speaks of his glorious and globally significant return to earth. In Matthew 24:30–31, he speaks of coming in the clouds, accompanied by the trumpet call of the angels. Then, in 25:31, Jesus speaks of coming "in his glory" and sitting on his glorious throne. The picture of his return that Jesus presents to us is one of complete glory, power, and rule over all the earth. He came once as a humble baby to die on a cross for sinners; he will return as the conquering and ruling King and Judge over all creation.

In fact, it is the judgment that will bring Jesus back to earth. He will come to reign over his people forever, but first to judge all the peoples of the earth in a final way. The end of Matthew 25 offers a picture of the final judgment, which will happen before the great throne of God. Those whom Jesus knows will be given the gift of eternal life, and those whom he does not know will be sent away to eternal punishment. Jesus is the King, and he will make the final determination regarding the eternal destiny of every human being.

We must be ready. The main application of Jesus's words, which he keeps repeating to his disciples throughout all his teaching about the final days of the world, is to "stay awake" (Matt. 24:42) and "be ready" (v. 44) for his return. In every age, this application is the same for faithful followers of Jesus. We do not know exactly when all these things will come to pass. We see "birth pains" (v. 8) of the end in every age—wars, natural disasters, famines, and persecution of Christians at varying levels. But God alone knows the timing of all these things that are to come. Our response, as faithful followers of Jesus Christ, is to stay awake in faith—to keep holding on to the truths of God's word and making the hope of the gospel of Jesus Christ known in all the world.

SECOND THESSALONIANS AND THE FINAL JUDGMENT

We have seen that the final days will be ones of chaos, suffering, and persecution. But Jesus will come in the clouds and will judge the world with glory and power as the risen and reigning King of all creation. The call to believers, from Jesus himself, is to stay awake and be ready for his return.

Another portion of the New Testament that offers insights about the conclusion of God's story is the little letter of 2 Thessalonians. Paul wrote this epistle to an early church that was struggling with how to think about the end times. As we will see, some of the believers in this church thought that they might have missed the return of Jesus Christ. Paul wrote to correct their thinking and to help them understand a terrible figure who will come in opposition to the gospel. As we will see, though, God will not leave his people without hope!

READ!

Read 2 Thessalonians 2—a chapter in which Paul deals with the character of the "man of lawlessness," whom he obviously wants the Thessalonian believers to understand and anticipate.

In the opening verses of the chapter that you just read, we see what was happening in the ancient church at Thessalonica when Paul wrote to the believers there. It seems that some people had become worried that the "day of the Lord" (2 Thess. 2:2)—the return of Jesus and the beginning of God's eternity—had already come. The believers in this church were concerned that they had somehow missed the return of Jesus and had been left out of it.

Paul writes this part of his letter to reassure the believers in this city that certain things need to happen before Jesus will return and eternity will begin. One of these things is the coming of a figure whom Paul calls the man of lawlessness (2 Thess. 2:3).

What are some things we learn about God's eternity through Paul's teaching in this chapter of this letter?

God's gospel will be violently opposed. First, we learn generally that God and his people will be attacked, opposed, and battled in essentially every way until the return of Jesus Christ. Paul describes what is coming as a "rebellion" (2 Thess. 2:3), which will be led by the man of lawlessness that he goes on to describe. This passage connects with what Jesus says in Matthew 24–25 and with what John sees in his Revelation. The witness of all of Scripture agrees on this point. Until the very end—and probably with increasing intensity—the true gospel of Jesus Christ will be opposed by the evil forces of this world and by Satan himself.

Satan will seek to deceive the world. Second, we see that the role of Satan (the one who ultimately stands behind the man of lawlessness) is to deceive the world and make people worship something other than the Lord Jesus Christ. This figure that Paul speaks of will sit in God's temple and proclaim himself to be God (2 Thess. 2:4). Whatever the rule or reign of this man of lawlessness will look like, it seems that it will have at least some aspect of worship to it. He will attempt to draw the worship of the world toward him—and away from Jesus Christ.

Most people who study this passage equate this figure with the "beast" (also called the antichrist), whom John describes in Revelation 13—a passage that we will discuss in the next chapter. This is right!

Whether the man of lawlessness—the antichrist—will be just one man or a series of world leaders, the influence he will wield clearly will be that of Satan himself, who will raise up this great figure to deceive people and lead them away from the true faith of the gospel of Jesus Christ.

Believers in Jesus can—and must—stand firm. Finally, even though the figure that Paul describes in this passage is frightening, it is important to notice that God will not leave followers of Jesus without hope. Jesus, says Paul, will kill this lawless man with the "breath of his mouth" (2 Thess. 2:8)! His apparent power and his efforts to deceive will be brought to nothing when Jesus Christ returns. The final victory will never be in doubt; Jesus will conquer and will reign forever.

It is on this basis, then, that Paul calls God's people to "stand firm" in the final verses of this chapter (2 Thess. 2:15). The man of lawlessness will come; Paul wants the believers in Thessalonica to be aware of this fact. But they can also know that the gospel is true. Their faith is sure, and they need to hold firmly to all that they have been taught about Jesus Christ. We, too, need to hear this message today as we look ahead to all that will come, holding firmly to the truth of the gospel every day!

FIRST CORINTHIANS AND THE RESURRECTION

Earlier, we noted that the Old Testament Scriptures offer hints about bodily resurrection. King David pointed forward to the Messiah of God, who would never see "corruption" in the grave (Ps. 16:10). Job pointed forward to his future hope of seeing God in the "flesh," even long after his physical body had rotted in the ground (Job 19:26).

As we look at Paul's writing in 1 Corinthians 15, we see this future resurrection hope made much more explicit for us. Essential to our understanding of the conclusion of the Bible story is the doctrine of the resurrection of all people from the dead. As we will see, this glorious hope is grounded in the real bodily resurrection of Jesus Christ from the dead; his resurrection gives hope that, for God's people, death is truly not the final word!

📖 **READ!**

Read 1 Corinthians 15—one of the most complete and clear passages in all of Scripture regarding the future resurrection from the dead.

Perhaps you do not think about the resurrection very often as you go about your day. But for the apostle Paul, the reality of the resurrection—Jesus's resurrection and ours—was one of the central pieces of Christian faith and future hope. His example shows us that we would do well to think more often about this important future hope!

The resurrection from the dead is a key part of the final scene of the Bible story that we have been considering together: "God's Eternity." What do we learn from Paul about the resurrection, to which we look forward in faith?

Our resurrection is grounded in Jesus's resurrection. Did you notice where Paul begins his discussion about the resurrection? He starts by affirming, explaining, and proving the reality of the resurrection of Jesus Christ from the dead. For Paul, the hope of resurrection for believers in Jesus is completely grounded on the fact the Jesus himself really rose bodily from the dead. He is the "firstfruits" of believers who have died—the one who rises first and sets the example and the model for everyone who will follow him into resurrection life (1 Cor. 15:20). To put this in slightly different words, we have no hope that we will be raised from the dead someday if Jesus Christ was not truly raised first!

Paul even goes one step further. He says that if Jesus has not been raised from the dead, we are still in our sins (1 Cor. 15:17). If Jesus stayed dead, that means that his sacrifice for sin was not enough to be accepted by God. But that is not the case! Jesus *did* rise from the dead, proving that the sacrifice for sin that he made on the cross was accepted by the holy God. His resurrection was God's vindication of his Son and of the sufficiency of his sacrifice for sin; it proved that by Jesus's sacrifice, sin really is completely paid for and death has been defeated for all who put their faith in him.

Our resurrection bodies will be wonderful. Paul rebukes the Corinthians a bit for asking somewhat foolish questions about the resurrection body (1 Cor. 15:35–36). Paul goes on to explain that, much like a seed, which "dies" as it goes into the ground and then bursts forth into something far more beautiful, our mortal bodies will die, be buried, and burst forth in resurrected life that is far more beautiful and perfect (vv. 37–40)! Paul explains that "natural" bodies grow old, sick, and die; spiritual bodies, though, will live forever (vv. 42–46).

We can take from this teaching the simple fact that God has prepared resurrection bodies for his people that will be wonderful, strong, perfect, and incorruptible. The Bible teaches that, in God's eternity, human beings who have trusted and believed in Jesus will experience the new heaven and new earth in glorified physical bodies, which will never grow weary, old, or sick. This is the promise of resurrection life.

Our resurrection will happen at the end. Finally, we see that Paul teaches the Corinthians about the timing of the resurrection; it will happen at the "last trumpet" (1 Cor. 15:52), which is similar to the way Jesus speaks about his return in Matthew 24 (with the trumpets of the angels being blown). Even now, the physical bodies of many believers in Jesus still lie dead in the ground. But when Jesus returns, this passage tells us that "in a twinkling of an eye," these believers will be raised to life, will be given glorified resurrection bodies, and will prepare to spend eternity in the presence of their Lord and Savior, Jesus Christ.

Hope for us. So Paul teaches us about God's eternity as he explains the truth and reality of the resurrection. This is a future resurrection that will be connected to the resurrection of Jesus Christ—the "firstfruits" of all who will one day rise. When it happens, mortal bodies will be replaced by immortal resurrection bodies. It will accompany the great and glorious return of Jesus Christ in the clouds with the blast of the angels' trumpets. This is the hope, then, that believers in Jesus Christ can and must hold on to as they look ahead to God's eternity. Death is not the end; real resurrection will come.

DAVID AND THE "FOREVER KINGDOM"

Let's go back to the Old Testament one final time as we prepare for our final chapter, which will focus on the book of Revelation. We have seen how the Bible points us toward a final judgment, a future resurrection, a final place for God's people, and the perfect worship of heaven. As we look back at a very big promise God made to David, we will remember the Bible's teaching about the "forever kingdom" that is still to come.

READ!

Read 2 Samuel 7—the account of God's great promise to establish David's throne forever.

We will not spend much time on the context of this great promise now; we walked through the story of David and Solomon earlier. Instead, we will simply focus on the content of this great promise that God made to David and what it means for our understanding of what to expect about God's eternity.

The content of the promise. So what was the content of this promise that God made to King David as he began to see his reign over Israel grow firm and secure? God promised to establish the kingdom of the offspring of David. He promised him that his "house" and his "kingdom"—his throne—would stand forever before him (2 Sam. 7:12–13). There were no qualifications or conditions to this promise. It was simply a promise, from God to David, that his kingly line would never go away. God would raise up a descendant of David who would establish this kingly line over God's people in an eternal way. This is why we call this a promise of a "forever kingdom."

The expectations of the people. Because of this promise to David, it is not surprising that many of the people of Israel came to expect that another human king would rise to lead God's people and return the nation of Israel to the glories of the days of David and Solomon. Even after the exile, many of them held out hope that God would restore power and glory to Israel through a great "Son of David" who would come one day. What they did not realize was that the kingdom of God—the "forever kingdom" that he had promised to David—would be much greater and far more glorious than the earthly city of Jerusalem. In fact, it would be eternal.

Partial fulfillment. Jesus, then, was not the "Son of David" that many of God's people expected. He was, humanly speaking, descended from David, but he came saying very clearly that his kingdom was "not of this world" (John 18:36). Here was God's King, but he was no earthly king. Jesus came humbly—to serve God's people and save them from their sins by dying on a cross for them. Here was a King who would not reign from a palace in Jerusalem, but would reign from a bloody cross, where he would fight the greatest battle on behalf of God's people— a battle against Satan, sin, and death. This King would rise again and return to heaven, there to begin reigning from the right hand of God the Father and waiting to finally establish the eternal kingdom of God after his return to judge the earth.

Final fulfillment. As we can see when we understand where we are in the Bible story, we are still waiting for the final fulfillment of God's great promise to David. The King—the great Son of David—has come to earth. Jesus, the King and Savior, "reigned" from the cross and conquered death forever through his resurrection from the dead. But as he builds his eternal kingdom through his people who put their faith in him, he is still waiting to finally reveal his glory and power at his return and the final judgment. He is still waiting to establish his rule forever over God's people in the perfect place that God is preparing for them—the new Jerusalem in the new heaven and new earth. God's promise to David is still "good." God is keeping this promise through his Son, the great King, and he will one day show us what this beautiful forever kingdom will look like!

REVIEW

The Old Testament Scriptures, as well as the New Testament books, point to the glorious eternal future for God's people who have placed their faith in God's Son. What lies ahead for them is resurrection life in the new heaven and new earth, where they will reign with Christ and rejoice forever in the presence of their Savior. That part of the story is yet to begin; we await the return of Jesus as King and Judge.

⬤ PRAY!

As you close this chapter in prayer, begin by giving thanks to God that he has made known his plans to his people in his word. Ask him to help you understand his purpose for his people, which will be finally fulfilled when Jesus returns, judges the world, and begins his eternal reign over them. Pray that your hope for eternity would rest on Jesus Christ—the only true Savior, Lord, and King!

Chapter 16

GOD'S ETERNITY
PART 2

We are living in the scene of God's big story that we have called "God's Church" and waiting for the next (and final) scene—"God's Eternity"—to begin with the return of our Lord and Savior, Jesus Christ. As we began thinking about eternity in the previous chapter, we looked at many different parts of Scripture—Old Testament and New Testament—that give hints, glimpses, and clear teaching about all that God has in store for this world and for his people as he brings his plan for his creation to completion. But to get the best possible picture of what lies ahead, we need to turn to a study of the book that gives the largest and most complex explanation of this final scene in God's saving work in the world: Revelation.

That is what we will be doing in this chapter. While we will not study every single passage of this wonderful book, we will seek to get a solid and thorough overview of what Revelation teaches about the last things and about what God's people can expect at the conclusion of God's big story.

> **Remember!**
>
> Your suggested memory verses for this chapter come from Revelation 21—the very end of God's story, for which we are still waiting.
>
> *Then I saw a new heaven and a new earth, for the first heaven and the first earth had passed away, and the sea was no more. And I saw the holy city, new Jerusalem, coming down out of heaven from God, prepared as a bride adorned for her husband. And I heard a loud voice from the throne saying, "Behold, the dwelling place of God is with man. He will dwell with them, and they will be his people, and God himself will be with them as their God. He will wipe away every tear from their eyes, and death shall be no more, neither shall there be mourning, nor crying, nor pain anymore, for the former things have passed away. (Rev. 21:1–4)*

A REVELATION OF THINGS COMING "SOON"

Hopefully you are not too intimidated by the prospect of spending some time in the book of Revelation. Many people—even Christians—avoid careful study of this book. It is seen as challenging, confusing, and even mysterious. There are, of course, some very difficult parts to Revelation. Some of John's visions are hard to understand, and many godly Christian people have different opinions on exactly what John means in certain sections. But these are not reasons to avoid studying Revelation. This book is a gift from God to his people, and it is meant to teach us about his work and encourage us to live faithfully for Jesus in this world.

READ!

Read Revelation 1:1–3—a short but important passage.

What do we learn from the opening words of Revelation? Amazingly, a lot is packed into these three short verses.

A revelation of Jesus Christ. First, we learn that what we are about to study is a direct "revelation" from the Lord Jesus Christ (Rev. 1:1). In other words, John did not come up with all of this on his own—it was revealed to him by Jesus. This vision is a gift from God himself to the apostle John, who was exiled on an island during this time because of his faith in Jesus. Through John, it is a gift from God to his church.

Things that will happen soon. Second, we learn that Jesus gave John the vision of Revelation to show God's people the "things that must soon take place" (Rev. 1:1). Clearly there is a future-oriented focus in Revelation. God is showing his people, through John's vision, his plans for the future. John's vision gives the church a glimpse into the conclusion of God's story.

A promise of blessing. Third, this "introduction" to John's Revelation concludes with a promise of blessing to all who read this book aloud, hear its teaching, and obey what it calls God's people to do (Rev. 1:3). This is a wonderful and important word for us to hear today as Christians! Here is a simple and strong call to read the book of Revelation carefully, study it, seek to understand all that it teaches, and strive to obey it well and remain faithful to Jesus Christ according to what it tells us. God's people will be blessed as they study and obey this book (as well as every part of God's wonderful word).

The time is near. Finally, the introduction to the book of Revelation tells us with utter clarity that "the time is near" (Rev. 1:3). What time? The time of the days of tribulation, Christ's return to earth, the final judgment of God, and the beginning of eternity in the new heaven and new earth. It is true that we do not know if "near" means ten years, a hundred years, or a thousand years (this verse was just as true in John's day as it is now, for to God, a thousand years are like a day; 2 Pet. 3:8). However, we know that we are closer now to seeing the return of Jesus Christ than ever before. He is coming soon, and John's revelation reminds us that these things will one day really take place. God's story will really be completed, and eternity will begin.

GOD'S THRONE ROOM

Now let's skip forward a few chapters to the first major scene of John's vision. It is, as you will see, a look into the very heavenly throne room of God. The drama that happens in this scene is very significant for everything that will happen during the rest of this book.

READ!

Read Revelation 4–5.

There is much we need to understand in this passage. Our primary goal is to understand what these chapters are describing, but we also need to see the way they set up the rest of the visions that John will soon receive.

The setting. As you probably noticed, Revelation 4 sets up the scene for the drama that occurs in chapter 5. What is the setting for this drama? It is the throne room of God the Father in heaven. In his vision, John is taken into the very presence of God and actually sees the infinitely holy God enthroned in heaven. He is surrounded by angelic creatures, who continually sing songs of praise, worship, and adoration to him. They praise him, most fundamentally, because he is holy and is the *Creator* of all things. This praise should help shape our vision of our most holy and infinitely powerful God.

The drama. As John continues to look, the drama begins in Revelation 5. He sees a "scroll" in heaven (v. 1), which we should take to represent all the purposes of God in the world for both judgment and salvation. This scroll, in other words, contains the full story of the work of God in the world; it contains everything that God intends to do—both in the judgment of sin and in the final salvation of his people.

There is a problem, though. No one is found who is "worthy" to open this scroll (Rev. 5:2)—to actually execute all of God's purposes for both judgment and salvation in the world. John begins to weep. Why? Because he wants God's plan to be accomplished; he wants salvation to be completed.

Finally, the problem is solved. Jesus Christ is identified. John sees him as the "Lion" (Rev. 5:5)—that is, the King—and also the "Lamb" (v. 6)—that is, the Savior who has been slain for the salvation of sinners. This one is worthy to open the seals of the scroll and bring about its contents. The chapter ends with a "new song" (v. 9), which all of creation eventually joins in to sing. This is a song not about the glory of God as Creator, but about Jesus as the *Redeemer* and *Savior*!

The meaning. So what is the meaning of all of this? We have already seen that the scroll pictured here should be understood as God's purposes and plans for the judgment of the world and the eternal salvation of his people. We have seen that no one except Jesus is worthy to open the scroll. Here, then, is the meaning, and how this scene connects to the rest of what we will discuss:

- This passage is showing us that Jesus Christ is the one who will bring about all of God's eternal purposes for both *judgment* and *salvation* in the days to come. He will judge evil as the great King and will assure the salvation of God's people forever.
- Everything, then, that comes after this in Revelation, as confusing as it may seem, is part of God bringing his purposes to pass through the leadership and activity of Jesus Christ, his Son. All that follows shows us how God's judgment of the world and his completion of salvation for his people will unfold.
- Most fundamentally, as we see from this passage, Jesus will accomplish the eternal salvation of God's people through what he

has already done. He is praised and worshiped, as Revelation 5 closes, for his work on the cross. He was slain—and he ransomed a people for God by his blood (v. 9). This "Lion" and Judge is also the "Lamb" who died for God's people. Jesus will be *both* these things as he brings God's story to its conclusion.

Revelation 4–5, then, shows us all that is coming in the story of God's work in the world. Jesus is preparing to bring about—and complete—all of God's sovereign purposes for perfect judgment and for final salvation of those who belong to him by faith.

THE SEVEN SEALS

The scroll that John sees in his vision is sealed with seven seals. As John's vision continues, he sees Jesus beginning to open these seals one by one, bringing about the great judgments of God on the earth. These judgments are fierce, brutal, and very real. But as we will see, God's people are not left without hope amid these judgments.

READ!

Read Revelation 6:1–8:1—the account of the Lamb's opening of the seven seals of God's wrath.

Let's now seek to understand all that is recorded for us in this amazing portion of John's vision and to see what it means for our understanding of the conclusion of God's story. Here are several important points:

God's righteous judgment. The seven seals are the first set of three remaining "sevens" in the book of Revelation. All these series of sevens are meant to describe the perfect and full judgment of God on the earth. The seven seals come first, then the seven trumpets, and then finally the seven bowls of God's wrath that are poured out on the earth. Each series of seven ultimately represents the same thing—God's judgment—but each series also seems to build on the previous ones, progressively becoming more intense and global (the final bowls, for example, seem to describe judgments that would each make a complete end of the entire earth). The first four seals are judgments symbolized by horses, which probably signify God's judgments that come through the forces of war, death, disease, and famine. The fifth seal shows the need for judgment as God's faithful martyrs wait to see his perfect judgment revealed. The sixth seal brings about the vanishing of the sky itself as the rulers of the earth grow aware of the coming wrath and judgment of the Lamb.

We need to stop here and recognize that these judgments are a central part of the end of God's story. Throughout all of history, God has been promising his people that he will one day make a complete end of sin. This world is sinful and fallen, and it will come under the final and awful judgment of the holy God of the universe.

A hanging question. Just as it seems that judgment has become almost unbearable, something happens in the narrative that is meant to be a great comfort to believers in Jesus. Did you see where the seventh seal is finally opened? While the first six seals are opened by the Lamb in Revelation 6, the seventh seal is not opened until 8:1. Why is this? What is going on here?

There is a "hanging question" at the end of Revelation 6, which introduces chapter 7—an interlude that is meant to give comfort and hope to God's people even as God's terrible judgment is described. As the earth-dwellers are judged by God, they cry out, "The great day of . . . wrath has come, and who can stand?" (6:17).

A word of comfort and salvation. Revelation 7, then, is the wonderful answer to the question that ends chapter 6. Who can stand in the day of God's wrath and judgment, which will be poured out in the last days against sinful people and the sinful world? The great multitude of God's people, who belong to him by faith in Jesus Christ, will be able to stand in that day!

John shows us this multitude in two parallel and complementary pictures in Revelation 7. The first is of a great number of people—144,000 "servants of our God"—who are meant to symbolize the fullness of God's people, the church (vv. 3–4). Those who belong to Jesus are the true Israel, so they are now represented as the fullness of the tribes of Israel. The next picture is of a great multitude that no one can number (v. 9). They are God's people who have been "washed" in the blood of the Lamb (v. 14), and they are ready to sing praises to their God and Savior for all eternity.

So as John's vision points us to the judgment of God that will be poured out at the conclusion of God's story, it also points us to the hope that God's true people will stand amid the judgment because of the blood of Jesus Christ. All those who are washed in him will be safe and will praise their God forever.

THE SEVEN TRUMPETS

Everything in the story of the Bible has been moving toward the final days that we read about in the book of Revelation. The coming of Jesus was foretold—beginning in Genesis 3:15 and then throughout the Old Testament in the promises of God and the words of his prophets. When Jesus came, he died on a cross for sins, rose again from the dead, and returned to reign in heaven until his second coming to judge the world. In Revelation, John gives us glimpses of all that is still to come in the story. The next important milestone we must consider is the seven trumpets of God's judgment.

READ!

Read Revelation 8:6–9:21—another account of the judgments of God against the earth.

The theme of judgment is a big one in the final scene of God's story— "God's Eternity." As you have already gathered, this theme is especially prominent in the book of Revelation. We've already looked at one account of judgment (the seven seals), and now we will consider another. As part of this study, we must consider the sad reality of the response of sinful people even after they have been given a glimpse of God's terrible judgment against sin.

The seven trumpet judgments. We mentioned that Revelation contains a theme of "sevens" as the judgments of God against the earth are described. The number seven usually symbolizes perfection or fullness in some way, so we should probably take this to mean that John's vision is showing God's perfect and full judgment being poured out on the earth. As the angels blow their trumpets and the next series of seven judgments unfolds, we can make the following observations:

- The trumpet judgments have very interesting similarities with the *plagues on Egypt*, which God brought down through his servant Moses. We see hail falling, water turning to blood, and the sun being darkened, just to mention a few. These judgments clearly are meant to mirror those ancient plagues.
- Because of their similarities with the plagues on Egypt, we should take the trumpet judgments of Revelation 8–9 to be against people who choose to trust the *things of this world* for their security rather than God. In these judgments, God affects everything that people might be tempted to rely on for security. He is shaking the very foundations of the earth and showing sinful people the foolishness of trusting anything other than him for security and lasting salvation.
- While the first four trumpets bring judgments that seem to affect the earth generally, the fifth and sixth trumpets bring judgments that particularly affect those who have chosen to follow Satan instead of Jesus Christ. Both have to do with the influence of demonic beings—Satan's evil and violent servants in the world. They torment and abuse their followers, and then lead demonic armies in wars that take thousands and thousands of human lives. We cannot

get into the depth of this interpretation, but it is enough now to simply say that God is allowing Satan to torment and torture those who have chosen to sinfully follow him rather than Jesus.

The lesson about total depravity. The huge surprise of this passage, though, comes in the final two verses of Revelation 9. Read verses 20–21 one more time, keeping in mind the terrible description you have just read about the judgments that are being poured out on the entire earth and specifically on the servants of Satan. What jumps out at you about these verses? Notice that the people who are not killed by these plagues *still* refuse to repent and turn to God in faith. They *still* choose sin and opt to follow demons, worship idols, and reject the God and Savior of all mankind.

Most likely, John wants to show us here that some people will reject Jesus no matter what. This is a defense of "total depravity"—the theological teaching that human beings are fallen, sinful, and depraved in such a way that they are incapable of choosing God unless he makes them alive spiritually by the miraculous work of the Holy Spirit. It is sad to see people being exposed to the fierce judgment of God against sin and the full reality of the terrible abuse that Satan gives to his followers, and then still choosing to reject Jesus and worship the very demons who torment them. This is a reminder to us to praise God for the gift of faith and to keep sharing the gospel of Jesus Christ with sinful people who, apart from faith, are under the judgment of the holy God of the universe.

SATAN RAGING

How often do you think about Satan? Hopefully you are not obsessed with him because your focus as a Christian should be on God, not Satan. But hopefully you recognize that he is a real and powerful spiritual being—one who is opposed to God's people and God's work in this world.

The passage from Revelation that you will read next gives us insight into Satan's work in the world throughout history—and into the future.

For centuries and centuries, Satan has opposed God's work in the world, and he will continue to rage against God's people until the very end. In Revelation 12, John wants us to be aware of this even as we continue to trust in one whose power is much greater than that of Satan.

READ!

Read Revelation 12—a passage that gives us insight into the past activity of Satan as well as his continuing activity and influence in the world until the very end.

Probably the most common error that followers of Jesus fall into is not believing that Satan exists. They forget that the Bible teaches that his influence and power in this world are very real. There is a real Satan, and he is fighting against God's work in this world with every bit of strength and power that he has. It is important that, as we consider the conclusion of God's great story, we understand rightly the influence of Satan and his future defeat. So what does Revelation 12 tell us about this great dragon—Satan?

Satan—opposing God's people. The first part of the passage you read—Revelation 12:1–6—shows Satan's opposition to and attacks against God's people. The woman that John sees represents the people of God. She is Israel, and the child that she is seeking to bring forth is Jesus, God's Son in human flesh. Satan, then, not only opposes God's people, but actively and violently opposes God's great saving work, which comes through the incarnation of Jesus, and his death and resurrection. But God sustains this work and protects his people, so Satan is ultimately unable to stop the salvation that God is bringing into the world through his Son.

Satan—thrown from heaven. In Revelation 12:7, John's vision takes us back in time before the fall of Adam and Eve. He sees Satan's fall from heaven, when the angel Michael defeated him and threw him from the presence of God. This fascinating account tells us two important things about Satan:

1. His power is not equal to God's! Satan is not a worthy opponent for God in the world. In fact, long before the fall of Adam and Eve (when Satan showed up in the garden of Eden in the form of a serpent), another of God's angels, Michael, defeated him. We must never see Satan as an equal opponent to God.
2. Satan is a created being. He is a fallen angel—created by God but guilty of the great sin of rebelling against God's perfect word and rule in heaven. Satan is not omnipotent, omniscient, or omnipresent; as a created being, his powers are limited.

Satan—his time is short. Though he is not omnipotent, Satan is very powerful, and we see his influence and activity in the world described in the rest of this chapter that you read. After he is thrown from heaven, he comes down to earth in great "wrath, because he knows that his time is short!" (Rev. 12:12). Satan's response to his defeat (and his knowledge of his inevitable judgment by God) is to devote himself to creating as much violence, sin, and destruction on earth as he can. God has allowed him a certain amount of time before his final judgment, and Satan is spending that time making war on all those who belong to Jesus.

Even during this powerful activity of Satan, though, God's people continue to be "nourished" and protected by God (Rev. 12:13–14). Those who belong to Jesus Christ should acknowledge and understand the activity of Satan, but they do not need to be terrified or tormented by him. His time is short, and he knows it. As we will see later in the book of Revelation, there will come a day when he will finally be thrown down forever by Jesus, never more to torment or attack the people of God.

THE ANTICHRIST

There is another evil force or person that Christians are to expect as the return of Jesus and the final judgment of the world draw nearer. In your next reading, you are going to be considering the antichrist. There are many interpretations of this striking passage, but there is ultimately one application for Christians, who are called to stand firm until the end.

◤ READ!

Read Revelation 13—a passage that describes the rising of two beasts who will have a great influence for evil in the world in the days before the return of Jesus Christ and the final judgment of the earth.

The first and most important thing that you need to recognize about the beasts that are described in Revelation 13 is that both are linked to the work and influence of Satan. Look back at how chapter 12 ends. Satan stands on the edge of the sea—the symbol of evil and chaos. Now look again at how chapter 13 begins; the beast rises out of the sea. Satan—the great "dragon" and enemy of God's people—is behind these beasts that are rising up to seek to bring evil, sin, and deception to the earth. Let's spend a few moments seeking to understand all that John tells us about these beasts to better know what to expect as God's story draws to its conclusion.

The first beast—a political ruler. You might remember that we mentioned this passage during our discussion of Daniel 7—the chapter in which Daniel receives a vision of four beasts that rise up out of the sea during future days. The first beast we see in Revelation 13 is a composite of the four beasts that Daniel saw—a terrible combination of all their powers. This means it is probably best to see this beast as a great world leader or ruler, one who is greater than all the mightiest world powers of all time. This is a political ruler—an antichrist who will exalt himself over all the world and seek to bring all peoples to serve and worship him.

The second beast—a religious leader. A second beast comes up in the second part of this chapter. This beast is distinct from the political ruler, the antichrist. His role seems to be specifically religious, as he seeks to direct all the world in the organized worship of the antichrist. This vision should cause us to picture a kind of new world religion organized around the idolatrous worship of the first beast. People everywhere are marked with the symbol of allegiance to this beast, and they cannot buy or sell anything unless they are under that mark. The goal of both beasts, who are in service to Satan, is obviously total domination of the lives, hearts, and souls of humanity as they oppose God and demand human worship and allegiance.

Different interpretations, one application. There are many interpretations of what John means in this vision. Are these literal world rulers, which we should expect to see in the days and years to come? Quite possibly. Will there be multiple beasts or antichrists, who will rise up in the coming years to seek to deceive the people of the world? That is possible too. Is this simply John's way of picturing the continuing deceptive influence of Satan in the world through political leaders and false prophets? That is another interpretation. You should commit to studying Revelation—and the entire Bible—even more diligently on your own so that you can be more informed about these things.

No matter your interpretation of this chapter, though, the application is the same. There is one group of people who are safe from the deceptive influence of these beasts. One group refuses to be marked by allegiance to and worship of the antichrist. It is the group of people belonging to God through faith in Jesus Christ. They are not marked. They are not deceived. The application for us today, even as we consider the terrible power and influence of these beasts, is to cling to Jesus Christ and resist deception as we believe God's good word.

THE CONQUERING LAMB AND KING

Now let's skip ahead to the final four chapters of Revelation (and the Bible). Next, you will read a portion of Revelation 19, which contains a very vivid picture of the marriage supper of the Lamb and the "feast" of those who are judged by Christ.

As you have already seen in many passages of Revelation, Jesus Christ is the Savior and the Lamb, but he is also the conquering King and the eternal Judge. His coming will mean salvation for some and horrible judgment for those who have not accepted his rule over their lives and hearts. Passages like the one you will now read are not easy, yet they remind us of the seriousness of the need for people to accept Jesus now.

READ!

Read Revelation 19:6–21—the account of John's vision of two great "suppers."

In Revelation 14–18, which we are skipping, John records his vision of the final series of seven—the seven "bowls" of God's wrath (16:1), which are poured out on the earth. After that, he tells of seeing "Babylon"—the great enemy of God—judged and thrown down (18:2). But when we come to Revelation 19, we finally begin to approach John's vision of the very last things. Soon we will move to the very good ending of the story of Scripture—and of the whole world.

The passage that you just read gives us a very different picture of Jesus than we are used to seeing. This Jesus is the same Savior that we have learned about, but he is also the glorious, holy, and powerful Judge of those who reject him. We have much to learn from this passage and the two "meals" that it describes.

Meal #1—the marriage supper. The first meal that is described, in Revelation 19:6–9, should be very encouraging to believers in Jesus Christ. Again, as he has done before, John puts before us the multitude of people who have confessed Jesus as Savior and now gather in praise to him. These people have been invited to the great "marriage supper of the Lamb" (v. 9). This image—a marriage supper—has appeared in several places in the Bible story. It is always a beautiful and climactic feast—one that a person does not want to miss. Jesus uses this imagery several times when he teaches about the final gathering of God's people.

We should note that those who attend this marriage supper are dressed in "fine linen," which, John explains, is the "righteous deeds of the saints" (Rev. 19:8). These good deeds are, of course, gifts from Jesus Christ; no one can earn saving favor with God by his or her own strength. Yet it is true that the right clothing for this meal is righteousness; no one gets in without the right outfit!

Meal #2—the feast for the birds. The second meal is a bit grotesque—and it is meant to be! The picture that concludes this chapter is intended to wake us up to the awful reality of sin and the terrible judgment that it brings. As the passage ends, an angel calls out to the birds overhead to gather for the "great supper of God" (Rev. 19:17), which comes as he judges sinners who have rejected Jesus as Lord and Savior. The description of these people covers everyone—from kings down to ordinary people—who has refused the rule of Jesus. The two beasts are defeated and devoured as well. All in all, there is no real battle—the enemies of God are simply destroyed, and the birds that gather overhead devour their flesh (v. 21).

Jesus—Savior and Judge. As we near the end of the Bible story, we should take seriously the picture of Jesus that John gives to us in Revelation 19:7–10. This is, of course, the same humble Savior who came as a human baby and laid down his life on a cross for sinners. But when he returns, he will come with powerful judgment. He will ride in with might and authority—and will trample God's enemies with the fury of his righteous anger against sin. When we picture Jesus, we must see him like this as well as our humble Savior; he is both Savior and Judge! On the final day of the world, everyone will either be safe in Jesus and invited to his supper or will face the wrath and judgment of the truly righteous King.

THE MILLENNIUM

The next chapter of Revelation gives us John's description of the millennial (thousand-year) reign of Jesus Christ. As you will see, there is more than one way to interpret this passage, yet the different interpretations come together in the final verses of this chapter, which take us before the very throne of God in the final judgment of all the world.

READ!

Read Revelation 20—the account of the millennium and the final judgment of all people.

Revelation 20 is one of the most hotly debated passages in all of Scripture, so we will seek to study it carefully and see how it leads us into the rest of the story, which has not yet begun.

The millennium. We are going to discuss some of the interpretations of this passage in the Christian church today. First, though, we will very simply summarize what seems to be taught in the first ten verses of this passage—an extremely key passage in the book of Revelation. Here is what John sees:

- Before the millennium. In verses 1–3, we read about the key event that signals the beginning of the millennium. It is the binding of Satan so that he is unable to "deceive" the nations any longer. Satan is pictured as being bound with a chain and then thrown into a pit, which is closed and sealed over him.
- During the millennium. Verses 4–6 describe the thousand-year reign of Christ on earth. Satan is bound during this time, and it seems that Christ rules on earth with the resurrected saints of God, who have been raised to share in his reign. This is a time of peace on earth as Jesus Christ visibly and powerfully manifests his reign as the rightful King of all the world.
- After the millennium. Finally, verses 7–10 tell us that Satan is released to make one last attempt in battle against God the Father and his Son, Jesus Christ. Amazingly, even after the visible reign of Christ on earth for a thousand years, many people still flock

to follow Satan in his battle. It does not go well for Satan and his army, though; they are consumed with fire from heaven and then thrown into the lake of fire to be judged eternally.

Different interpretations. Many people who have read and studied Revelation 20:1–10 take the teaching here very literally. They see John's vision as a picture of the future, with Christ visibly reigning on earth. Satan will be bound during this time—unable to deceive people in the world as he currently does. This is a legitimate way to understand this passage—and it comes from the most straightforward reading of the text.

Other faithful Christians, though, have understood this passage to be a kind of metaphor—a symbolic way of describing how Jesus Christ is *even now* reigning on the earth, having bound Satan through his death on the cross and his resurrection from the dead. They teach that we are already living in this millennium, reigning with Christ as his people, as the gospel is freely proclaimed around the world without hindrance by Satan.

As you study this passage—and all of Revelation—on your own, you should work hard to come to your own conclusions about how to interpret John's visions.

Final judgment before the throne. The different interpretations of the millennium come back together in the final five verses of Revelation 20. After the millennium (whether real or figurative) is over, all people, from all ages, gather before the throne of God to face the final judgment. "Books" are opened (v. 12), which probably symbolize the deeds that all people have committed during their lifetimes on earth. However, those who are saved are judged according to another book that is opened at this point: the "book of life" (vv. 12, 15). Those whose names are written in this book, because of faith in the Lord Jesus Christ, are saved and accepted into God's eternal kingdom. Those whose names are not in this book are sent to be with Satan in the lake of fire.

This event—the final judgment—will be the last act of history, the very final event in the story of the Bible and of this earth. There will be no second chances after this point. God's people will be brought in and his enemies will be judged.

Next, we will see how a new era begins once the final judgment is over.

A GOOD ENDING

The judgment of every human being before the throne of God will be the final scene of history before the end of this world as we know it. Afterward, the new world will begin, and that is what John shows us in the passage that you will read next.

As you conclude your study of Revelation and your trip through the story of the Bible, you will see that God's story will have a very good and very complete ending. Everything will be wrapped up; there will be no loose ends. The way the story will end is another indication that this is no human story; it is God's story, and it will end with great blessing for all who are truly his people through faith in his Son.

READ!

Read Revelation 21–22—the very good ending to the story of the Bible and the story of the world.

What a great gift it is to know the end of the story of the world! God has not left his people in the dark, but has graciously given to them, through his servant John, a picture of how it all will end. After the final judgment of all people before God's throne, something new will come—something wonderful for all who truly belong to God through faith in Jesus. As we end by looking at Revelation 21–22, this material should fill you with great hope and anticipation—if you truly know Jesus Christ.

Everything new. The focus for John in Revelation 21:1–8 is the newness of everything that he sees. The old heaven and earth are gone; they have finally "passed away" (v. 1). God has made an end of this fallen world and has initiated his new creation—a new heaven and new earth for his people.

His people, too, are new; they are "adorned" like a bride for him (Rev. 21:2), no longer stained with sin but made ready to live in eternal and perfect relationship with him. In fact, "all things" are new (v. 5). God's salvation of his people is finally complete in this future scene, just as judgment is final for those who have rejected him.

Promises and prophecies fulfilled. As you read Revelation 21:9–22:5, hopefully you noticed at least some of the Old Testament "echoes" in this passage. The overwhelming sense that we get, as John begins to describe the people and place of God (the holy city), is that God is perfectly fulfilling his great promises to his people for all time. Here are just a few examples:

- John's use of the number *twelve* in his description of the holy city is an indication that this is the place for the fullness of the people of God (Rev. 21:12–14, 21; 22:2). There were twelve tribes of Israel and twelve apostles of Jesus, and now the city is organized with measurements of twelve. This is the place that God has built for his people.
- The description of the *wealth* and *splendor* of the city (note John's mention of gold and jewels—Rev. 21:15, 18–21) reminds us of the splendor and wealth of Solomon's kingdom. John is telling us that this city will far outshine the glories of the height of Israel under Solomon.
- The city itself is in the shape of a *cube*. The only other cube-shaped object in Scripture is the Most Holy Place in the tabernacle—the place where the presence of God dwelt with his people. John is telling us that the entire new heaven and earth will be a Most Holy Place—a place for the dwelling of God with his people in holiness.
- The descriptions of the tree of life and the river running through the city (Rev. 22:1–2) remind us of the *garden of Eden*. This will be a place like Eden in its beauty and life—but even better.

A new story begins. As we close the story of the Bible, we should notice that a much greater and more eternal story begins in the new heaven and new earth. For God's people, the ending of this world will signal the beginning of new and eternal life with him. There is great hope ahead for those who trust in Jesus. Are you looking forward to an eternity with him?

REVIEW

John's vision in the book of Revelation gives us the Bible's most extensive teaching on the last days, the end of the world, and the triumphant return of Jesus Christ as Savior, King, and Judge. We know that there is a good ending to the Bible's big story, as God's redeemed people will witness the end of sin and death—and Jesus's final defeat of Satan. This world will end, and Jesus will make all things new. Believers in Christ await that day with joy, faith, endurance, and hope.

PRAY!

Close this chapter—and this book—in prayer to God. Consider praying in the following ways:

- Thank *God for all that you have learned about his word—in all its unity and beauty.*
- Ask *God to help you continue to have a hunger to know the Bible more and obey him better.*
- Praise *God for his grace and mercy to you in his Son, Jesus Christ.*
- Confess *to God the ways that you still struggle with sin and unbelief— and ask him to forgive you and help you keep growing in him.*

CONCLUSION

My hope and prayer is that this book has helped you get a better sense of the storyline of the Bible—and confidence that we as Christians truly can study God's word as one unified story that has its climax and central point in the redeeming work of Jesus Christ. What a gift God's word is to us: sixty-six books composed by more than forty human authors over thousands of years, but with one divine author inspiring all of it! My encouragement to you, reader, is to keep studying God's word. Make it your life's mission, passion, and worshipful work. One day we will walk together, by faith, into the conclusion of the story.

GENERAL INDEX

Aaron, 107, 108
Abel, 57
Abijam, 161
Abraham, 14, 16, 22, 65–72, 75–79,
    82, 89, 90, 95, 96, 130, 214, 263,
    267, 269
abstract thought, 32
Adam, 15, 28, 32, 38, 39, 47, 53, 58–59
adultery, 147, 148, 153, 242
Ahab, 161, 162, 163, 167–89
Ahasuerus, 178
Amalekites, 142
Ammonites, 141
Ananias, 265
Ancient of Days, 195, 304
angels, 23, 229, 293, 327–28
animal sacrifices, 13, 50–51, 69
Anna, 222–24
announcements, 225
anointed one, 198, 233–34, 305
antichrist, 304, 311, 328–30
apostles, 5, 260, 287, 296
Areopagus, 268
arrogance, 284
artistry, 31
Asa, 161–62
ascension, 297
Assyria, 165, 169, 197, 207
Athens, 268–70
Augustine, 10

Baal, 122, 166, 168
Baasha, 161, 162

Babylon, 165, 170, 175–76, 194, 199, 331
baptism, 72, 230–31
barrenness, 136–37
Bathsheba, 147–48, 149, 153
beauty, 27, 31, 32, 300
betrayal, 245
Bible
    as about Jesus, 4
    scenes of, 19
    story of, 134, 251
    unity of, 2, 7–9
biblical theology
    definition of, 1
    foundations for, 2–9
    and the gospel, 12–14
    "journey" of, 10–12
    and personal Bible study, 14–16
    value of, 9–10
birth narrative, 98–99
blame, 48–49
blessing
    hints of, 97
    to the nations, 85, 91, 129, 153, 175,
        214, 267
    promise of, 64–66, 74, 319
    under Solomon, 155–57
Boaz, 128–29
book of life, 334
born again, 202, 228

Cain, 57, 295
Caleb, 109–10, 115
calling, 40, 119–21, 137, 232, 253, 291

SCRIPTURE INDEX

Theology Basics Series

The Theology Basics series is a collection of books,
workbooks, and videos designed to provide an accessible
introduction to the study of biblical truth—systematic
theology, biblical theology, and biblical interpretation.

For more information, visit **crossway.org**.